Québec

A French Colonial Town in America, 1660 to 1690

Rémi Chénier

Translated from the Original French

Studies in Archaeology
Architecture and History

National Historic Sites
Parks Service
Environment Canada

Available in Canada through authorized bookstore agents and other bookstores, or by mail from the Canada Communication Group, Publishing, Supply and Services Canada, Ottawa, Ontario, Canada K1A 0S9.

Published under the authority
of the Minister of the Environment,
Ottawa, 1991

Translated by the Department of the Secretary of State.
Editing: Jean Brathwaite
Design: Suzanne Adam-Filion.
Production: Suzanne Rochette and Rod Won.

Parks publishes the results of its research in archaeology, architecture, and history. A list of publications is available from National Historic Sites Publications, Parks Service, Environment Canada, 1600 Liverpool Court, Ottawa, Ontario K1A 0H3.

Canadian Cataloguing in Publication Data

Chénier, Rémi

Québec, a French colonial town in America, 1660 to 1690
(Studies in archaeology, architecture and history, ISSN 0821-1027)
Issued also in French under title: Québec, ville coloniale française en Amérique.
Includes bibliographical references.
ISBN 0-660-13630-9
DSS cat. no. R61-2/9-51E

1. Québec (Quebec) — History. 2. Urbanisation — Quebec (Province) — Québec — History. I. Canadian Parks Service. National Historic Parks and Sites. II. Title. III. Series.

FC2946.4C43 1990	971.4'47101	C90-098690-5
F1054.5Q3C43 1990		

Cover: Detail from "L'Entrée de la Riviere de St Laurent, et la ville de Quebec dans le Canada," *circa* 1670, anonymous
Bibliothèque Nationale, France

CONTENTS

PREFACE

This book was written under the direction of one of my colleagues, Marc Lafrance; it is one of the many works the Canadian Parks Service has devoted to the Town of Québec. Having been introduced to the type of urban studies currently being carried out, particularly in France, England, and the United States, I was attracted by the approach advocated by certain geographers and by historians like Pierre Goubert, Fernand Braudel, Roland Mousnier, and Jean-Claude Perrot.

To my knowledge, Canadian historians had produced few such studies, and only in recent years had urban history begun to enjoy some popularity. Articles that had been published, notably in the *Revue d'histoire urbaine*, dealt primarily with the 19th century and neglected the French régime. This work, as well as meeting the needs of the Canadian Parks Service, provided an opportunity to fill that void by studying a town under the French régime. The phenomenon of urbanization thus provided a very specific framework for this study.

The period between 1660 and 1690 was of paramount importance in Québec's history; it was marked by profound administrative changes, an influx of immigrants, a boom in housing construction, and an attempt at labour self-sufficiency. By looking back over these years, we shall develop a definition of the town as it existed in New France and learn of the policies and people that governed it; we shall also become acquainted with its inhabitants, their houses, and the day-to-day environment in which they lived and worked; and we shall examine the labour force.

ACKNOWLEDGMENTS

This book would not have been possible without the cooperation of the staff at the various archives consulted. I am particularly grateful to Gilles Langelier of the Cartographic Records Section at the National Archives of Canada. I also wish to thank several people from the Quebec Regional Office of the Canadian Parks Service: Louis Richer, Chief, History and Archaeology, for having made completion of this book possible; Jean Audet, for his excellent service provided in the photographic reproduction of maps; and Robert Gagnon and François Pellerin, for redrawing certain illustrations and the graphs.

Part of this book was submitted as a thesis at the University of Ottawa in 1979 under the direction of Jean-Claude Dubé. I am grateful to him for his support and judicious advice.

However, above all, I wish to stress the role played by three of my colleagues, André Charbonneau, Yvon Desloges, and Marc Lafrance. They helped with compiling some of the tables and provided both useful information and constructive criticism. Above all, I appreciate their unfailing friendship and constant encouragement.

INTRODUCTION

As a rule, urbanization is not considered to have appeared in Canada until the 19th century, yet, like town planning, it existed in New France as early as the 17th century. But what do the two terms mean?

Urbanization is a phenomenon that lets us identify various states of urban life according to time and place. Whether on a provincial, national, or global scale, this movement reflects a reality: that of settling and living in a city or town. It presupposes population concentration in urban environments that differ from the countryside. It takes into account the proliferation and vitality of cities and the expansion of their functions. These functions in a sense constitute the very reason for the existence of cities; they represent their distinguishing features, whether commercial, administrative, religious, political, or other. Urbanization engenders its own form of social organization and fosters a particular kind of landscape. It gives rise to institutions, a way of life, a culture, and a set of activities that, usually, distinguish the urban from the rural.

In a colonial context, urbanization takes on a special character, as is shown by a petition from some of the inhabitants of Québec to the Conseil Souverain in 1683. In it the town's merchants complained that the regulations protecting the privileges enjoyed by the inhabitants of New France were not being enforced. These privileges, granted in 1645, gave the permanent residents of the colony exclusive rights to the fur trade with the Indians. Thus they were the only ones authorized to open shops and stores in the towns and to sell retail goods between 15 June and 15 August each year, at the height of the trading season.[1] In their petition the merchants reminded the council why the privileges were granted:

Note to Readers

Unless otherwise indicated, the old French units of measurement are used in this book:

1 *toise* = 6 *pieds*	1 *perche* = 18 *pieds*
1 *arpent* = 180 *pieds*	1 *lieue* = 84 *arpents*

The following can be used for conversion:

1 *pied* = 1.06575 feet	1 foot = 0.9383 *pied*
1 metre = 3.28 feet	

> *Having left Their homes in Old France, Their relatives And friends, and built houses Here, Worked the Land, sailed by various means in the ships of Old France to this country And the Islands of North America; And had built many ships And boats in this Country; Which have attracted a number of inhabitants, sailors And tradesmen of All kinds; And thus having made a notable contribution to increasing the Settlement of this country of which they have borne And still bear All the Burdens, And where they use Their own possessions, And those they have acquired through Their toil, not only for Themselves alone, but also to assist The inhabitants, to whom they provide large advances in order to help Them with Their ventures And relieve Them when in Want, as for Example was seen in the Fire in the Lower Town of Quebec, after which it was possible to rebuild only through mutual help on the part of the inhabitants who have nowhere else to turn, And in the Example of the war with The Iroquois, now behind us, which was waged And endured only by the habitants, together with his Majesty's troops, to which many officers And Soldiers now belong; his Majesty having in consideration of this Intended together with the Governors And Intendants, And this Court, to Grant privileges to the said inhabitants, as the only means of augmenting the country with families of honest folk who will Always contribute to the well-being And Good of the Colony.*[2]

Although the petition was signed by Québec merchants, it reflects the conceptions of a significant portion of the town's inhabitants and covers almost all aspects of urban life. It suggests that the urbanization of New France was an artificial process. Cities and towns did not develop spontaneously, but were created; people left France and settled on a new continent. The petition mentions certain elements of this urbanization: settlement, housing construction, trade, shipbuilding, administration, and privileges granted to the townspeople. Settlers built houses, tilled the soil, and traded with France and the West Indies. Industry, particularly shipbuilding, attracted sailors and labourers. Finally, the petition indicates that there was a feeling of solidarity among the town's inhabitants, who helped each other through hard times caused by fire and war.

The term *urbanisme* (town planning) must now be defined. According to Gaston Bardet, it was used for the first time at the London Congress of 1910. This French town planner believes that *urbanisme* and urbanization emerged in the 19th century. He even describes "urbanification" as the application of the principles of town planning and suggests that *art urbain* should be used instead of *urbanisme* in dealing with earlier periods.[3] Whatever the case may be, and without denying the apparent anachronism, I shall adopt the definition given in general dictionaries such as the *Petit Larousse*, according to which *urbanisme* consists of the technical, administrative, economic, and social measures underlying the harmonious, rational, and human development of agglomerations. Such measures, whose purpose is to improve inhabitants' well-being, are found in the techniques and ideas put forward by the administrators, theorists, and engineers of the 17th century. This form of town planning, which was born in Europe and reached its peak in France, was transmitted to the colony, where administrative and commercial regulations attest to its presence, particularly in Québec.

This monograph studies Québec between 1660 and 1690. The choice of Québec is easy to explain: as the oldest settlement in the St. Lawrence Valley, it was likely the one that reached the highest degree of maturity in New France in the 17th century. Furthermore, it was the capital, the seat of government, and the colony's religious, cultural, economic, and military core. In brief, Québec is the site *par excellence* to study in New France. Although the period is arbitrary, it is easily justified. Since my purpose was to describe a case of urbanization in New France, my attention was immediately focused on the second half of the 17th century, during which the town reached a level of development suited to such an analysis, which would have been pointless had a level nearer the time of the town's foundation been chosen.

Our starting point, 1660, falls just a few years prior to the profound changes that were to mark New France. In 1663 the Compagnie des Cents-Associés was abolished and the king once again took control of the colony. The final years of the Cents-Associés régime were included in this study in order to emphasize the administrative changes brought about when the Crown resumed the management of New France. This enabled me to contrast the two administrations and to determine their effect on the town of Québec.

The terminus is 1690. That year marked a major change in the character of the town, as it was then that Major Provost built the first defensive wall for Québec. A network of fortifications, even a primitive one, imposes many constraints on a city or town: crowding, reduction of inhabitable space, cost of maintaining and repairing the ramparts, presence of a larger garrison, and so on. I did not wish, and indeed was unable in the time allotted, to analyse all of these elements.

Theorists see a city as a whole in which all the components — administration, economy, demography, physical evolution, religion, and the military — simultaneously come into play. All of these dimensions of urban life were present in Québec and all have to be considered to reach a comprehensive overview of life there during the second half of the 17th century. However, as it was impossible to cover all these elements, four were chosen: the concept of *ville*, administration, physical evolution, and demography.

Thus, the military, religious, and commercial aspects have been left aside. Up to 1690 the military played a very small part in Québec; furthermore, many works are already underway in this field. Although the religious aspect was of major importance to the capital of New France, time constraints prevented me from studying in depth the religious community (its establishment, recruitment, and so on), its architecture and land holdings, and its impact on all facets of town life (cultural, economic, political, and social). And the focus of the research was such that trade could not be explored beyond the regulations governing it as set out in the bylaws.

Chapter I
THE CONCEPT OF *VILLE*

Modern usage of the word *ville* (town or city) differs from that prevailing in the 17th century. Following a brief overview of definitions used by contemporary geographers and town planners and a discussion of the notion of urban function, we will trace the evolution of the concept of *ville* in France from the Middle Ages to the 17th century in order to determine what the term means, what it encompasses, and what it implies. The city is a reality, but how was it perceived and what did it comprise during that period?

Québec was founded at the dawn of the 17th century and eventually came to be considered a city. As a product of colonization, can it be compared to cities and towns of Frence? Did it evolve in the same way as its sisters across the Atlantic? And what did it represent in the 17th century?

A Modern Definition

Despite the disagreements that arise among historians, sociologists, and others over the definition of *ville*, we can turn to the field of geography to gain an understanding of the general principles of urbanization and master the terminology specific to the study of this phenomenon.[1] Geographers' specialized vocabulary is generally applicable only to the contemporary world. This is true of the concept of "urban," which is defined first and foremost as opposed to "rural": a settlement where inhabitants generally earn their living through occupations that are not related to agriculture, but primarily to commerce and industry.[2] This differentiation between urban and rural areas, based essentially on livelihood, is further refined by the notion of lifestyle and by criteria of density and territory. This means that city-dwellers do not live as countryfolk do and that a city or town is defined only in terms of its population and land area. These two elements, population and area, are the essential factors for certain geographers, who view the town as "an urban settlement generally with a population of not less than about three thousand persons, below which in England, it is usually termed a 'village'. In the United States, when a village or town exceeds five thousand population, it usually becomes a city."[3]

In modern urban dialectics, a further notion is frequently introduced: urban function. The function is the purpose of the city's or town's existence: it is first and foremost the activities of the city as an organ, performing a function as a whole, that is, its outward-looking activities.[4] The essential element of this definition is the idea that the city looks outward. Beyond its physical limits, a city's function defines its primary "occupation" as an entity. For instance, today Ottawa is perceived primarily as the national capital, while Montréal is considered a financial and economic centre.

Yet the city also exists for its own sake. In fact, the activities that take place within it, such as residential construction and consumption, are not externally focussed functions. Rather, they transmit an image of the city and are linked to its role.

Five categories of function are generally identified (military, commercial, religious and cultural, administrative and political, and industrial), and each can correspond to a particular type of city or town. However, there is no reason why more than one of these functions cannot be carried out by a given city. This was true of Québec, which had most of the functions mentioned above.

While the notion of function can be used as an analytical tool in studying Québec in the 17th century, the same cannot be said of the modern concept of the city, which cannot be applied to that era. Current criteria for defining a city or town (area, population, etc.) are virtually inoperative, which is why it is necessary to trace the evolution of the urban phenomenon and familiarize ourselves with the connotation of the word *ville* in the 17th century.

The Legal Evolution of the Concept of *Ville* in France

In order to understand fully what was meant by *ville* in France during the *ancien régime*, we must go back to the Middle Ages, since urban emancipation superseded seigneurial control and administration. From a legal standpoint from the Middle Ages onwards, urban France can be divided into three regions: in the north the communes were predominant; the south was home to the *consulats* and *collèges de magistrats*; while the *villes de franchises*, *villes de simple bourgeoisie*, and certain kinds of communes co-existed in the central regions.[5] In tracing the evolution of the concept of *ville* through etymological and legal definitions, we will examine only the communes and *villes de franchises*, since they arose in the area of France that most strongly influenced the colonization of New France.

French communes were first created in the 11th century to combat banditry and the exactions of feudal lords, who frequently abused justice and imposed arbitrary taxation. From Poitou to Picardy the communes survived until the French Revolution.

The commune did not, a priori, constitute a form of autonomous municipal government and did not necessarily abolish serfdom as it existed in the Middle Ages. The commune was originally a confederacy in which admission and expulsion were regulated and where the inhabitants or *bourgeois* of a town pledged allegiance to one another in order to ensure peace and security in the community. This confederacy usually took shape with the consent of the lords and was underwritten by the *bourgeois*. It did not always entail the drafting of a charter setting out political prerogatives and the administrative organization of the commune. The bestowing of a commune was often an opportunity to confirm ancestral customs or to grant new freedoms to its inhabitants. Among these privileges, the most common were those of administering justice, levying taxes, coining money, and raising a militia.

"Commune" refers exclusively to the permission granted to the inhabitants to work for the common good and to swear a mutual oath. It does not imply the bestowing or tolerance of independence and municipal institutions. Although not prerequisite to their foundation, many communes did have charters that set out their privileges.

The *serment commun* (common pledge) differentiated communes from free cities or *villes de simple bourgeoisie*, which required an inhabitant to reside there a year and a day and own real property in order to be considered a *bourgeois*. The free city could be defined as one with privileges such as tax advantages, reduction or abolition of seigneurial taxation, exemption from forced labour, etc., guaranteed by a charter and with no common pledge. This city was always administered by a *prévôt* (provost) who rendered justice and managed its finances. Such authority was extremely infrequent in the case of communes.

Between the 11th and 13th centuries, communes played a critical role in the fight for municipal freedoms in France. According to French historian Charles Petit-Dutaillis, the communal movement was the catalyst that drove the burghers of free cities to demand greater political autonomy. Free cities and communes evolved in similar ways.

The original notion of the commune began to shift, particularly in the 13th and 14th centuries. In the 13th century it was perceived as a vassal by kings and lords, who called on the communes to defend their lands. In the late 13th century and early 14th century the legal definition of the commune started to change. Ignoring the original confederation, modern legal experts now consider the existence of a charter and the bestowing of privileges to be the essential characteristics of a commune. Among these privileges, the enjoyment of municipal freedoms was a predominant factor; no commune could be said to exist without a municipal body and a mayor. These changes in the perception of the commune, symbolized by external signs such as the city seal, the charter chest, and the belfry, allow comparison with the *ville de franchises*. By the 13th century there was essentially no difference between *villes de franchises* and communes. From the reign of Louis XI onwards (late 15th century), the only consistent notion was the *ville à échevinage* (aldermanic city).

In the 13th and 14th centuries, municipal authority passed to a *bourgeois* oligarchy that came to dominate the judicial system. What with their exactions and the upheavals of the Hundred Years' War, cities ran heavily into debt, which is why the Crown's attitude toward them began to change. As early as the reigns of Louis XI and Henri IV, certain towns, such as Poitiers, saw their privileges curtailed. In the 16th century, urban centres began to come under state control. In June 1555 an edict created the office of *surintendant de l'administration des deniers des villes* (city coffers) in order to control mayors, aldermen, and municipal administrations. Moreover, as a result of the complexity of laws and procedure, and given the increasing numbers of disputes, legal experts began to take control of municipal offices.

In 1635 Louis XIII directly attacked urban administrations with an edict creating the offices of *procureur du roi* (king's attorney) and *greffier* (city clerk). By so doing he sought to keep closer watch on aldermen and to preclude any possibility of embezzlement. The king also wanted to change electoral practices and reduce the ranks of aldermen. Under Louis XIV, as a result of his minister Colbert's actions, upheavals in city administrations became even more profound.

In his efforts to expand commerce, Colbert relied on the cities and towns to revitalize French industry and develop trade outside the kingdom; however, early in his administration he was confronted with the cities' financial ruin, resulting from poor money management by municipal authorities and unrestrained borrowing, wars, and troop billeting. In 1683, in an effort to remedy these problems and to eliminate municipal debt, Colbert issued an edict giving control of municipal finances to the intendants. He also reduced cities' judicial powers, created presidials, and enacted many administrative trusteeships. Since they were set over mayors and aldermen, intendants became the actual municipal administrators. Four times a year they had to examine city revenues and set budgets. Without their authorization, cities could not borrow, sell, or prosecute.[6]

There were early signs of the innovations that would become entrenched after 1690: purchasable municipal office was established in 1692, and the office of *lieutenant de police* was created in all cities and towns under royal jurisdiction in 1699. These changes reflected the transformation of the legal concept of *ville* in the 17th century. Communes, *villes de privilèges*, *villes de franchises*, and others came to be regarded as being at the service of the state and of the communities that composed it.[7]

The French *Ville* in the 17th Century

The concept of *ville* in France also evolved from society's changing perception of urban reality. In 17th-century France this reality was one of urbanization dominated by medium-sized towns. Apart from the three major cities of Paris, Rouen, and Lyon, as well as about 15 other large towns (Toulouse, Orléans, Bordeaux, etc.), most French *villes* were just small local or regional capitals. With close links to rural districts and active in agriculture and crafts, these market towns and county towns constituted the strong thread of the French urban fabric.[8]

Outside the legal framework, it is difficult to say how the French city or town was perceived by the people of the 17th century. Even French dictionaries of the time, such as that of Antoine Furetière, show that the definition of *ville* remained vague and that the legal aspect was overlooked:

> *A place inhabited by a considerable Number of people, ordinarily enclosed by walls; assembly of many houses arranged in streets & sharing a common enclosure, generally walls & trenches. It is difficult to provide a good definition of the word, since usage has still kept the words Bourg or village for places that Are actually villes. For example, The Hague in Holland, which has everything to make a ville except a defensive wall, is not yet able to call itself a ville.*[9]

A first observation is that in the 17th century, demographic strength — the number of inhabitants — did not a city make. The essential element that confirmed the existence of a city was its *enceinte*, its defensive walls, a symbol of the primacy of military principles over legal notions of a city.[10] For that reason, concentrations of a few hundred inhabitants held the title and privileges of cities if they had, or at one time had had, a system of fortifications.[11]

Walls both protected and bounded the city. Erected to afford security to the inhabitants and to safeguard territorial integrity, they hemmed in the city's expansion and, through their gates, controlled entrance and egress. But they also delineated economic and social divisions, since the most noisome trades and industries were relegated to outlying districts.[12] The walls also marked the city's legal limits, outlining the physical area within which its many privileges and its jurisdiction were exercised.

Ramparts profoundly affected a city's physical aspect, primarily because of their imposing presence and also because of the land area they occupied. In addition, they influenced the inhabitable urban space. By blocking city expansion, they brought about crowding and encouraged multi-storey construction. Fortifications also influenced city layout by requiring wide military roads for manoeuvres and other defence needs, which affected street grid patterns as well as lot divisions.

The 17th-century city was not solely defined by the presence of defensive walls or fortifications. Privileges, the most important of which was the endowment of a municipal administration, continued to characterize the city. The city exercised certain rights over civil and criminal law, either in conjunction or in conflict with seigneurial or royal jurisdictions. It also retained military powers aimed at preserving fortifications and recruiting militia. All cities and towns enjoyed financial powers: each administered a budget and levied taxes, owned land and buildings, recruited municipal employees, maintained roads, provided sanitation, and cared for the poor. The most flourishing had a college or university.

Cities of the *ancien régime* were also distinguished by their physical aspect. Except in the case of newer cities, fortress-cities, or cities expanded and renovated by military engineers, it would be hard to detect any set plan. Deeply marked by the Middle Ages, they almost invariably had a *cité*, the original fortified nucleus from which they developed and which included the church, the convent or monastery, the castle, and the older, wealthier homes. Added to these were the public square and market that housed merchants and shopkeepers.

These two basic cells of the urban fabric were augmented by a complex network of streets, neighbourhoods, and parishes whose limits often overlapped. In addition to the crossroads, squares, and cemeteries, there were many areas not built up. Even within a city's walls, one frequently encountered meadows, vineyards, decorative or vegetable gardens, and sometimes even fields in cities that had common herds. Religious communities also occupied large tracts of land, and the many convents and monasteries that were established in cities and towns after the Counter Reformation of the 16th century gave them decidedly ecclesiastical airs.

Along their main access roads or near their gates, most cities and towns developed *faubourgs*. These urban extensions showed where the jurisdiction of the city and that of its immediate *banlieue* ended. The *banlieue* was an area extending about one *lieue* from a city and was subject to the *ban*, the proclamations affecting the city. Beyond this point began the true countryside, "the economic, seigneurial, financial and mental fiefdom of the town," for the city provided the countryside with commodities, shops, and entertainment, and imposed on it its weights and measures, its legal authority, its moneylenders, and its institutions.[13]

The 17th-century city was a reflection of its society, a place where inhabitants identified and ordered themselves into groups (orders, guilds, corporations, etc.), leading to social stratification and spatial segregation. There were neighbourhoods and streets full of tanners, cobblers, and butchers, and a clear demarcation existed between poor neighbourhoods and affluent ones. The *bourgeoisie de statut* existed only in cities and towns. This group, the wealthiest of the middle class, formed true oligarchies, imposing their will on small property owners and the ordinary people, and dominating the urban proletariat, a mix of largely illiterate tenants, in debt and without trades, who constituted the mass of a city's population.[14]

Québec
A French Town in North America?

"Wherever it may be, a *ville* is a *ville*." This apparent redundancy, borrowed from Fernand Braudel, certainly expresses Québec's situation on the North American continent. It was a new town, created quite deliberately at a time when the concept of *ville* in France and the monarchy's attitude towards cities were undergoing change. Although it started out as a company town, Québec was to become a royal town, particularly after 1674.

When Champlain built the Lower Town Habitation in 1608, he founded a trading post there and his choice of Québec was dictated by trading considerations. His decision to establish it there was undoubtedly based on its potential as a centre of supply (given its resources in agriculture, drinking water, and lumber, and its natural harbour) for newcomers and its potential for control of the fur trade. Of course, the promontory's defensive characteristics had not escaped him, but only in 1620 did he build a fort in Upper Town. In 1617 and 1618 Champlain proposed establishing a town, Ludovica, "almost as big as Sainct-Denis," not on the site of the trading post, but on the banks of the Saint-Charles River. However, his plan never came to fruition.[15]

Québec remained an outpost until well into the 1650s. Indeed, the town was known as a *habitation*, which, according to Furetière, meant a small colony, a settlement in a deserted and uninhabited place. Interestingly, the examples he gave were taken exclusively from New France: "the people of Québec have established *habitations* in Montréal, at trois rivières, and among the Yroquois."[16]

Under Governor Montmagny, Québec received a new title: that of town. According to historian Lucien Campeau, the Compagnie des Cents-Associés decided to establish the town on Cap-aux-Diamants and the riverbank below in January 1636.[17] The town plan was certainly drawn up before August of that year: in the *Relation de 1636* Père Lejeune reported: "Monsieur de Montmagny our Governor has drawn up the plan, as I have said, of a fort to be built according to regulations.... The building alignments of a town have been laid out so that everything to be built henceforth shall be in good order."[18] Even as early as 1637, there was mention of "the site designated for the building of the town of Quebek."[19]

Soon after his arrival, Montmagny went ahead with a physical reorganization of urban space. At the expense of the religious communities and the Couillard family, he took back part of the land in Upper Town and thus successfully fought the geographic division, caused by their ownership of vast tracts of land, that threatened to paralyse the town's future development.[20] The governor was then better able to plan the town's organization. In so doing, he referred to the principles of military and urban planning then in vogue in France where, since the Renaissance and following the Italians' example, French engineers and theoreticians had relied primarily on two types of town plans, radial and chequerboard or grid.

Looking at the way Upper Town is depicted on the 1660 and 1664 plans drawn by the engineer Jean Bourdon (Figs. 1 and 2), one is struck by the apparent disorder; however, upon closer examination a concern for orchestration and symmetry characteristic of a radio-concentric plan, something like a spider web, is evident. Mont-Carmel, Saint-Louis, and Sainte-Anne streets, which converge on the château, fan out; the cross streets, des Jardins and du Trésor, tend to form concentric circles. Because of the topography and existing concessions, the overall plan cannot be mistaken for a radio-concentric plan; it is more an adaptation of a radial plan. In Lower Town we see a different style: an irregular chequerboard with streets crossing at right angles to form squares and rectangles. This grid came about not only because the town planners wanted it so; it was also dictated by the layout of the land and the narrowness of the riverbank at the promontory.[21]

Thus was Québec founded and even given the title of town without a common oath being taken by the *bourgeois* or any particular privileges and exemptions being granted to its inhabitants. Legally speaking, apart from the fiefs of Sault-au-Matelot and that of Notre-Dame *fabrique* (parish council), the town was a *censive*; that is, lots that could not be sub-conceded were granted for a token payment to the *procureur fiscal* acting for the Compagnie des Cents-Associés, which was to be replaced by the Compagnie des Indes Occidentales in 1664.

Theoretically, until the abolition of the Compagnie des Indes Occidentales in 1674, Québec was a company town. These companies appointed or presented to the king the governors and officers of justice, maintained the garrison, defrayed administrative costs, and owned the land on which the town was established. When the monarchy took back control of New France in 1663, Québec became a royal town and its importance within the colony grew. The king appointed a governor, created the office of intendant, and established a court *de justice souveraine* in the town. He also forced officeholders and town notaries to obtain royal commissions and reserved the right to appoint them. Almost every aspect of town administration was to be controlled by royal officials.

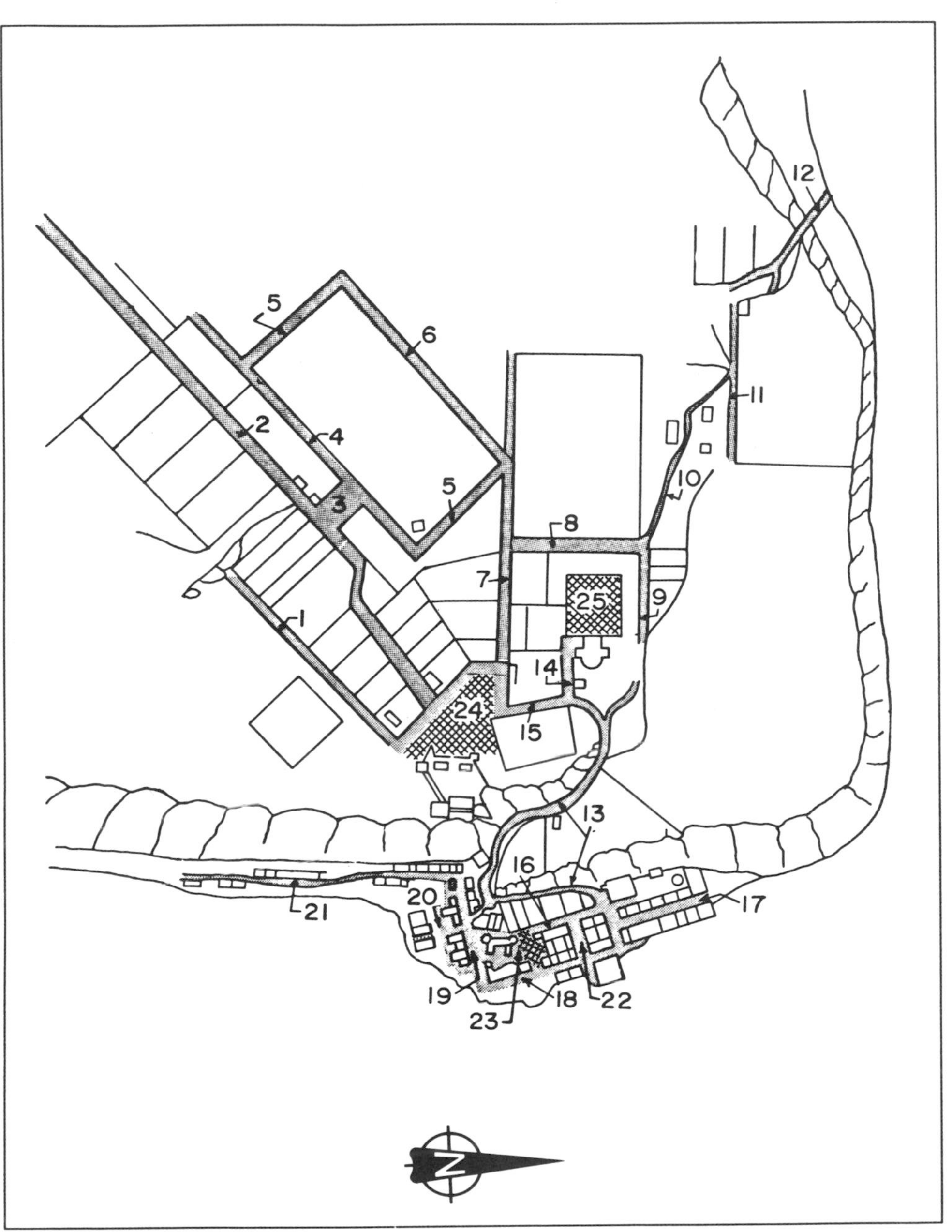
1
2
3
4
5
6
5
7
8
9
10
11
12
13
14
15
16
17
18
19
20
21
22
23
24
25
N

1 Québec streets in 1660

This drawing, based on Jean Bourdon's, clearly shows that Upper Town was built on a radial plan, while Lower Town was laid out in a grid, as is demonstrated by streets' right-angled intersections and the presence of irregular rectangles. In addition to the vacant lot in front of the château (24), there were two public squares: one adjoining the cathedral (25) and one bordering Notre-Dame and Saint-Pierre (23). I have attempted to identify the streets by their modern names despite changes in location and orientation, and have added a few of the names used in the 17th century (*see* legend). Some of the streets Bourdon showed no longer exist or are difficult to locate (Nos. 5 and 6), and the same is true of the many paths and lanes.

Drawing by François Pellerin

Streets in Upper Town

1 - Mont-Carmel (road to Mont-Carmel)
2 - Saint-Louis (street from the fort to the Grande Allée)
3 - Du Parloir (not identified as a street)
4 - Des Ursulines (including Donnacona)
5 - No longer exists; Bourdon did not identify the road running along the northwest of the Ursulines' estate as a street
6 - No modern equivalent
7 - Sainte-Anne and Cook (street leading to the Jesuits' estate)
8 - Des Jardins (street from the Jesuits' estate to the Ursulines')
9 - Garneau?
10 - De la Fabrique (road from the church to the hospital)
11 - Charlevoix?
12 - Côte du Palais (road leading down from the hospital to the riverbank)
13 - Côte de la Montagne (street leading from Lower Town to Upper Town)
14 - Buade (identified as a road on Bourdon's plan)
15 - Du Fort (road)

Streets in Lower Town

13 - Côte de la Montagne
16 - Notre-Dame (northern extension closed around 1655)
17 - Du Sault-au-Matelot (street leading to the Sault-au-Matelot)
18 - Saint-Pierre (or d'Argenson)
19 - Sous-le-Fort
20 - No longer exists (street leading to the Cul-de-Sac)
21 - Petit Champlain (street leading to the Champlain Fountain)
22 - Du Porche (rue Neuve)

Public Squares

23 - Place Royale
24 - Place d'Armes
25 - Square in front of Notre-Dame church

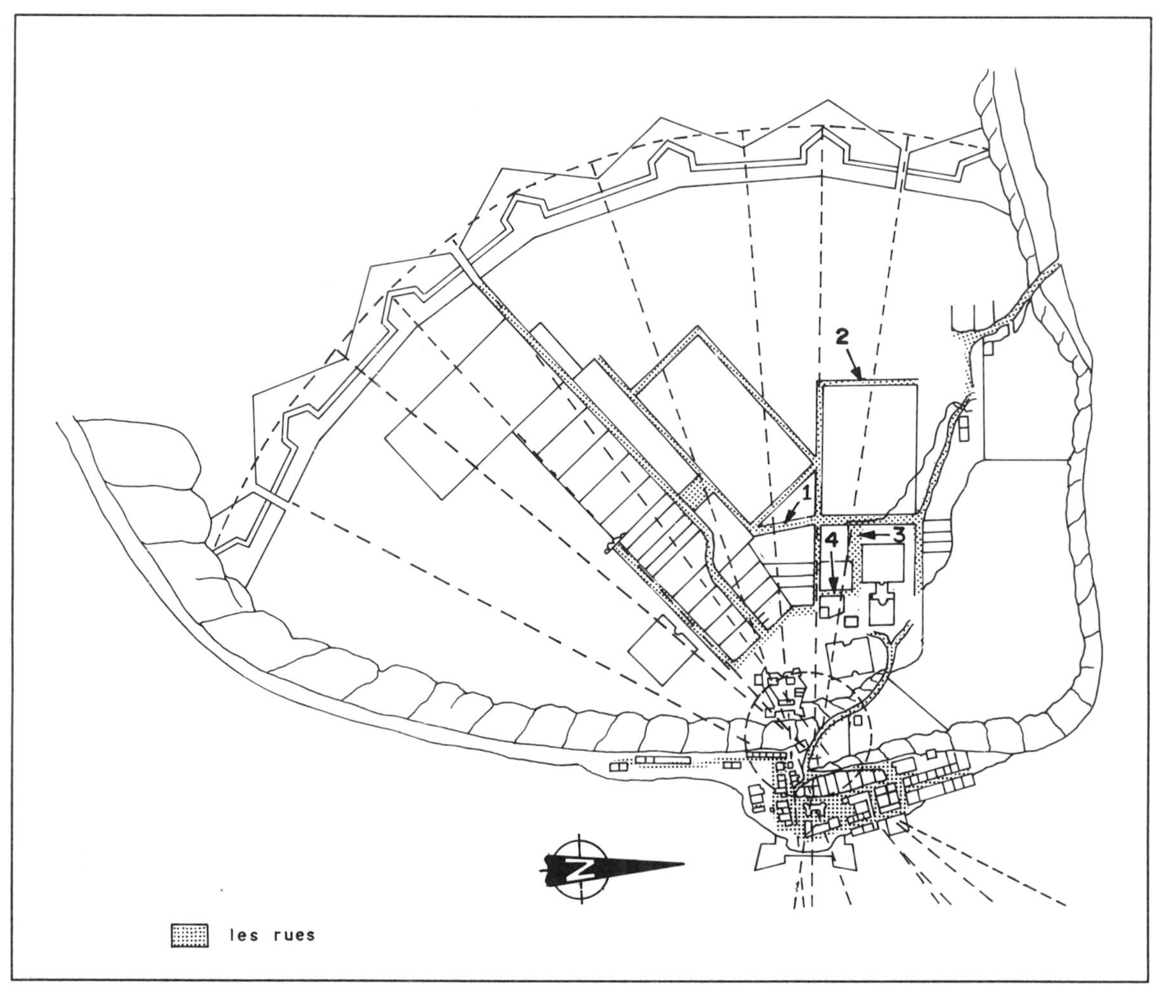
2
1
3
4
N
les rues

2 Québec in 1664: radial and grid plans

Except for the fortifications there are a few differences between this plan and Figure 1: (1) rue des Jardins has been extended; (2) a street that may be rue Saint-Stanislas has appeared; (3) Buade has been identified as a street and meets des Jardins; and (4) rue du Trésor is indicated.

Drawing by F. Pellerin

The lands of the Québec *censive* were directly incorporated into the king's domain after the company system was abolished. Indeed, even before the abolition of the Compagnie des Indes Occidentales, Louis XIV clearly set out his claim to the territory of New France and particularly its capital. As early as 1672 his sense of possession was evident in documents where the king, in referring to the town, used such expressions as "*my* town of Québec" or "*our* town of Québec," reminiscent of the classic designation of the kingdom's premier city as "our good city and viscountcy of Paris."[22] This idea reaffirmed Québec's vassalage rather than doing away with it.

With the arrival of Frontenac, who landed in Québec in 1672 with his own stock of knowledge and ideas about urban affairs, intentional affinities with French cities and towns grew. His primary concern was administering the town.

> *We have Determined that one of the first things to be attended to upon our arrival in this government, after having apprised ourselves of all necessary Information regarding the State of these regions, is the establishment of some kind of administration, Beginning with the town of Quebec, which is the foremost town of the country, And attempt to make it worthy of the prominence It will Without doubt some day enjoy as Capital of a very great Empire.*[23]

To do this he decided to establish an aldermanic system, a market, and municipal archives: he also wanted to obtain revenue for the town and create municipal offices.[24] Frontenac therefore saw the town as inheriting franchises and privileges. But reaction was swift and Colbert made it clear to the governor that it would be dangerous to introduce such doctrines, which ran completely counter to the centralization Louis XIV advocated.

At the conceptual level, there was not a perfect match between the kind of colonial town that Québec was and towns or cities in France; however, certain traits were common to both. Québec was first and foremost a Catholic capital in a Catholic colony, but it was also a town of refuge (with its poor), a military town (with its fort, its garrison, its own governor, and its militia), and a trading town (with its public squares, its markets, and the privileges afforded its own citizens but denied to nonresidents).[25] Too, the town was increasingly becoming a place of retirement; people were retiring there to live a quieter, easier life than was possible in the country.[26]

Québec was nevertheless similar to French towns and cities in terms of its physical characteristics. Despite Montmagny's initial plan, its streets still evoked the layout of medieval towns, and its many open spaces gave it a rustic atmosphere (Figs. 3 and 4). In Upper Town a multiplicity of convents, monasteries, and churches (the seminary, the buildings housing the Jesuit, Ursuline, and Récollet orders, the Hôtel-Dieu, and the cathedral) pervaded the urban landscape, while in Lower Town, where a number of merchants had set up shop around the Place Royale, a certain amount of crowding could already be seen.

There was one major difference. Québec had no defensive walls nor fortifications other than the Upper Town fort, the château battery, and another battery in Lower Town. And yet the military element, as seen in the presence of ramparts, was certainly not foreign to the concept of *ville* applied to Québec. In fact, throughout the period beginning with Montmagny's initial plan in 1636 and until the actual completion of a defensive wall by Major Provost in 1690, the idea of fortifying Québec was ever present and plans to do so abounded (Figs. 5 and 6).

In 1663 Governor Davaugour proposed that the town be enclosed by a rampart (Fig. 7). The following year, an engineer named Bourdon drew plans for proper fortifications (Fig. 8). One by one, several administrators laid plans to fortify the town: Minister Colbert in 1667, Intendants Talon in 1669 and Demeulle in 1683, Governors Frontenac in 1672 and Denonville in 1689, and the engineer Villeneuve in 1688 and 1689. The absence of true fortifications at Québec can be attributed to special factors, such as the war with Holland that broke out in 1672, and insufficient funds. Also, until 1690 the colony's main enemy was the Iroquois, who did not pose enough of a threat to justify erecting conventional fortifications at Québec. Town authorities therefore contented themselves with only temporary and expeditious measures: additional work at Fort Saint-Louis, building redoubts in Upper Town, and constructing batteries.[27]

The absence of fortifications did pose some problems as far as the town boundaries were concerned. The latter had been set by Montmagny as early as 1636. In their respective plans, though, Governor Davaugour and the engineer Bourdon also wanted to set town boundaries, just as Frontenac did in 1672, when he declared that he would like the king to rule on the *enceinte* to be given to the town. And yet in 1655 mention is made of a line of circumvallation for Québec, and later, in 1667, one of Bishop Laval's pastoral letters refers to the town's *enceinte*.[28] These ambiguities probably resulted from the fact that no continuous rampart marked the town's limit. Over the years the original boundaries had likely become blurred, which would explain why repeated attempts were made to reset them.

This lack did create some difficulties with respect to the actual area considered to be part of Québec's urban jurisdiction. It also had some impact on the concept of *ville*. Ramparts were an important aspect of the

A
B
D
E
H
K
L
M
N
O
P
R
S
T
V
Y
Z
17

3 & 4 "L'Entrée d
bec dans le Canada,
This beautiful drawi
Brulé to Cap Rouge.
d'Orléans, and a sect
spective and obvious
town of Québec, its r
from the seigneurie d
Sainte-Foy (13), the F
(16) are too close to
Louis (x), the Upper
college (7), the Ursu
(5) can be seen. The
character: streets give
in town, and some lots
Bibliothèque Nationale, Fr

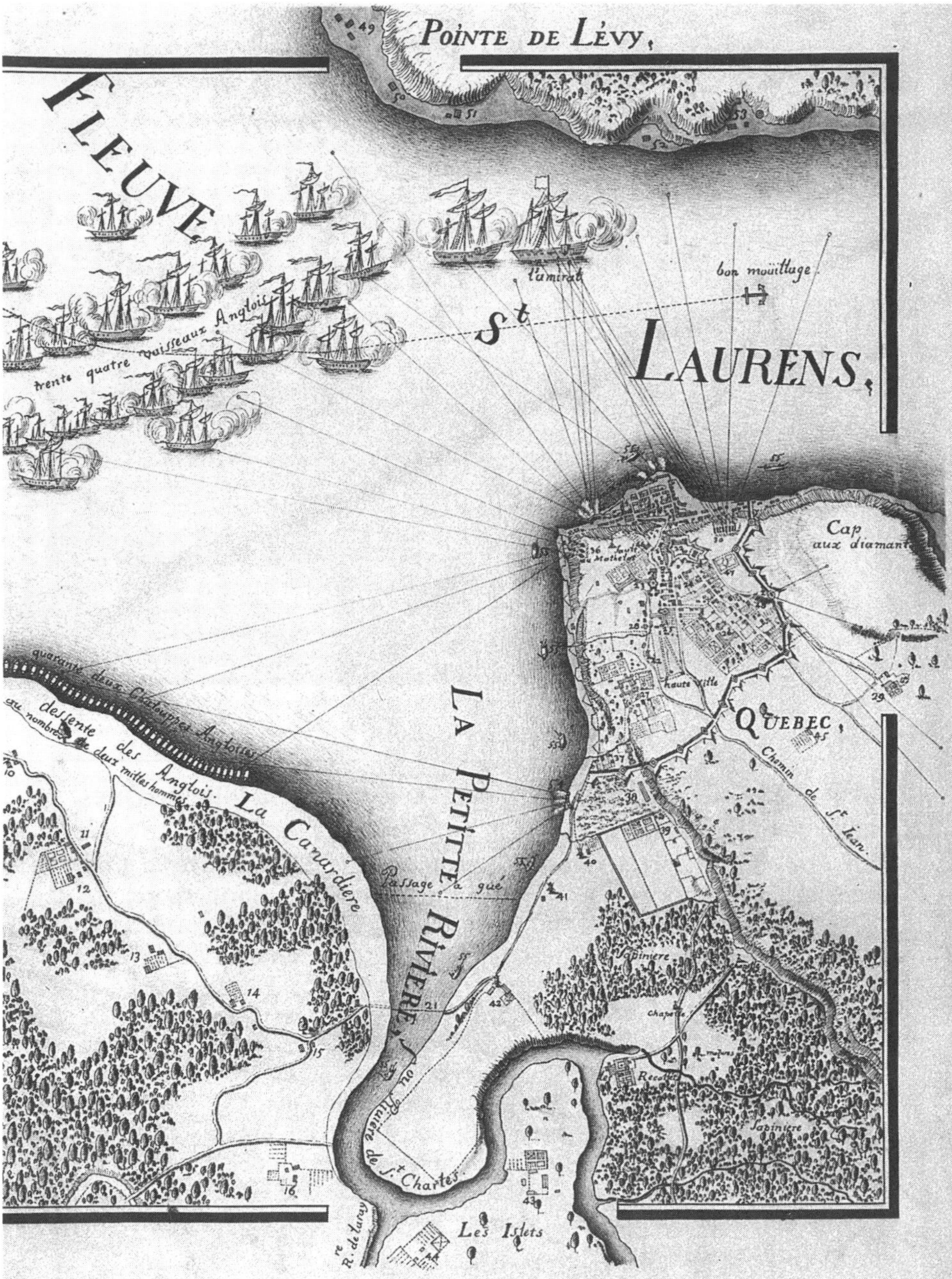

Pointe de Lévy

Fleuve St Laurens

trente quatre vaisseaux Anglois

l'amiral

bon mouillage

Cap aux diamant

haute ville

Quebec

Chemin de St Jean

quarante deux Chaloupes Angloises

dessente des Anglois au nombre de deux milles hommes

La Canardiere

La Petitte Riviere ou Riviere de St Charles

Passage a gué

Sapiniere

Chapelle

Recol

Sapiniere

Les Islets

R. de Lary

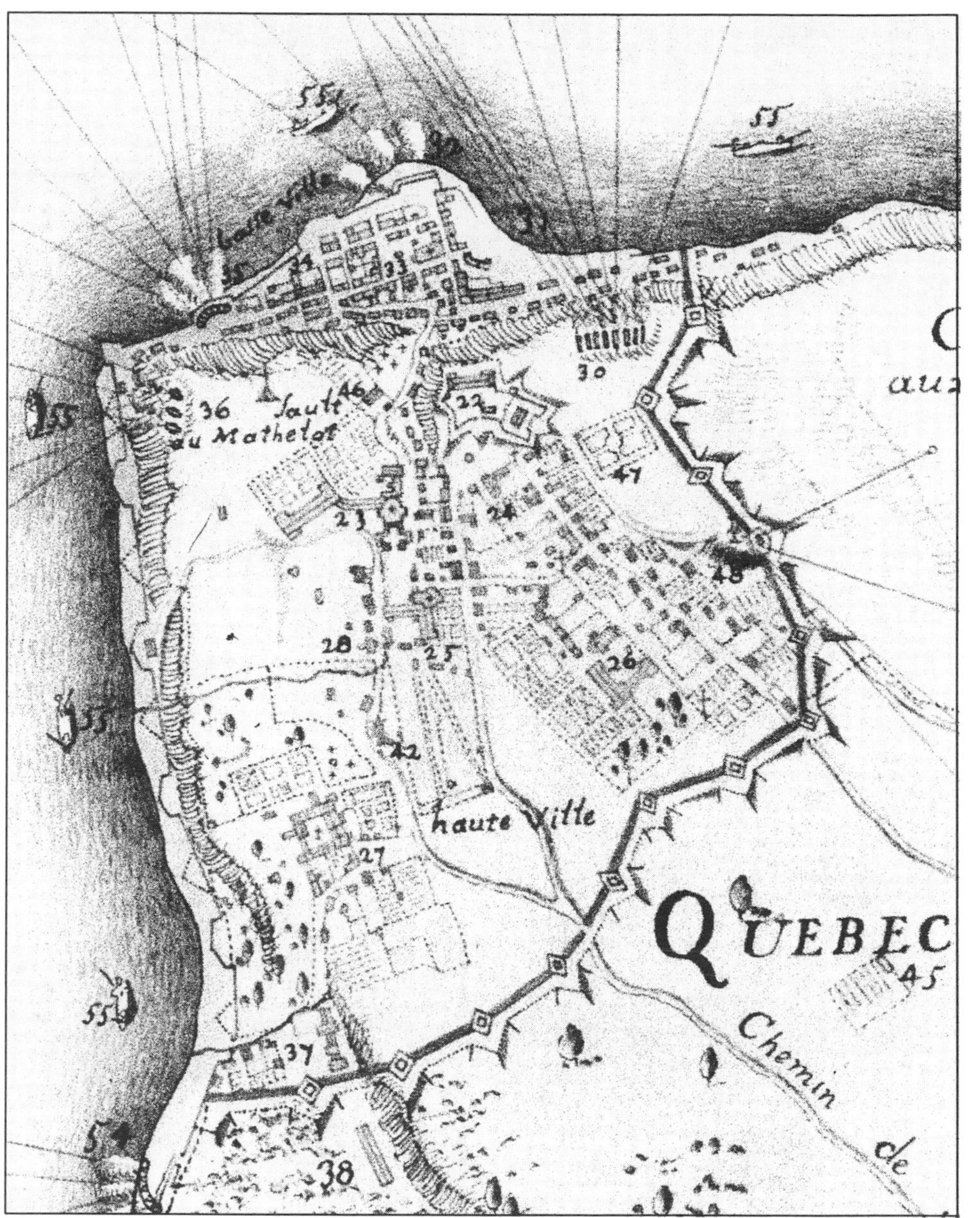

5 & 6 "Plan de Québec en la Nouvelle France, Assiégé par les Anglois, le 16 octobre 1690," Robert de Villeneuve

This plan of Phips' siege of the town shows the fortifications built by Major Provost. The detail gives an even better view of the fortifications: the wall surrounding Upper Town and the batteries near Fort Saint-Louis and in Lower Town.

Archives Nationales, France; copy on file, National Archives of Canada, C-15835

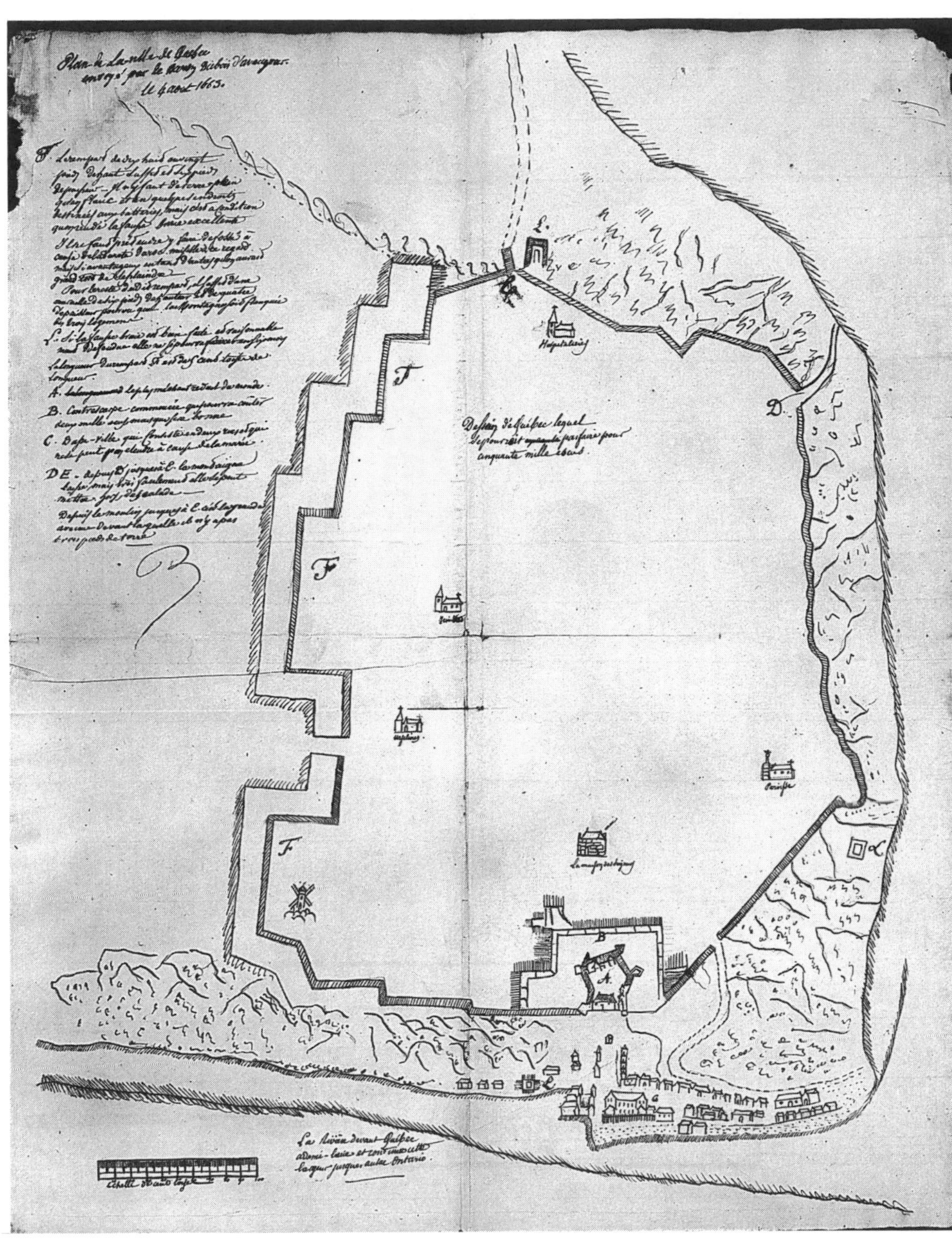

7 "Plan de La ville de Quebec envoyé par le Baron Dubois d'avaugour le 4 aout 1663"

This illustrates a plan for fortifying Québec's western flank. It also shows the major buildings in Upper Town, the Château Saint-Louis, and the houses of Lower Town. The plan does not follow the cardinal points: the fortifications should appear in the west (toward the top of the plan) and not in the south (or left) as they have been drawn.

The Newberry Library, Edward E. Ayer Collection, Chicago

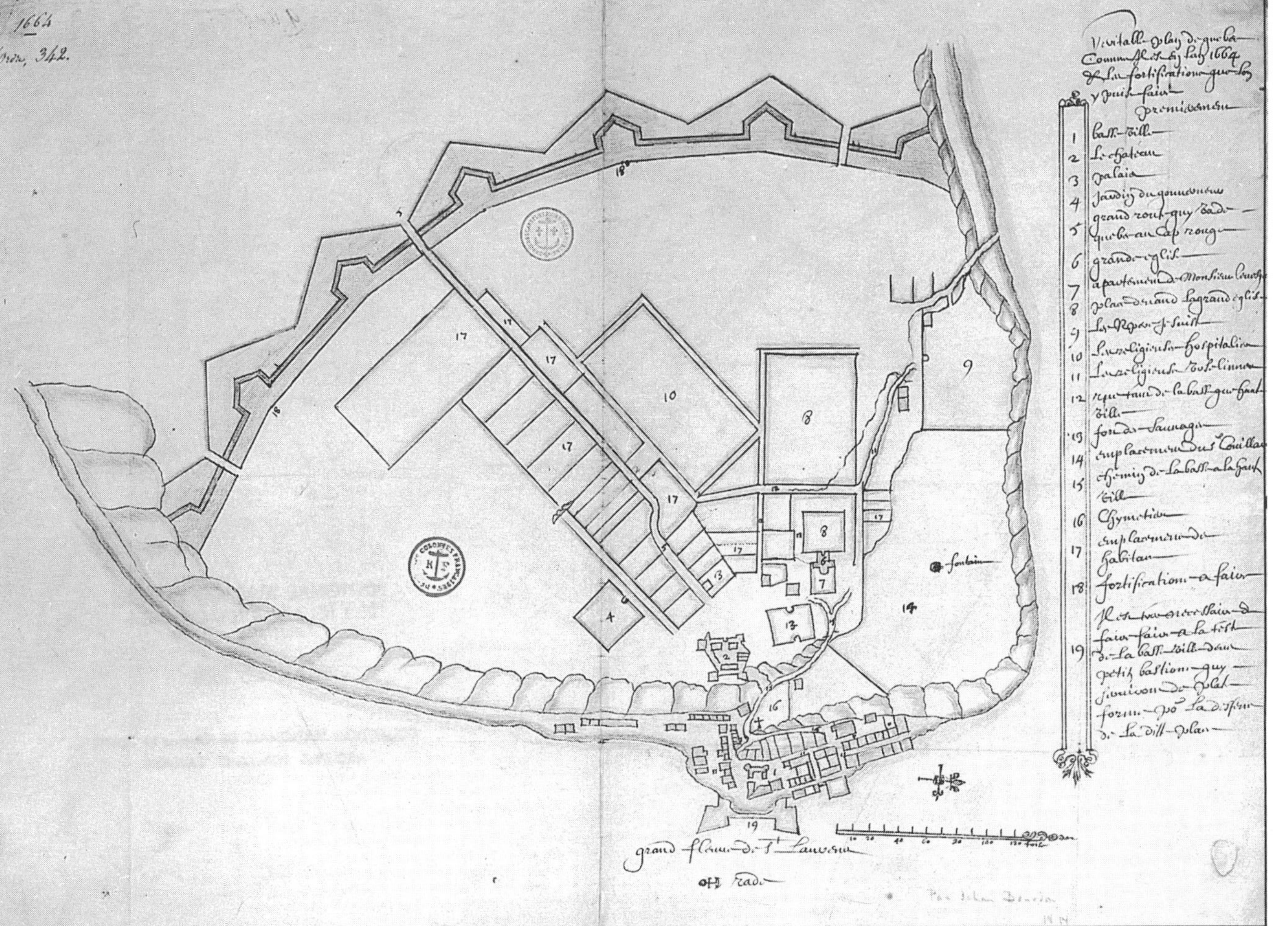
1664
grand fleuve de St Laurent

8 "Veritable plan de quebec Comme Il est En lan 1664 & les fortifications que lon y puise [*sic*] faire," Jean Bourdon

This plan shows the major concessions in Québec in 1664. A few errors appear in the legend: the number 8 is assigned both to the square in front of the church and to the Jesuits' land; 10 in fact corresponds to the Ursulines' land, 9 to the Hospitalières', and 11 to the streets of Lower Town. In this plan Bourdon proposed a defensive wall for Upper Town and two bastions in Lower Town.

Archives Nationales, France; copy on file, National Archives of Canada, C-21758

French concept of a town, but in Québec this particular concept underwent a slight change, or at least, was applied differently: Québec was given the title of town even though it did not have defensive walls.

Another similarity with French towns that could be seen in Québec was a certain spatial segregation (butchers, masons, and merchants in Lower Town; officials in Upper Town), although it was not as apparent as that prevailing in France. Indeed, colonial society was less hierarchical than that of France; the urban oligarchy hoping to dominate the town was not yet on a solid footing in a colony where social mobility did not encounter as rigid a socio-economic order as existed in the parent country. Finally, despite its small population (547 inhabitants in 1666; 1407 in 1688), Québec, like other urban centres overseas, dominated its surrounding countryside, whence it tapped part of its manpower and whose products as well as raw materials it consumed. Even though the town was still too new to have officially recognized *faubourgs*, it did have its own *banlieue*, and its jurisdiction in fact extended westward by a *lieue* and a half.

* * *

Québec was neither a commune nor a free town. Attempts by Frontenac, in particular, to make it resemble such towns were not successful. The fact is that Québec came into being in a particular context, at a time when kings, especially Louis XIV, were trying to take control of municipal administration and reduce the privileges French cities and towns enjoyed. That is probably why the aldermanic system was not particularly successful in the capital during the 17th century.[29]

The concept of *ville* was modified and adapted at Québec. Before 1690, at least, it lacked ramparts, certainly one of the essential features of a town as classically defined. In spite of that, Québec was indeed a town, and certain comparisons could be made with urban settlements in France. But, more importantly, it was the capital of the colony, and its situation does, albeit to a lesser degree, bring to mind Roland Mousnier's comment about Paris:

> *a town that is to the State as the head is to the body, a town that is, in principle, the seat of consciousness, thought, and political reason; the place where those organizations that regulate all the activities of the inhabitants of the State guarantee them justice and security, and convey to them orders, decisions, and advice to that end; indeed, a town that is the seat of government, the law and the central administration, and which sets an example for the State as a whole.*[30]

Chapter II
THE ADMINISTRATION OF THE TOWN OF QUÉBEC

Québec and its history cannot be understood without some knowledge of how and by whom it was administered. The town evolved in a world with a complex and strongly hierarchical administration where, paradoxically, identical powers and similar responsibilities rested with various officials and different organizations.

Between 1660 and 1690 Québec, like the colony, experienced three forms of administration. The final years of the monopoly of the Compagnie des Cents-Associés lasted until 1663, followed by the monopoly of the Compagnie des Indes Occidentales from 1664 to 1674. During the latter period the Crown became increasingly involved in the government of the colony and constituted an all-pervading presence after the removal of the Compagnie des Indes Occidentales.

The colony's administrative system exercised a particular influence in Québec, probably because it was the capital of New France. The town's administration lay mainly with the principal officers of the colony (governors, intendants, and *grand voyers* [overseers of roads]) and certain judicial bodies, the most important of which was the Conseil Souverain. However, the town itself did have some institutions and administrators of its own: a *prévôté* (provostship), a syndic, and for a certain time, a mayor and aldermen.

The Colonial Administration and the Town Division of Power

The power of the colony's different administrative levels and how their functions evolved will not be detailed since that work has already been done.[1] But in considering how the town was administered, we must look at the division of power. We must also analyse municipal regulations and have a precise idea of the actual roles played by the numerous officials active in town affairs.

France

All power emanated from the king, upon whom it was conferred by divine right, the basic principle underlying the doctrine of absolutism. The monarch attended to the administration of the kingdom through the appointment of ministers at his pleasure.[2]

The Secrétaire d'État à la Marine, known as "ministre" in New France, exercised control over the colony from France: on the king's behalf he sent despatches setting out policy to be followed by the local administration. He decided on promotions, bounties, and any matter his clerks drew to his attention. Such delegation of power enabled the minister, rather than the king, to effectively direct Canada's destiny. The king was not, however, removed from such decisions, since he was kept informed about what was happening in the colony by summaries of extracts the minister prepared for him, and he took this information into account when issuing orders in his *mémoire du Roy*. Nonetheless, the instigator of France's colonial policy was the Secrétaire d'État.[3]

France's activity concerning the town of Québec had three aspects: concessions, bylaws, and what could be described as direct action. In the first case, the king and the minister enacted legislation, attended to distribution of lands, and set policy.

France's control over grants was exercised pursuant to the concept of "corporate domain," whereby all property was held by the king, including fiefs, public sites, fortifications, and the royal *censive*. In New France the first application of this principle is found in decrees on grants, the first of any interest being dated 21 March 1663. Noting that the vastness of landholdings constituted an obstacle to their settlement and clearing, Louis XIV ordered that the holdings be brought under cultivation within six months of the decree's publication. Failure to do so would result in their confiscation and redistribution by the governor, bishop, and intendant. In a second regulation, dated 4 June 1672, modifying the previous one, the king charged Talon to draw up a register of landed property from which half of the land left uncleared since 1662 was to be removed. The intendant was also empowered to distribute the land taken away in this fashion and instructed to ensure that it was exploited within four years. Failure by new titleholders to meet this requirement automatically cancelled their ownership. A further change in 1679 stipulated that a fourth of the land granted before 1665 and left uncultivated would be returned to the royal domain. As of 1680 this decree also provided for the annual withdrawal of one-twentieth of the unimproved land grants.[4] The stand taken by French authorities softened, since instead of being revoked in their entirety, only a quarter of the concessions would be taken back.

In addition to its concern with productive use of land, the French government also looked after the distribution of seigneuries and lots. Thus in 1669 Talon received the power to grant concessions to habitants, subject to royal confirmation. In 1676 Frontenac and Intendant Duchesneau obtained similar rights. The letters patent sent for this purpose stipulated that the concessions had to be made jointly by the governor and the intendant, then confirmed by the king within a year, failing which they would be declared void; they were to be revoked if they were not improved within six years. Lastly, it was recommended that these land grants be distributed one lot after the other, so that new grants would be contiguous to existing ones.[5]

This power was passed on to successive governors and intendants, who were required to send the list of concessions granted to France for confirmation. That procedure guaranteed *donataires* secure enjoyment of their property and sanctioned the clauses in the deeds of gift, particularly with respect to payment of fees and compliance with the conditions attached to land ownership, one of which, as the king decreed, was the obligation to build as soon as possible.

The king's involvement in concessions was not limited to confirmation alone; he by no means renounced his prerogatives in this matter. Firstly, the distribution of fiefs and lots was made in his name. Religious orders obtained letters of amortization from the king and sometimes received deeds of ownership directly from him. The registers of landed property (*papiers terriers*, lists of documents relative to the ownership of a piece of land) were prepared on the king's orders and in accordance with his instructions. In a *mémoire* addressed to Duchesneau in 1679, one learns that the king alone could change the custom to which the land was subject and that the transformation of a fief into *rotures* (concessions of land which could not be sub-conceded, held by *censitaires* from a seigneur) was an exclusive royal power.[6]

This legislation dealt only with the countryside. What of the towns? The presence of fiefs and seigneuries in Québec, and particularly in its immediate vicinity, warranted the application of the different decrees concerning concessions. Lots that were part of the king's *censive* were subject to the same regulations. In this connection I have found only one case illustrating the revocation of a lot in the town of Québec;[7] however, it does demonstrate that decrees on the revocation of concessions applied to urban sites as well, since it was under those decrees that the failure of Simon Denys de la Trinité, the titleholder, to build on his land resulted in its reversion to the Crown.

Clearly Versailles set the policy to be followed on concessions. From 1679 to 1690 it remained constant and reflected France's unchanging concern with improvement. Throughout the period under study a series of directives insisted that lots be distributed one next to the other, and orders were given to create towns and villages, with emphasis on the requirement to build.

French authorities also saw to general administration and the maintenance of law and order. The latter may be described as the regulation of towns, whereas general administration concerned all of New France, relating as it did to the colony's finances, cultivation of land, and commerce. Very active roles were played by the king and the minister. They empowered colonial authorities to pass bylaws and assigned the lieutenant-general of the Prévôté the responsibility of enforcing them in the town of Québec. They also retained veto power; thus, the various regulations had to be submitted to them for approval, as Colbert made clear to Duchesneau in 1679 when he issued instructions requiring the regulations made by the Conseil Souverain to be sent to him every year. On a number of occasions administrators in France did not hesitate to reprimand a governor or the Conseil Souverain for exceeding the limits of their jurisdiction, whereupon Versailles issued the appropriate directives. Intendants were requested to observe the best policed towns in France and to copy their legislation. Since the lack of law enforcement was seen as an obstacle to immigration, France ordered that appropriate measures be taken in the colony.[8]

There is no need to elaborate at length on France's direct involvement in town affairs. The king was present not only through his personal representative, the governor general, but also through public buildings, particularly the Château Saint-Louis and the palace of the intendant. His action was also felt in the physical evolution of the town, for examples, the refusal of the projected expansion of Lower Town submitted by Demeulle in 1683 and the urban development resulting from the location of the intendancy in the Brasserie area. Too, assistance was provided to religious orders and gifts were made for various buildings in the town (the cathedral and the Lower Town chapel).

Certain decisions, such as quartering soldiers in Montréal rather than the capital after 1687,[9] influenced Québec's evolution. It is apparent that France regulated both the life of the capital and that of the colony as a whole through the appointment of officers, the creation of administrative bodies, and the control of commerce and immigration. State direction did nonetheless leave room for a made-in-New-France administration adapted to colonial requirements. This applied both to the colony and to Québec, which had its own administration.

Trading Companies

On 29 April 1627 Richelieu established the Compagnie des Cents-Associés, granting it plenary property, justice, and seigneurial rights to New France. In return for promising to undertake settlement and take charge of administration costs, the company was given a monopoly on the fur trade and, with the exception of cod fishing and whaling, enjoyed priority in all other commerce for 15 years as of 1628. Under the 1627 agreement, on presentation of candidates by the company, the king reserved the right to appoint officers of justice (*officiers de justice souveraine*) and also required thc Cents-Associés to swear him an oath of fealty and homage for New France.[10] The colony was to remain under this company, also known as the Compagnie de la Nouvelle-France, until 1663, although the trade monopoly was turned over in 1645 to the Communauté des Habitants in return for their taking over the administrative expenses of the colony and the settlement obligations.

In theory the functions of the Compagnie des Cents-Associés were as described. In fact, even before 1650, the monarchy involved itself in the company's affairs; powers and responsibilities were shared between the king and the Cents-Associés. As of 27 March 1647 a royal regulation changed the colony administration through the creation of a Conseil de traite, that, in addition to its responsibility for annually appointing officers, was charged with providing statements of account and setting wages and emoluments and "all other matters necessary to the Trade and the good of the said country." In 1648 and 1657, following representations from the habitants and the Cents-Associés, the composition of the Conseil de traite was changed by two decrees, but its functions remained the same.[11]

The duality of power, vested both in the governor and in company officers, was also found in judicial matters. Endowed with a royal commission since Montmagny, the governor was empowered, in the absence of judges, to judge without appeal and in last resort, with the assistance of officers and leading citizens in difficult cases. In 1651 the Cents-Associés set up in Québec a lower seigneurial court, the Sénéschaussée, made up of a lieutenant-general for civil and criminal cases, a *lieutenant particulier*, and a *procureur fiscal* (financial and judicial administrator). However, the governor's prerogatives in matters of justice were not restrained by this tribunal nor by the setting up of the 1647–48 council, which was endowed with judicial powers. Only in 1659, with the decree of 13 May, was a limit imposed on his role. As a result of this regulation, the governor heard only appeals, with the exception of those coming under the Parlement of Paris; even more significant, he was no longer empowered to suspend officers of justice, that right being reserved to the king.[12]

The influence of company management and colonial administration on the town of Québec may seem very slight. Except for the appointment of a syndic in 1647, the town did not have an independent administration that might be described as municipal. There was the Sénéschaussée, but it is not known whether its lieutenant-general, as would later be the case for the lieutenant-general of the Prévôté, was responsible for enforcing law and order in the town. In fact, the general administration of the colony also took in the town, and in addition to the sharing of powers between the company and the monarchy, there was a process of delegation and a hierarchy was established. At the top was the governor, nominated by the company and appointed by the king, followed by a joint creation of the king and the Cents-Associés, the Conseil de traite; in last place, coming under the sole jurisdiction of the company, was the Sénéschaussée.

Even though decisions, such as that of the company to establish the town of Québec in 1636, were made at all levels, the real municipal administrator remained the governor, who held most of the legislative and executive power. As early as 1659 the limitation imposed on his authority to dispense justice gave some indications of the changes that were to occur because of the king's decision to resume control of the colony. On 24 February 1663 the Compagnie des Cents-Associés renounced, on behalf of the king, its possession of New France and all rights conferred upon it under the charter of 1627.[13]

In May 1664 Louis XIV created the Compagnie des Indes Occidentales, granting it ownership of New France and, for 40 years, exclusive rights to trade, except for fisheries. Its powers were basically the same as those of the directors of the Compagnie de la Nouvelle-France: the appointment of governors, clerks, and officers of justice, the nomination of members of the Conseils Souverains, and control of trade.

The administrative organization of the Compagnie des Indes Occidentales was similar to that of the Cents-Associés. There was, however, a new official, the agent general of the company in New France, with a significant role and extensive powers: inspection of all officers and clerks appointed by the company, distribution of merchandise and management of warehouses, rendering of accounts, and distribution of land.[14]

By 9 September 1666 Agent General Le Barroys was making several requests of Lieutenant-General Tracy, Governor Courcelle, and Intendant Talon, asking that the company be granted possession of the country and that it be entitled to appoint officers to the Conseil Souverain and judges wherever necessary. In addition, Le Barroys called for several measures aimed at guaranteeing the company's monopoly of the fur trade. In accordance with his commission, he also demanded to be allowed to sit as a member of the Conseil Souverain and called for the installation of a lieutenant-general for civil and criminal cases in Québec, along with a *procureur fiscal* and a lieutenant-general's *greffier*. Lastly, he proposed that the register of landed properties (*papier terrier*) begun by Talon be continued on behalf of the company and that in future, concessions be granted by the intendant, but in the presence of the *commis général*.[15]

Theoretically, by 1664 full responsibility for the management of New France, both military and civil, had passed to the Compagnie des Indes Occidentales. In fact, by 1665 Louis XIV was undermining the administrative control it was supposed to exercise: he appointed a lieutenant-general, governor, and intendant without asking company directors for nominations. The intendant, for whom no provision at all was made in the 1664 charter, was endowed with almost unlimited powers vying with those of the company: he was authorized to judge without appeal and to deal with matters of law enforcement, and was responsible for financial administration. The king's representatives, particularly Talon, were quick to oppose the company's monopoly: they alone appointed members to the Conseil Souverain;[16] Talon alone distributed land and set fees and rents; he was also the one who obtained freedom of the fur trade and then overall free trade in 1669.[17]

Thus control of the colony was lost to the company, which nonetheless retained an essential right relating to administration of the town: the appointment of subordinate officers of justice. In 1666 a court of first instance, with various officers, was set up for Québec. Louis-Théandre Chartier de Lotbinière received the commission of lieutenant-general with civil and criminal jurisdiction on 1 May 1666, and Le Barroys requested that he also be granted cognizance in matters of law enforcement and navigation. On the same day, Jean-Baptiste Peuvret Demesnu received a commission as *procureur fiscal* of the seigneurie of the town of Québec, thus becoming company receiver responsible for collecting fees and rents. As *procureur* of the lower court of the Prévôté he played an identical role to that of the *procureur général* of the Conseil Souverain. As well as being company receiver, he was also concerned with the company's interests in judicial matters. On 5 May Gilles Rageot was appointed *greffier* of the Prévôté, and in 1667 René Robinau de Bécancour was named *grand voyer*.[18]

The company retained very little of its initial monopoly: the ownership of New France, the Tadoussac trade, the import trade, and the collecting of taxes on merchandise and fur. Far more significant is the fact that colony administration was taken from the company and transferred to the governor, the intendant, and the Conseil Souverain. Therefore it is no surprise to learn that the charter of the Compagnie des Indes Ocidentales was repealed in December 1674, its debt having reach three million *livres*.[19] The colony reverted to the status of a royal possession: henceforth, all officials came under the king and justice was dispensed in his name. The edict abolishing the company also did away with the Prévôté, thc power to hear cases as a court of first instance returning to the Conseil Souverain and the concession of land in Québec coming directly under the king (*censive du roi*).

The trading companies played very minor roles in town management. The direct influence of the Cents-Associés was felt particularly in matters of concessions and the courts of first instance. Their indirect influence extended throughout the colony, since it affected both immigration and control of commerce. However, had the charters been respected, the situation would have been quite different. Québec would have undergone the domination of these companies which, particularly after 1664, would not have given way to royal administrators.

Governors and Intendants

From 1660 to 1690 seven governors were appointed to New France; one of them, Frontenac, held office for two terms (*see* Appendix A). For the most part their commissions were modelled on those of Lieutenant Tracy, who was sent to Canada in 1665.

The governor was the king's representative in New France. He had authority over all other governors and lieutenants-general, over all officers and the Conseils Souverains, as well as all French vessels, both warships and merchant ships. In military matters, including troops, the militia, fortifications, and relations with the Indians, the governor had absolute power. All habitants were under his orders, he could instruct them to take up arms, and he decided on the establishment of garrisons, on war, or on peace. However, he did not have control over moneys allocated for paying troops and for defence work. He played only a minor role in financial administration, his participation being limited to the preparation, with the intendant's assistance, of the colony's annual budget. In religious matters, along with the bishop, he was responsible for the propagation of religion — and was to be particularly careful to prevent Protestants from entering the colony. Missionaries were to enjoy his protection, and with the bishop and intendant he was responsible for assessing tithes and assigning livings. His other duties included stimulating the expansion of commerce and increasing the population and the land under cultivation. As well as being empowered to assemble the people, he also concerned himself with enforcing law and order.[20]

The governor's enforcement powers seem to have been rather theoretical, since Louis XIV made a point of instructing his representatives not to encroach on established tribunals' jurisdictions. This was made clear in a letter to Frontenac in 1676. The king reminded him that although he was the head and the presiding officer of the Conseil Souverain, the administration of justice and policing were to be left to that tribunal. Cases of abuse were to be settled in cooperation with the intendant or, should they fail to reach an agreement, referred to the king.[21]

At the most, the governor retained the right to be consulted. That was also the case for bylaws, as Secretary of State Seignelay noted to Governor La Barre in 1684: general matters of law and order were the Conseil Souverain's prerogative and only in exceptional circumstances were the governor, and the intendant, to deal with them. Nevertheless, this directive did not forbid the governor to draw up bylaws, since these were to be enacted by the Conseil Souverain in his presence and that of the intendant, and it was up to the governor to see to the maintenance of law and order and to the establishment of an administration where there was none.[22]

The intendancy in New France was a late creation, since under the monopoly of the Compagnie de la Nouvelle-France, the governor, the company's agent, and the Conseil de traite seemed to meet the need. Only in 1665 was the colony provided with an intendant, who was succeeded by four other administrators until 1690 (*see* Appendix A).

Jean Talon was the first intendant in New France. His commission empowered him to deal in the areas of justice, administration, and finances. As for his military responsibilities, he was entitled to attend councils of war, hear habitants' and soldiers' complaints, and dispense justice to them. His financial functions included managing the funds set aside for the maintenance of troops and distribution of supplies and munitions as well as for repairing fortifications. A further military duty was the obligation to be aware of musters and reviews because of the payments to be made. In judicial matters the intendant was to be informed of all crimes and offences and was to pass final sentence, with the number of magistrates specified by the ordinances. In the absence of the lieutenant-general and the governor, he chaired the Conseil Souverain, and in civil matters he was empowered to judge alone and without appeal. He was authorized to issue ordinances having the force of law since his mandate as intendant enjoined him to order everything as he might think just and proper in the king's service. The intendant controlled finances as the person responsible for the "management, handling & distribution" of funds directed to the colony.[23]

Talon's commission served as a model for the intendants who followed him in New France. During his second stay in the country, Talon was given additional powers. Under France's control, he was allowed to effect the provisional distribution of land to the habitants, although this was theoretically a prerogative of the Compagnie des Indes Occidentales; he could choose to appoint subdelegates to carry out business when he was unable to attend. The intendant's functions were extended through a number of decrees. In 1665 Talon's role was limited to general administration (finances, cultivation of land, and commerce), but beginning in 1672 he was given the power to draft specific bylaws on the administration of the *habitations* or settlements, such legislation being provisionally applied until royal approval was obtained.[24]

This sums up the main powers of the governor and intendant. It is often difficult to dissociate the actions of these two administrators, who exercised a preponderant influence on Québec. Not only were they active in urban planning, but they were also involved in roads and harbour administration.

Urban Policies and Town Development

The governors' and intendants' efforts to develop Québec were inspired by prevalent ideas on town planning in France. Between 1660 and 1690 the administrators originated a number of projects for expanding the town; their influence on its evolution would be decisive.

Little information is available on the kind of town planning Talon practised.[25] Before his departure for France he established the alignments (officially approved lines of position to be followed when buildings, streets, etc., were constructed) for concentrating the city's ironworks in côte de la Montagne. Frontenac noted in 1673, "the forges of the Ironsmiths, and other similar craftsmen that Are in the lower Town of Quebec Will be transported and Built Along the hill from the Lower Town to the upper, on The Lot set aside by M. Talon and In Accordance with the alignments given by him before leaving For france."[26] The evident purpose of these alignments was to limit the danger of fire by bringing the ironworks together in an area where fire was unlikely to spread. Another of Talon's achievements was the design of a water-supply system for the Hôtel-Dieu. As shown in the 1708 document and plan, he had conduits installed, at an unknown date, from the Bourreau spring (outside the Porte Saint-Jean) to the Hôtel-Dieu.[27] Also part of the water system was a canal that acted as a sort of sewer main emptying into the Saint-Charles River (Fig. 9). It may seem unusual to consider this project an achievement of town planning, but it was an important technical development and indicates a concern for hygiene.

Frontenac is perhaps the administrator who best symbolizes town planning in Québec in the 17th century. He informed Colbert of his impressions and ideas on his arrival in 1672:

> *Nothing has appeared to me to be so fine and magnificent as the situation of the town of Quebecq, which could not be better located were it to become the capital of a great empire One day, but I find, or rather it seems to me, that a very grave error has been committed in allowing private individuals to build houses to suit themselves, and Without any order, because in settlements such as this, which one day may grow to a great size, I believe that one should Consider not only the present situation, but also the future state of things. Thus, I do not Know whether you will deem fit, before this disorder increases even more, to indicate roughly, On the plans Mr Talon may have already sent to you, or which he is bringing you (since I have not had time to have a new one drawn up) the sort of enceinte you consider should be given to the town and to mark thereon the streets and squares that would be laid out, so that Subsequently when some individual wishes to build, he will do so with*

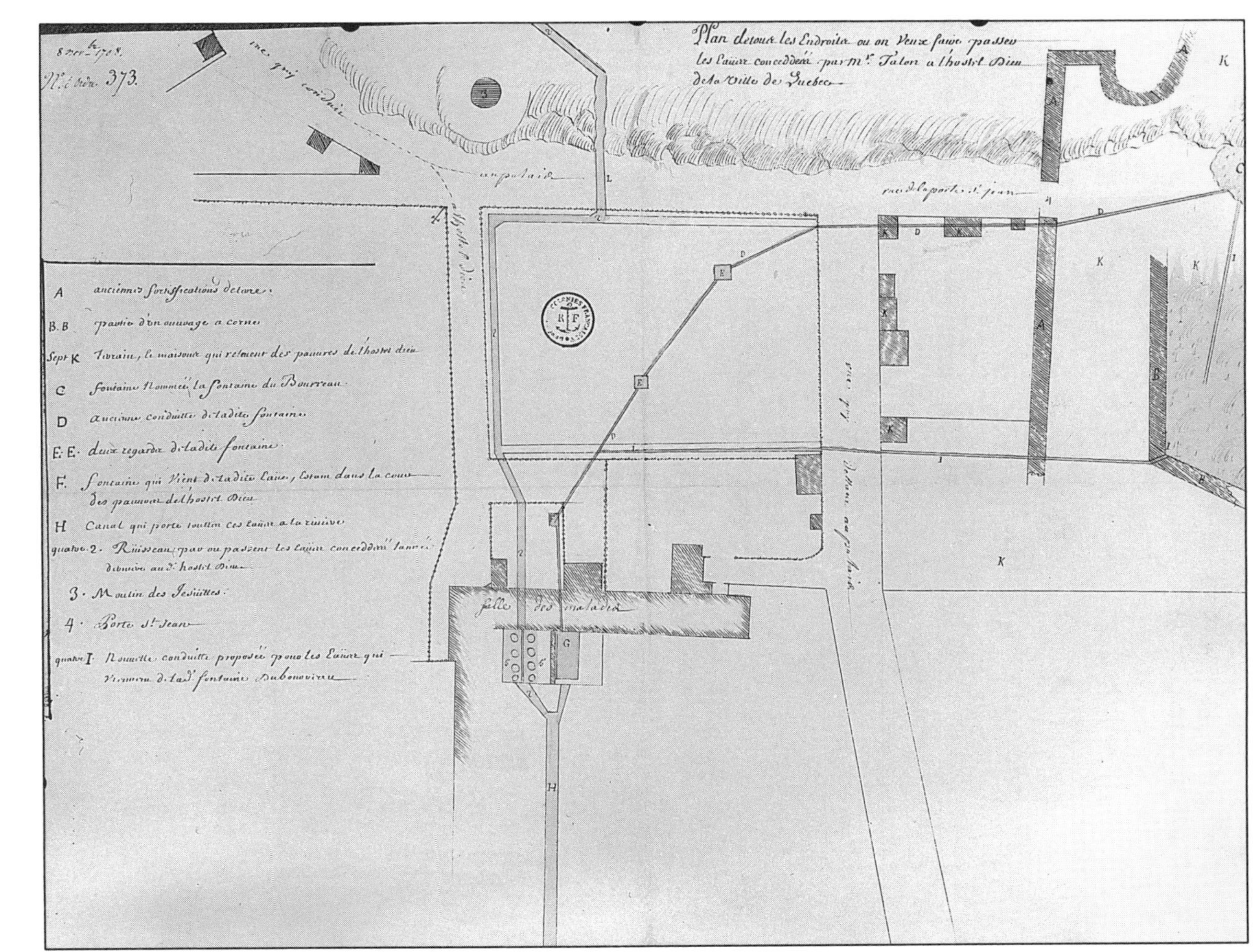
8 nov[bre] 1708.
N.° d'ordre 373.
Plan de tous les Endroits ou on veux faire passer les Eaüx conceddées par M.r Talon a l'hostel Dieu de la ville de Quebec
rue de la porte S.t Jean
Salle des malades
A anciennes fortiffications de terre.
B.B partie d'un ouvrage a corne
Sept K Terain, et maisons qui relevent des pauvres de l'hostel dieu
C fontaine nommée la fontaine du Bourreau
D ancienne conduitte de ladite fontaine
E.E. deux regards de ladite fontaine
F. fontaine qui vient de ladite Eaüe, estant dans la cour des pauvres de l'hostel Dieu
H Canal qui porte toutte ces Eaüe a la riviere
quatre 2. Ruisseau par ou passent les Eaüx conceddées l'année dernière aud.t hostel Dieu
3. Moulin des Jesuittes.
4. Porte S.t Jean
quatre I. Nouvelle conduitte proposée pour les Eaüx qui viennent de lad.t fontaine du bourreau

9 "Plan detous les Endroits ou on Veux faire passer les Eaües conceddées par Mr Talon a l'hostel Dieu de la ville de Quebec" (Plan showing the changes to be made to the Hôtel-Dieu aqueducts), 8 November 1708, De Lajoue

The plan for the first water system developed by Intendant Talon was drawn from the perspective of côte du Palais, looking south. Several of the features on this plan, such as the Porte Saint-Jean and the fortifications, were built after 1690.

Archives Nationales, France; copy on file, National Archives of Canada, C-15787

> *symmetry and in such a manner as to contribute to the beauty and embellishment of the town.*[28]

This quotation describes a program the governor would try to effect. An attempt was made to transfer to the colony notions of town planning inherited from France. The 17th century in France was a time of conscious town planning based on concepts of symmetry, embellishment, and order. Frontenac began his administration with such concepts.

In the bylaws Frontenac drew up in March 1673 for the town of Québec are a number of sections dealing with town planning. Section 12 provided for the design of an overall town plan and required that buildings conform to the street alignment "to give by this means some form And Symmetry to A Town that one day Must Be the Capital of a great country."[29] The following section concerned latrine and house construction and required owners of houses already built or to be built to include latrines "in order to avoid the infection And stench issuing from Such filth when its presence on the streets is allowed." Section 14 provided for a survey of Lower Town streets for the purpose of having them cobbled by the inhabitants. A subsequent section dealing with house construction required owners to build masonry gable walls.

These are only some of the specifications in the 1673 regulations, which also dealt with commerce, trades, fire safety, stabling livestock, stray animals, hygiene, town meetings, roads, and harbour administration. The regulations mark a turning point in the administration of Québec because legislation was passed relating to the main sectors of urban activity. The governor would be reprimanded by the king and the minister for exceeding his authority and usurping that of the Conseil Souverain in drafting the 30 articles; nevertheless, the regulations were not repealed and most of them were re-enacted by the Conseil Souverain in 1676.

Intendant Demeulle initiated the first proposal for expanding the town of Québec. In 1683 he had Jean-Baptiste-Louis Franquelin deliver to the minister, Seignelay, a *mémoire* in favour of enlarging Lower Town.[30] In the intendant's view, the proposed expansion would be an advantage for the entire colony, "serving Both to attract New inhabitants to the Said Town to augment Trade and, through the increase in population, to Enable it to resist the efforts of Those who might have Designs Against This Colony." For these reasons he suggested taking a piece of land uncovered at low tide; one side measured 200 *toises* from rue Sous-le-Fort, another measured 100 *toises* back to Sault-au-Matelot, and the third was 80 *toises*. To protect the triangle thus formed they would build a dike 12 *pieds* high and 8 *pieds* wide at the base, tapering to 3 *pieds* at the top (Fig. 10). In addition to providing building land, the project was also for

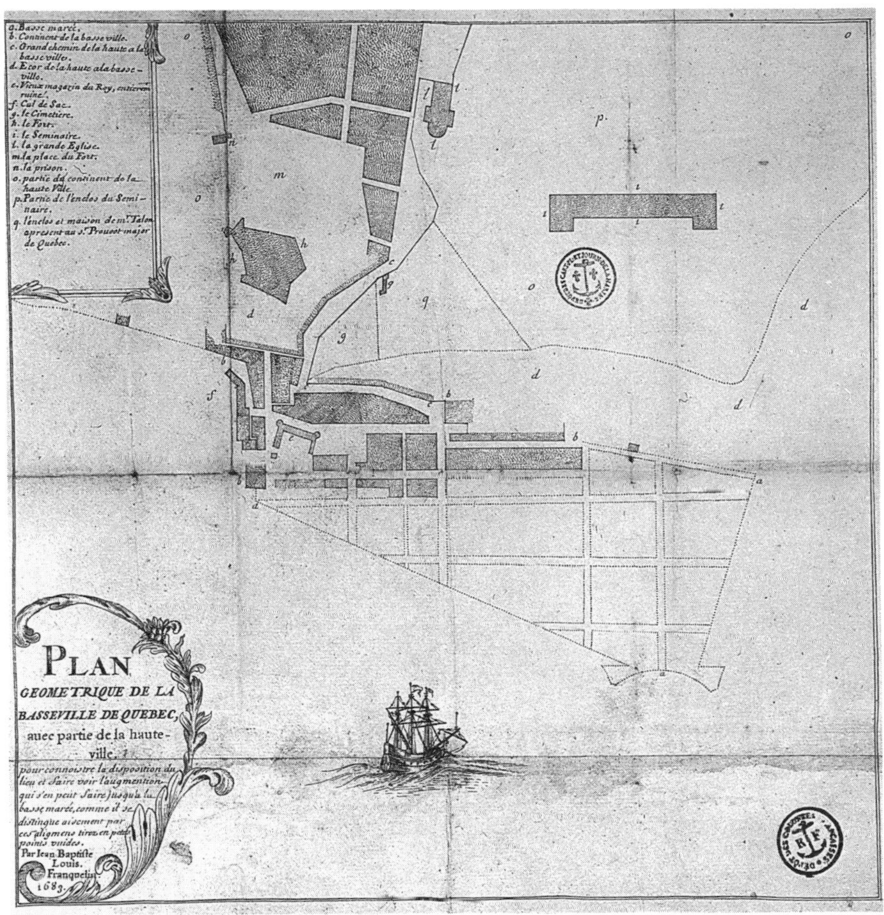

10 "Plan geometrique de la Basseville de Quebec, avec partie de la haute-ville," 1683, Jean-Baptiste-Louis Franquelin

This drawing was probably commissioned by Intendant Demeulle to illustrate his plan to extend Lower Town.

Archives Nationales, France; copy on file, National Archives of Canada, C-21759

defence, since on the northeastern tip of the triangle could be constructed a counterfort with room for 20 guns.

The total cost of this proposal would amount to some 30,000 *livres*. To pay for it Demeulle suggested that the lots created in this way be included in the king's *censive*. If the king were unwilling to bear such costs, the intendant offered to construct the dike at his own expense, but in that event he requested that Seignelay grant him a number of building lots in the projected expansion. For the completion of the project, which would increase the area of Lower Town by one-third, Demeulle wished to receive a payment of 10,000 *livres* and to be given free entry for 30 barrels of wine and 50 barrels of brandy for the workers to be employed on the site.

The project's worth in relation to the principles of town planning prevalent in the 17th century can be appreciated in a plan Franquelin drew in the same year (Fig. 10). The spaces allocated were modelled on already existing ones, at least with respect to length. The lots were of different forms (rectangular, square, triangular) and varying dimensions. Average sites occupied 25 *toises* by 20, and the largest were up to 60 *toises* long and 20 *toises* wide. The overall impression of the plan is an irregular arrangement with only three streets oriented south to north and five perpendicular avenues, all of these being only 18 *pieds* wide. The plan is not an example of good planning for Lower Town expansion in view of the pronouncedly irregular lots and narrow streets. Notably absent is an avenue along the sea wall. Military planning required that such a road, leading to a defence installation — in this case the gun emplacement — be wider than the other streets, whereas here the road is nonexistent.

On 10 April 1684 Seignelay wrote to Demeulle informing him that the king viewed the project with favour. However, himself unwilling to undertake the project, he left it to the intendant: "His Majesty could indeed grant the Land concession that you request for the enlargement of the lower town of Quebek provided you take upon yourself all expenditure necessary to construct the dike or wall that you intend to build. I shall await your communication before informing him of your intention." Demeulle must have informed the king and the minister the same year, since in a *mémoire* addressed to Seignelay he reported that the king was unwilling to accede to his request for compensation for the streets that would have been necessary.[31]

The project was therefore turned down, without doubt because of the heavy expenditure required. Nevertheless, Demeulle remained convinced that steps had to be taken to deal with the congestion of Lower Town, which was hemmed in along the shore and therefore unable to expand. For this reason, since the 1683 plan stood little chance of being implemented, he decided to draft a new one. This time his intention was to expand in Intendant Talon's Brasserie section of town. In addition to proposing the purchase of this land, he suggested that the plots adjoining the brewery be given to private citizens. Even then he imagined that "one Day this area would be joined with the lower town of quebec and would make an exceedingly fine enlargement."[32]

Demeulle took advantage of the opportunity to bring up the 1683 project once again. In response, the king answered in 1685 that he would decide on "your proposed expansion of the lower town of Quebek when the Sr de Denonville has examined it on the spot with you and the leading citizens and once you have sent me the plans, drawings and estimates and a *mémoire* on the most appropriate way of providing for this expense."[33] Although aware of the cramped conditions in Lower Town, Governor Denonville does not seem to have devoted much time to its proposed expansion.

Once again the Brasserie project was mentioned. Demeulle had great hopes for it:

> *I am sure that three years hence there will be as many houses here as in the lower town, And that in the Future it will grow into a Considerable town.... These two lower towns can be easily joined, since there is no doubt that two rows of houses will be built over time thus joining the One Another along the bottom of the hill, at least a quarter of the land is already built up Next to the lower town and it is starting to form a faubourg.*[34]

In 1686 the idea was submitted once again by Intendant Champigny; however, he added nothing to Demeulle's project.

Another two attempts were made, although we have little information on them. Apparently in 1686 the engineer de Villeneuve proposed a plan to enlarge and embellish Lower Town, but Denonville felt that "there remain a great many other things to do for the time being since the Security of the country is the main task. This project will keep." I know nothing more about the project and have been unable to find the plan. Then in 1686 the governor and intendant mentioned another of de Villeneuve's projects, this one to surround and extend Lower Town through the use of platforms.[35] This is probably illustrated in the 1689 plan (Fig. 11) in which we see Lower Town encircled by a wall provided with bastions, beginning at the far south end of rue De Meulles and ending below the intendant's palace. Its location indicates the firm intention to reclaim part of the intertidal zone as well as to enclose the Cul-de-Sac within this system of fortifications.

The various proposals to extend the town were not implemented; however, they do indicate that the typically urban problem of overcrowding

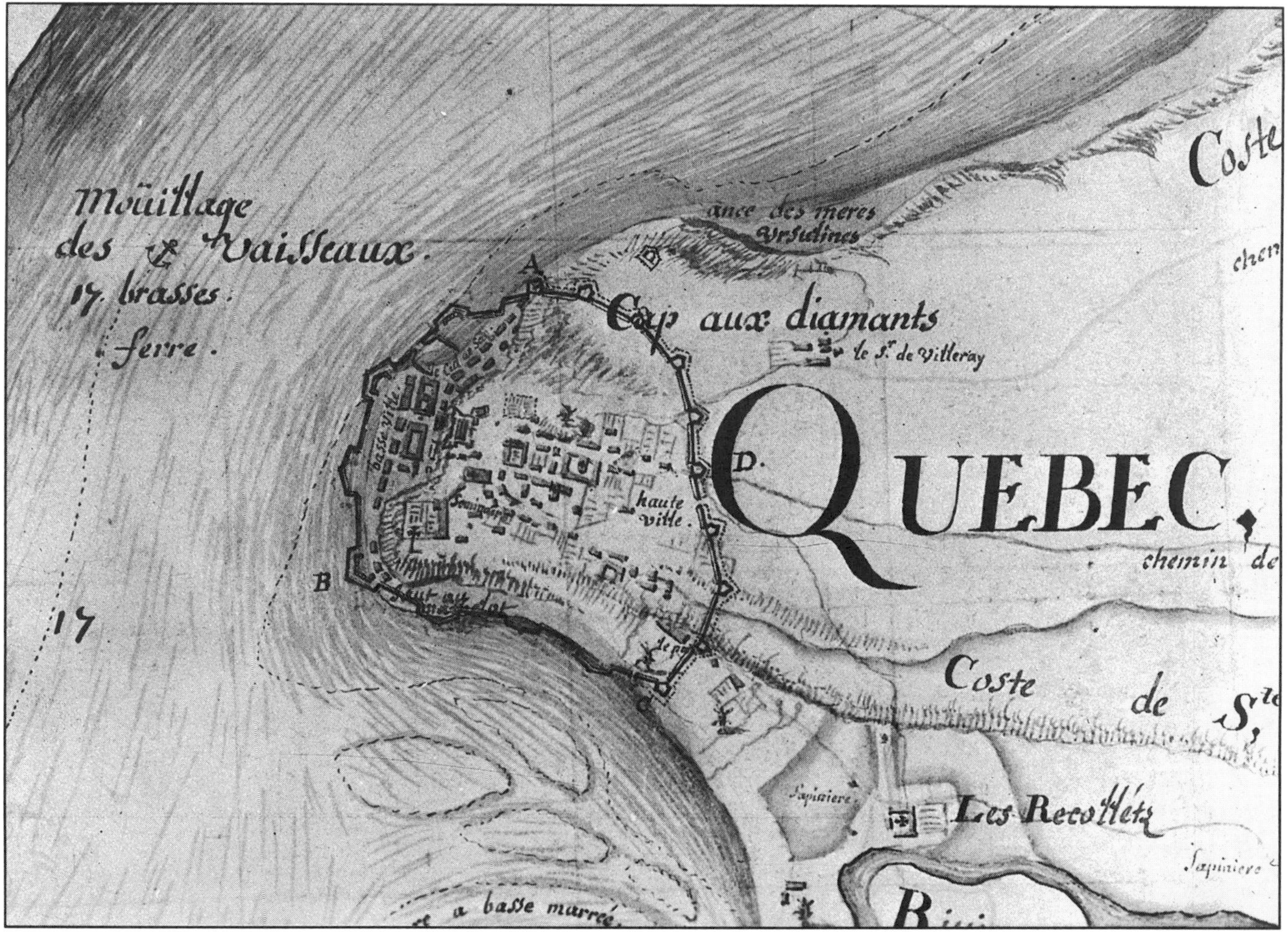

Moüillage
des Vaisseaux.
17 brasses.
ferre.
17
Cap aux diamants
le Sr. de Villeray
ance des meres
Ursulines
QUEBEC,
haute
ville
basse ville
Coste
Coste de Ste
chemin de
Les Recollets
Sapiniere
Sapiniere
a basse marrée
A
B
D.

11 Québec in 1689, Robert de Villeneuve

This detail of a map of Île d'Orléans shows the fortifications planned for Upper Town. There was also to be a system of fortifications for Lower Town, the engineer hoping to reclaim land that was exposed at low tide.

Dépôt des cartes et plans de la Marine, France; copy on file, National Archives of Canada, C-80600

began in Lower Town. The administrators were aware of the problem and attempted to solve it. In spite of the refusal of the projects, that area of the town did expand through the practice of filling in land left uncovered at low tide, as was prescribed by the concessions. Certain plans and views of the period show that there was some increase in lot area through land reclamation (Figs. 12 and 13). As for the area of the intendant's palace, even though the projects were not implemented, there was a slight increase in the town area because of the Jesuits' division of their property into lots as well as work done in the vicinity of the palace (Figs. 12 and 14).

The displacement of the Lower Town battery and Claude Baillif's concession in the Place Royale are two instances of state intervention practiced by the governors and intendants in matters of urban settlement.

In 1682, following the fire in Lower Town, La Barre and Demeulle visited the area opposite the Lower Town *magasin*, or warehouse, where Champlain had set up a battery (Fig. 27). The battery, "almost surrounded by Houses on all Sides And far from the Riverside," was poorly located and would be better removed to Pointe-aux-Roches at the foot of rue Sous-le-Fort. In this location the new artillery battery "would better command the Harbour and occasion much less discomfort to the houses of the lower Town."

A councillor of the Conseil Souverain, Charles Denys de Vitré, offered to build a terrace for the new battery, in exchange for which he wished to receive part of its previous location. La Barre and Demeulle granted him land measuring 72 *pieds* by 36 *pieds* between the lots of Sieur de Villeray and Nicolas Marion de la Fontaine (Figs. 15 and 16); however, the governor set a number of conditions for the grant: de Vitré was to complete the terrace by 24 June 1684, pay rent of 5 *sols* and *cens* of 8 *deniers*, and build on the land within a year.

In September 1683 the Jesuits offered to contribute to the cost of the terrace for the new battery on the same terms as de Vitré. They were given a lot 45 *pieds* long and 24 *pieds* wide on the east side of rue Saint-Pierre as well as a small parcel of land to the southeast. The clauses were identical to those in de Vitré's concession.[36]

On 23 October Governor de La Barre granted the Québec seminary the lot occupied by Champlain's Vieux Magasin, reserving a 56-*pied*-long lot for the construction of a *magasin du roi*. The seminary offered in exchange for this site another piece of land belonging to it between the properties of Marion de La Fontaine and Denys de Vitré. This was accepted by La Barre, who granted the seminary's land to François Pachot on condition that he build a warehouse on that lot (Figs. 15 and 16).[37]

But since these concessions had been made by the governor alone without the intendant's involvement, the king revoked them. In 1685 Denonville and Demeulle granted a new concession to the seminary for the erection of a chapel in Lower Town. Subsequently, in 1686, the seminary agreed to sell Pachot a piece of land the latter was anxious to acquire, discharging him from the obligation of building a *magasin du roi*.[38]

The contract for the Batterie Royale was concluded on 11 November 1683 by Claude Baillif *dit* Regnault and Denys de Vitré, the latter acting on behalf of the seminary. The parties had some difficulty paying for the construction work, which explains why La Barre issued an ordinance in 1684 ordering each of the buyers to pay 177 *livres* 10 *sols* for his share of the land, otherwise the lots were to be sold by public auction and under martial authority. The owners must have complied, since they were occupying the land in 1689, when Pachot, for example, received an alignment for the wall of his yard giving onto the site of the Lower Town chapel.[39]

These concessions granted in Lower Town at the time of the relocation of the battery well illustrate the state intervention that the administrators practised. Not only did the governors and intendants have roles to play, but France was also involved. The authorities made grants of land held under the principle of eminent domain in order to fund the construction of a new battery. They exercised full control over the division into lots of a very sought-after piece of land in Lower Town.

The Baillif affair began in 1684 and continued until 1686. Claude Baillif, a contractor and mason, received before December 1684 a concession measuring 15 *toises* long by four *toises* wide in the public square of the Lower Town.[40] The inhabitants immediately made known their opposition to the concession and on 31 December they presented a petition to Intendant Demeulle, who turned it down. On 4 June 1685 they came back with a second petition. In their *mémoire* to the intendant they put forward several grounds for revoking the concession to Baillif, the main reason being the need to conserve the square intact since it was there that the public markets and sales were held and executions took place and since it was a meeting place and a refuge in case of fire.[41]

The intendant's position remained unchanged and the 37 inhabitants who signed the second petition were condemned to pay individual fines. Faced with this intransigence, the inhabitants appealed to the minister to have the fines lifted and the square preserved; in 1685 they even sent him a brief of their grievances. This was probably the occasion when a very rough drawing of the Lower Town square was prepared, showing Baillif's plan for a building measuring 25 *pieds* wide and 15 *toises* long,

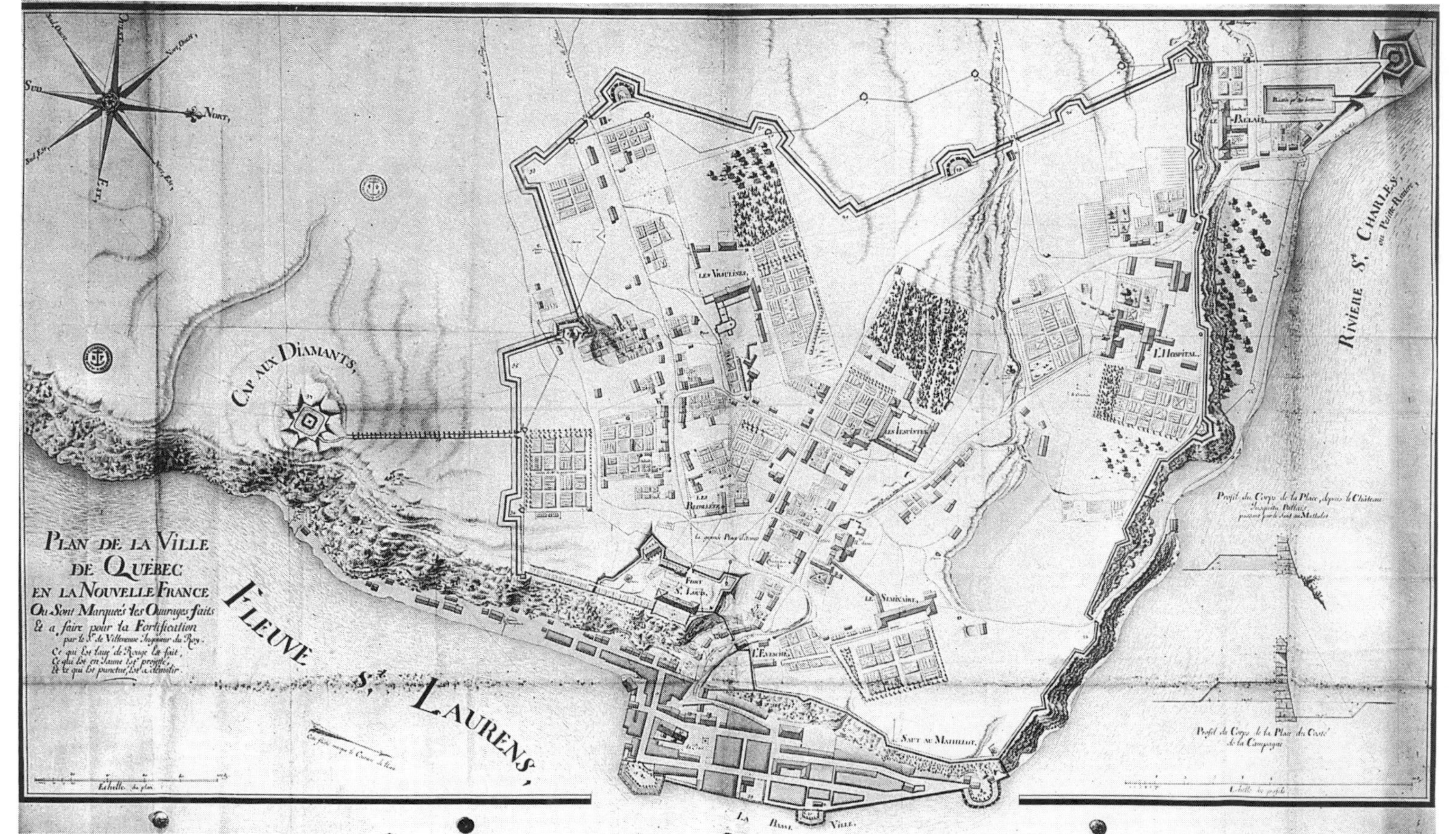

Plan de la Ville
de Québec
en la Nouvelle France
Ou Sont Marquées les Ouvrages faits
Et a faire pour la Fortification
par le Sr. de Villeneuve Ingénieur du Roy.
Ce qui est lavé de Rouge est fait,
Ce qui est en Jaune est projetté,
Et ce qui est ponctué, est a démolir.
Cap aux Diamants,
Fleuve S.t Laurens,
Riviere S.t Charles, ou Petite Riviere
Sud
Nort,
Est,
Ouest
Les Ursulines
Les Recollets
Les Jesuites
L'Hospital
Le Seminaire
L'Evesché
Fort S.t Louis
Le Pallais
Saut au Matelot
La Basse Ville

12 "Plan de la Ville de Québec en la Nouvelle France ou Sont Marquées les Ouvrages faits Et a faire pour la Fortification...," 1692, Robert de Villeneuve

This seems to be one of the most precise plans produced in the 17th century, second only to his 1685 plan (Fig. 28). Although it falls just outside the period under study, it shows the development that occurred in the sector surrounding the intendant's palace and along rue Saint-Louis in Upper Town and in Lower Town on rue De Meulles.

Archives Nationales, France; copy on file, National Archives of Canada, C-17764

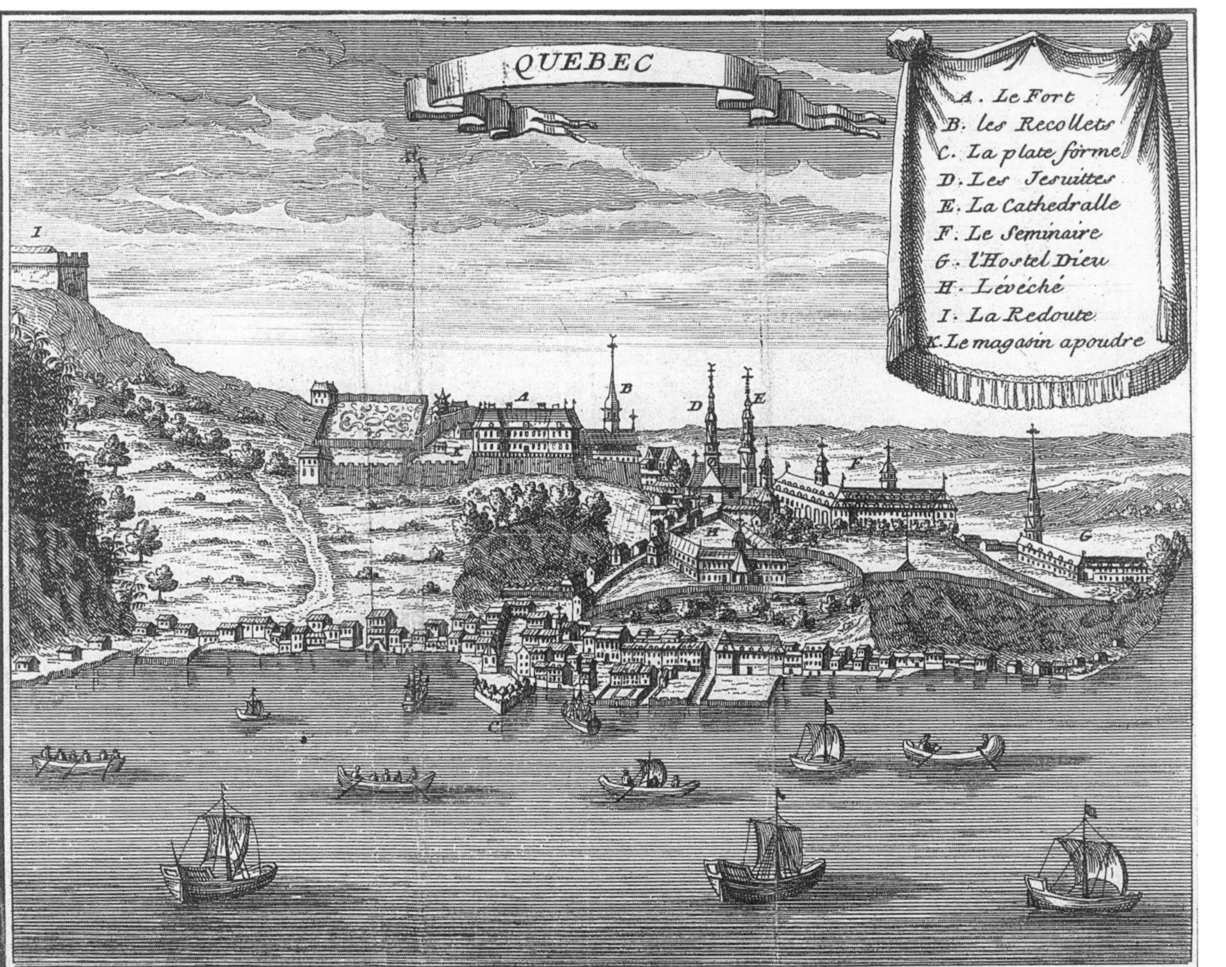
QUEBEC
A. Le Fort
B. les Recollets
C. La plate forme
D. Les Jesuittes
E. La Cathedralle
F. Le Seminaire
G. l'Hostel Dieu
H. Léveché
I. La Redoute
K. Le magasin apoudre

13 "Quebec," 1700, anonymous

A somewhat imaginative representation of Québec, it does indicate land use in Upper and Lower Town. In Lower Town part of the shore has been reclaimed at the foot of rue Saint-Pierre. Charles Aubert de Lachenaye's enormous home also stands out (in front of the empty space enclosed by a fence). In Upper Town the bishop's palace, begun in 1688, and the governor's garden, at the southwest end of Fort Saint-Louis, are noteworthy.

Original source unknown; copy on file, National Archives of Canada, C-4696

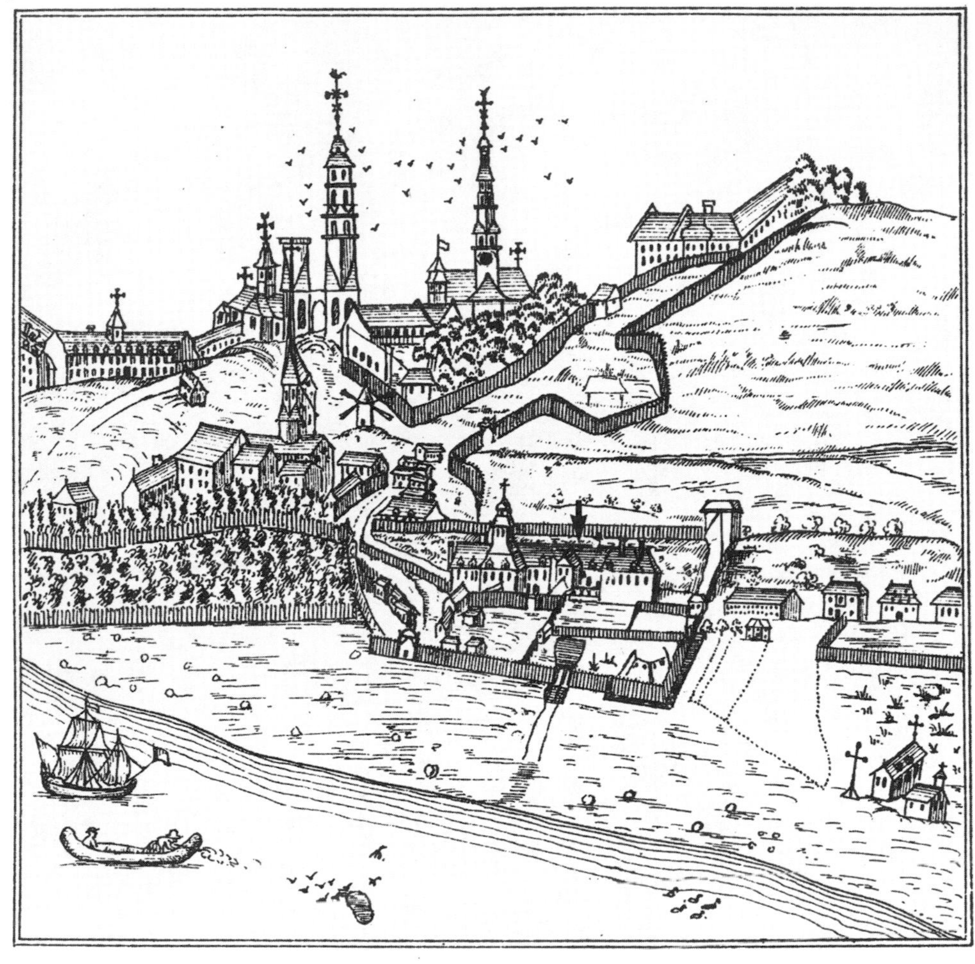

14 Quebec veu dv Nord Ouest," 1699, de Fonville

This engraving provides a good illustration of land use in the sector surrounding the intendant's palace (*see* arrow). The palisades, redoubts, and other defensive works were built after 1690.

Original source unknown; copy on file, National Archives of Canada, C-46450

with a carriage entrance onto the square. The building would have considerably reduced the square, which in any case was just 150 square *toises*.[42]

The inhabitants also submitted their grievances to the new governor, Denonville, who, writing to the minister in November 1685, took their part and asked that the concession be repealed. He went so far as to criticize La Barre and Demeulle: "I am surprised that these Gentlemen should have failed to note that the difficulty of This Town comes from its congestion, and that for the sake of a few private citizens the public is deprived of its sole refuge in case of misfortune, since This Open Space prevents the Spreading of fire and can be used to Save the people's belongings."[43] Denonville also had a plan of the Place Royale drawn up by the engineer de Villeneuve and sent it to Seignelay (Fig. 17).

The answer came in May 1686: the king, while confirming Baillif's concession, instructed Champigny and Denonville to study the matter. The monarch did not wish, by withdrawing the concession of a site to Baillif, to deter those wishing to build. The same year, the governor and intendant sent back to France the royal warrant confirming Baillif's concession, which was revoked because "the square is too small and It would be a great inconvenience to the public."[44]

The attitudes suggested by the Baillif affair are noteworthy. Demeulle was opposed to the inhabitants' petition because of his distrust of representations from the populace, but Denonville and Champigny were able to overcome this apprehension and see the problem in a fairer perspective. It was essential to preserve the square, particularly for refuge in case of fires. This second example of state intervention illustrates that in certain cases the common good came before private interests.

Roads

Frontenac is the best example of the role the governor played with respect to roads. On 3 January 1673, when the concession granted to Jean Maheust was enlarged, he had the *arpenteur royal*, Jean Guyon Du Buisson, establish the alignment. In his permit for Maheust to build a house, Frontenac ordered him to respect the alignments Guyon had set for both the new and old concessions. Maheust was also to follow the alignment for Charles Cadieu's house on rue Champlain and leave enough space for that street to be extended to the côte de la Montagne.[45]

Bylaws enacted in March 1673 reflected similar concerns on the part of the governor. Frontenac had wanted street layouts and house align-

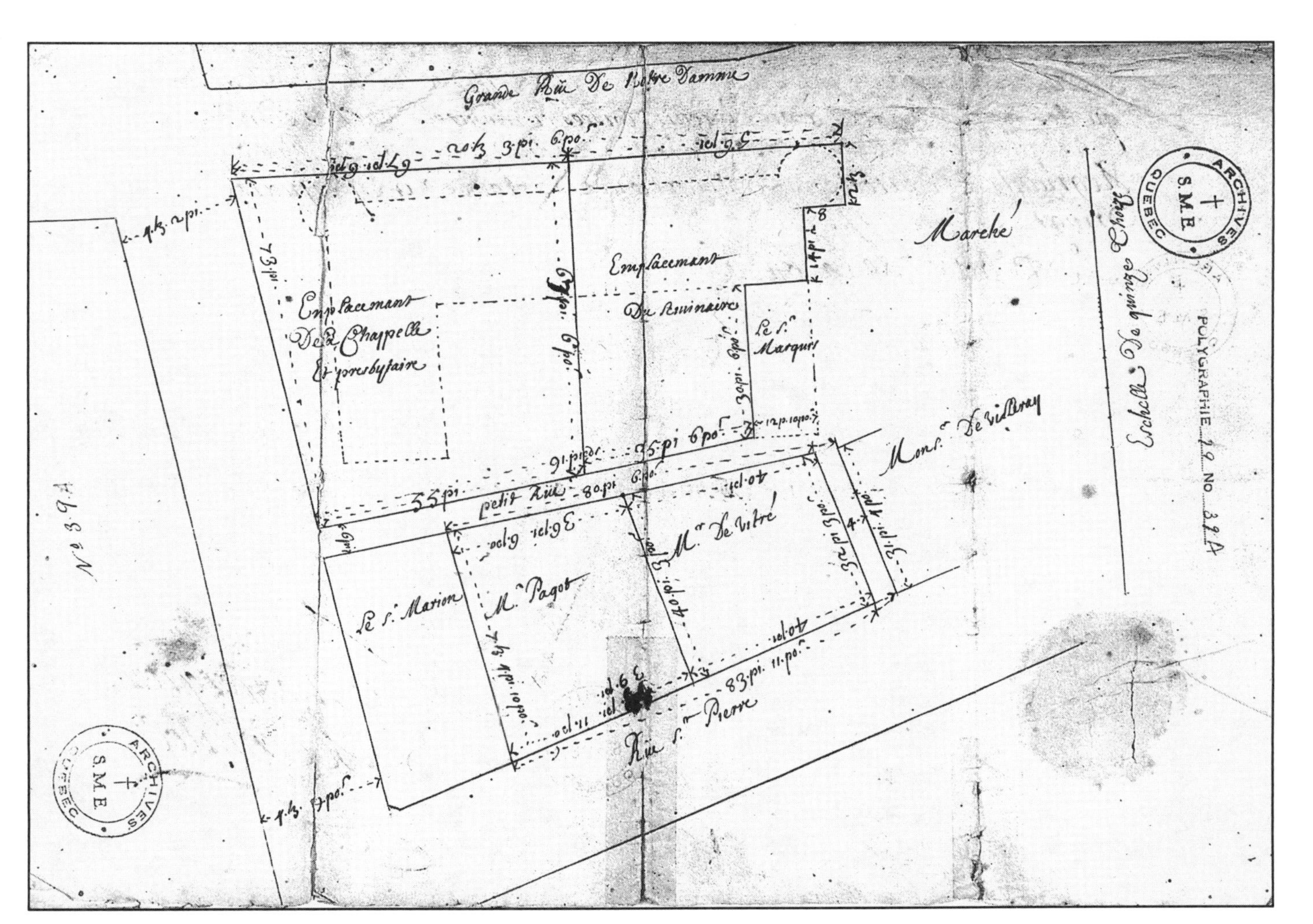
Grande Rüe De Notre Damme
Marché
Emplacement
Du Seminaire
Emplacement
De la Chappelle
Et presbytaire
Le Sr Marquis
Mons.r De Villeray
petit Rüe
Mr De Vitré
Mr Pagot
Le Sr Marion
Rüe St Pierre
73.pi.
35.pi.
80.pi. 6.po.
83.pi. 11.po.
40.pi.
ARCHIVES
S.M.E.
QUEBEC
POLYGRAPHIE 19 NO 39 A
ARCHIVES
S.M.E.
QUEBEC

15 "Plan des places du Vieux Magasin et de la vieille batterie de la Basse-ville," 20 October 1683, Claude Baillif

This plan was drawn at the king's command on 10 May 1682. The lots held by Pachot ("Pagot" on the plan) and De Vitré occupy the space in front of the old battery. The plan also shows the lot owners' names, the size of the Vieux Magasin (*see* dotted outline), and the widths of certain streets and lanes.

Archives du Séminaire de Québec

grande Rue de nostre Dame

20 toises 3 pi. 6 po.

9 toises

4 toises 2 pi.

Emplacement dela Chapelle et presbitere

72 pi.

Le S. Marquis

34 pieds

12 pi. 10 po.

10 pi.

13 toises 4 po.

Petitte Rue 80 pieds 6 po.

8 pi.

40 pi.

36 pi. 6 po.

Mons. de Vitré.

Monsieur de Villeray

31 pi. 11 po.

4 pi.

32 pi. 3 po.

40 pi. 3 po.

Le S. Marion

Emplacement du Seminaire

7 toises 4 pi. 10 po.

40 pi.

39 pi. 11 po.

83 pi. 11 po.

Rue S.t Pierre

4 toises 9 pou.

Echele de quinze toises.

Seminaire I, N.o 46

16 "Copie du plan du Vieux Magasin et de la vieille batterie de la Basse-ville," 11 August 1685, Claude Baillif

The surveying work for this plan was carried out by Baillif on orders from Denonville and Demeulle. There are only two changes in relation to Figure 15: the site of the Vieux Magasin (*see* dotted outline) was allotted to the Québec seminary for the construction of a chapel and rectory, and the seminary was also granted the lot next to the Sieur De Vitré's.

Archives du Séminaire de Québec

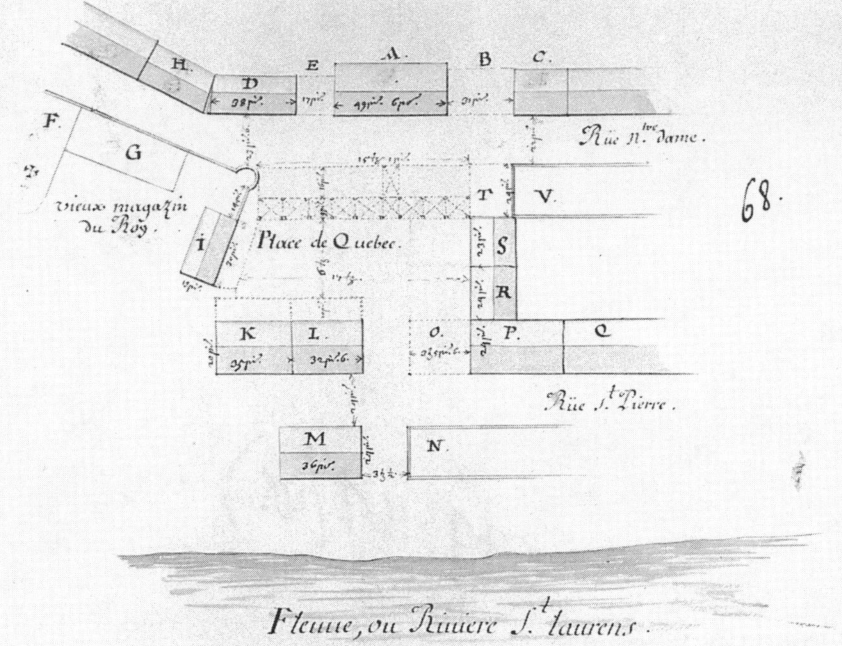

Ce qui Est laué de jaune Est la place ou le Sr Renault architecte pretend bastir. Et fe. des porches de neuf pis. de profondeur, Et vn passage a porte cochere, por communiquer de la rüe Nre dame a la place.
Ce qui Est laué de Rouge paste, sont les Endroits ou il faudra bastir, marqués, E, B, T, V, O, N.
Et ce qui Est laué plus fort, sont les maisons faittes

les Noms des habitans qui ont leurs Maisons prés lad. Place

A. Est la maison de Mr. a[illegible]
B. Est vne place a bastir qui appartient a Mr. pierre [illegible]
C. Est vne maison au Sr. de la [illegible]
D. aux Srs. pinguet, Et [illegible]
E. place a bastir, appartenant aux heritiers de Mr. vallon.
F. place ou lon propose fe. vne chapelle dans lannée 1686.
G. Est la place po. le presbitaire.
H. Est la maison de Mr. robert paue.
I. maison de Mr. le marquis, Marchand de vin.
K. maison a Mr. de villeray.
L. maison a Mlle. de la tesserie
M. maison de Mr. guyon.
N. maison de Mr. ~~rajot~~ le bert.
O. maison de Mr. rajot qui a esté bruslé, Et n'est pas restably.
P. Est vne maison aud. rajot qui a esté rebasty.
Q. maison de Mr. noland quil a fait rebastir
R. Est vne autre maison aud. noland quil a fait Encor rebastir.
S. maison de Mr. picart.
T. Est vne place a bastir appartenant a Mr. talon.
V. Est vne maison qui a esté bruslé, laquelle n'a pas esté restably, Elle appartient aussy a Mr. talon.

Par ordre de Monsieur Le Marquis de Denonville Je me suis transporté sur la place de la basse ville de quebec, pour En leuer le plan cy dessus, lequel Je certifie auoir mesuré tres Exactement, fait a quebec ce 10me Nouembre 1685. Villeneuue Ingenieur aud. quebec.

17 Plan of part of the Place Royale, 10 November 1685, Robert de Villeneuve

This survey is very useful for determining the ownership of certain concessions. It concerns in particular the concession (to the right of the Vieux Magasin) granted to Claude Baillif *dit* Regnault on the market square.

Archives Nationales France; copy on file, Ministère des Affaires culturelles du Québec, C 77-167/45

ments to be in keeping with an overall plan for the town which, after being submitted to the king, was to be stored in the municipal archives. Work was already being done on this plan in March 1673; Frontenac sent it to France on 13 November and asked the administrators there to settle the town limits. Unfortunately, it has been impossible to track down either this plan or the plan for the Château Saint-Louis sent at the same time; it would have shown the first proposal for regrouping land by lots in Québec and, according to Frontenac's remarks, projections for future streets and building sites. In section 14 the governor ordered that Lower Town streets be raised for easier cleaning and better runoff of water from Upper Town. Each inhabitant was required to raise the street level in front of his house and to cobble it, leaving space for a gutter in the middle. Frontenac also wished to establish a commissioner in charge of cobbling the streets.

On 25 June 1674 the governor approved a plan for the Ursulines' lot in Upper Town and gave them permission to set their alignments according to those shown on the plan. In it, rue Saint-Louis and rue du Parloir are shown as 36 *pieds* wide, and rue des Jardins, opening onto rue Saint-Louis, is 24 *pieds* wide (Figs. 18 and 19). The same year, Frontenac had the alignment of rue Buade drawn "so that individuals wishing to build there may have room."[46]

By 1672 Talon exercised certain powers over roads, and in 1681 Intendant Duchesneau drew up a document setting out the limits of the land granted to the Récollets in Upper Town. The alignment for the hospice the Récollets built in 1689 is shown on the plan that the intendant had had drawn up.[47]

With Demeulle the intendant's role became clearer. Following the 1682 Lower Town fire, which destroyed the beams supporting the côte de la Montagne, he suggested that a retaining wall two *toises* thick be built. Demeulle let a contract for building this wall on 23 February 1683 and instructed the *grand voyer* to see that the owners of houses and land adjoining the côte de la Montagne undertook the necessary preparations for the work.[48]

The restoration of the côte de la Montagne illustrates two points: the intendant was responsible, as La Barre noted, for major roads projects and had authority over the *grand voyer*. In 1685 Demeulle directed the continuation of rue Champlain, decided on the alignments, and set the width of the street and the lane. His ordinance applied only to one street in Lower Town, unlike the set of street regulations dated 28 July 1686, which applied to the entire town. On his return from Acadia, Demeulle visited Upper and Lower Town and noted that a number of townspeople had built houses during his absence without obtaining alignments from

Grand Voyer René Robinau de Bécancour or his clerk. This was a breach of their land-grant contracts, which stipulated that alignments must be observed. Further, a number had built and were still building, without permission, balconies, roofs, and covered vestibules.

To prevent such occurrences, the intendant ordered that in future the *grand voyer* (and in his absence his clerk) visit the sites to be granted in the town of Québec and along the roads to establish the alignments. His instructions were precise: "conscious always of The Width of the streets, so that no house projects farther than Another, And so that Fences, Yards and gardens do not extend Onto the streets or roads." Referring to legislation in effect in France, Demeulle brought in new penalties for offenders: fines and demolition of the misaligned building at their expense. He prohibited any construction projecting onto the street (balcony, porch, roof, covered vestibule, step, gutter, shutter) without the permission of the *grand voyer* or his clerk.

Demeulle is the only intendant whose activity concerning street regulation is well known. An ordinance issued by his successor, Champigny, in 1688 with respect to Montréal does give some information. In that document the intendant established street width at 30 *pieds* and required inhabitants to obtain their alignments from the bailiff. He also dealt with road repair and maintenance as responsibilities of landowners, even requiring that bridges be built over streams. That is the only ordinance of Champigny's I have found dealing with streets and roads; there is nothing on the town of Québec.[49]

Although the governor and intendant acted separately, they did share some functions relating to roads. Expectations of grantees reflect this collaboration. Before 1672, when grants were made by the governor alone, grantees were already required to build at the same ground level as their neighbours and were responsible for upkeep of the streets.[50] After that date these requirements were reiterated by both the governor and the intendant, along with property owners' further obligation to cobble the streets in front of their lots.

The administrators' role was not limited to such matters, they also had the power to change street alignments, as occurred in Lower Town in 1689. A transfer was made by Denonville and Champigny to François Charron de La Barre and Jacques De Faye of the land occupied by the lane joining rue Sous-le-Fort with the côte de la Montagne. In exchange Charron was to lay out a new five-*pied*-wide lane and look after its upkeep.[51]

Lastly, these two officials saw to the protection of public squares. On 25 April 1689, informed that Eustache Lambert Dumont had begun work on the foundation of a house on the Place Royale, Denonville and

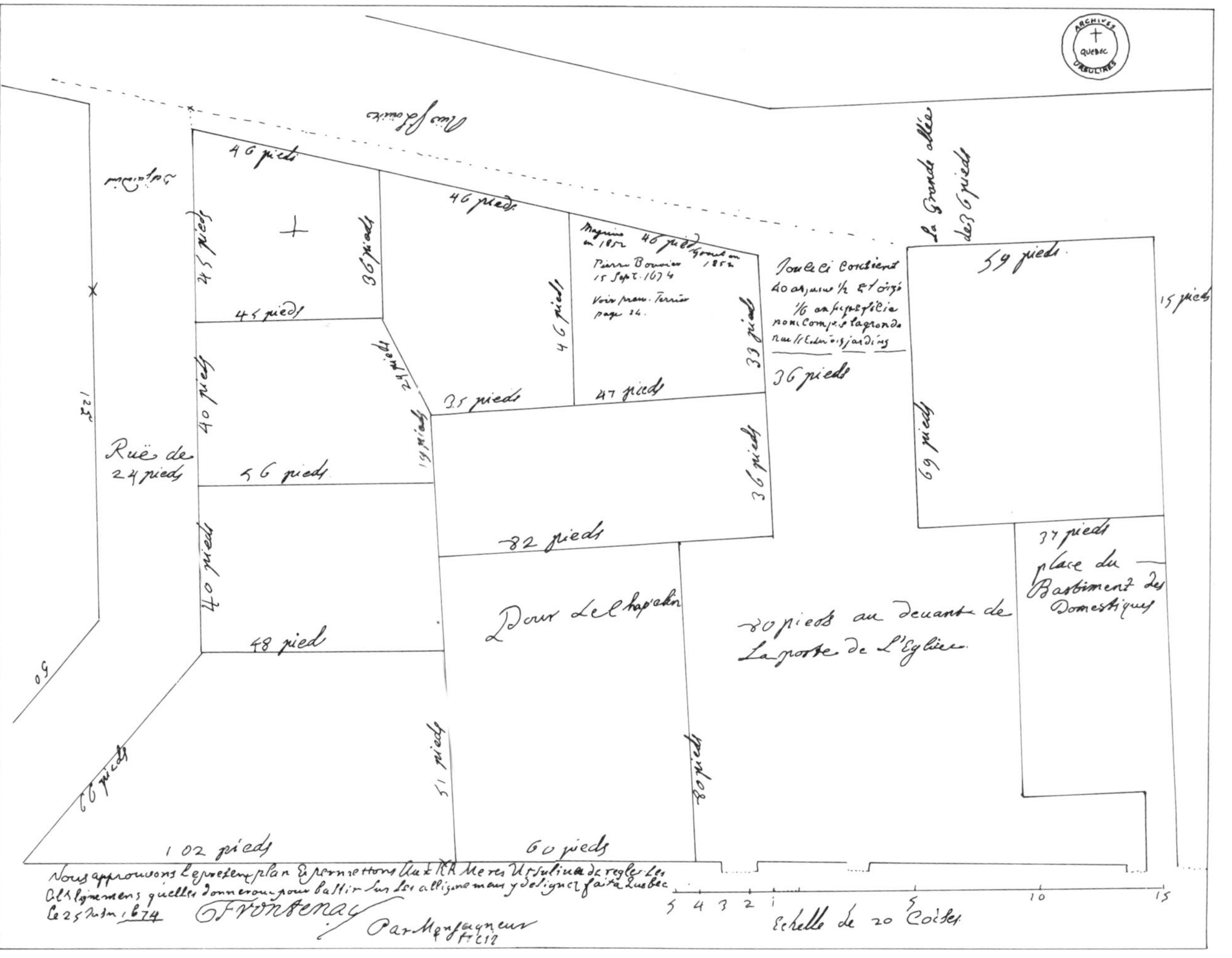

ARCHIVES QUEBEC URSULINES
Ruë de 24 pieds
125
60
La Grande allée de 36 pieds
46 pieds
45 pieds
36 pieds
46 pieds
40 pieds
56 pieds
24 pieds
19 pieds
35 pieds
46 pieds
47 pieds
33 pieds
36 pieds
82 pieds
40 pieds
48 pied
66 pieds
102 pieds
51 pieds
60 pieds
80 pieds
Magasin en 1852
Pierre Bouvier 15 Sept. 1674
Voir prem. Terrier page 24.
59 pieds
69 pieds
15 pieds
36 pieds
37 pieds
place du Bastiment des Domestiques
Dour Le Chapelain
80 pieds au devant de La porte de L'Eglise
Nous approuvons le present plan et permettons aux RR Meres Ursulines de regler les allignemens quelles donneront pour battir sur les allignemens y designez fait a Quebec le 25 Juin 1674
Frontenac
Par Monseigneur
5 4 3 2 1 5 10 15
Echelle de 20 Toises

18 Plan for dividing part of the Ursuline lands into lots, 25 June 1674, anonymous

This plan compelled the Ursulines to follow the specified alignments when subdividing their land. There are 11 lots, including the square in front of the church and the site of the servants' quarters.

Monastère des Ursulines de Québec; drawing by Rémi Chénier from a copy on file at the Archives Nationales du Québec, Québec

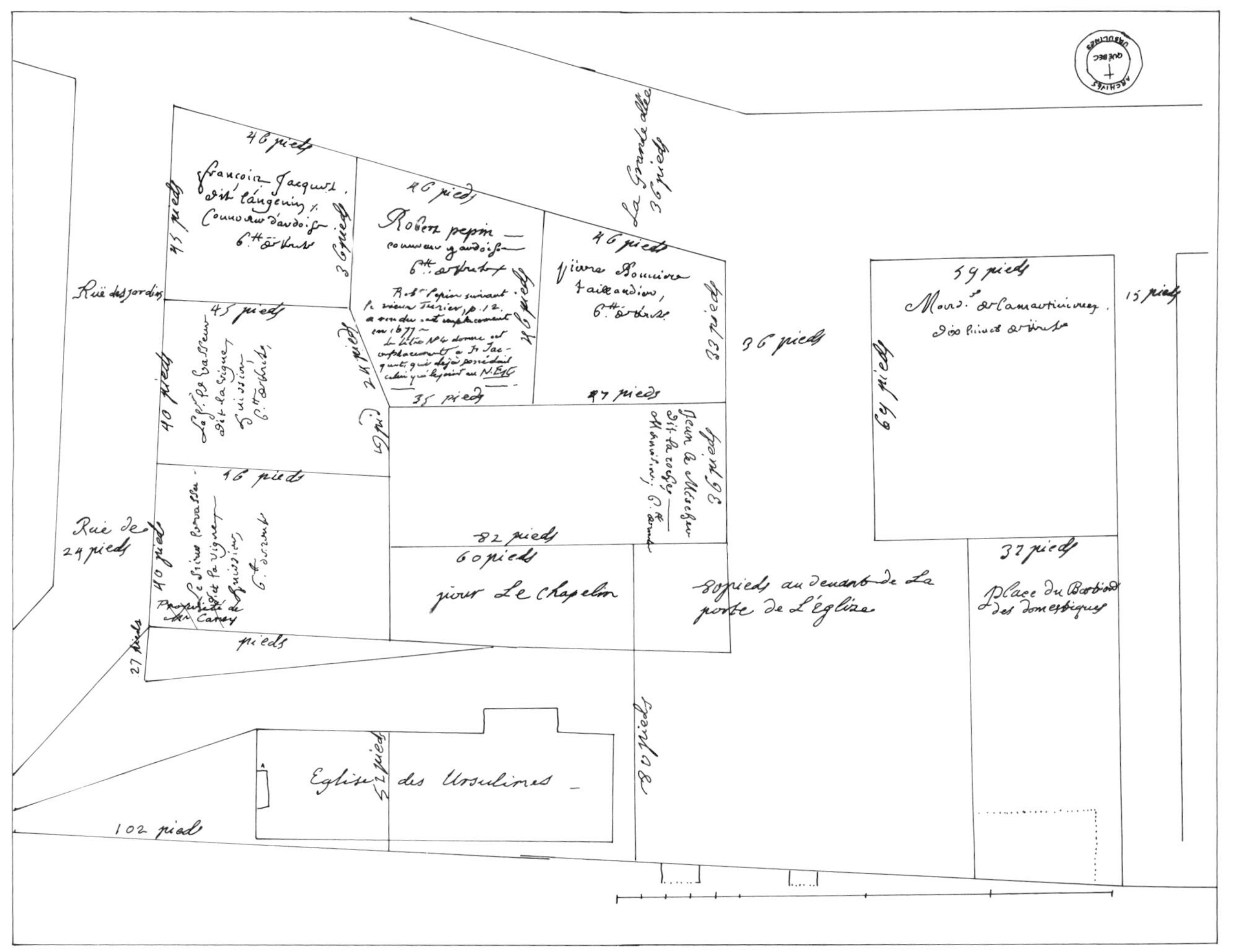

La Grande allée 36 pieds
Rüe des jardins
Rue de 24 pieds
François Jacquet dit Langevin, couvreur d'ardoise
Robert pepin couvreur d'ardoise
Pierre Bonnier taillandier
Jean Le Mercier dit La rochelle
Pierre Le Chapelain
80 pieds au devant de La porte de L'église
Place du Bâtiment des domestiques
Eglise des Ursulines
102 pied
36 pieds
15 pieds

19 Plan of the division of part of the Ursuline lands, with the owners' names, 25 June 1674, anonymous

This drawing accompanies Figure 18. It shows the Ursulines' church, the servants' building, and the lots granted as concessions. Some of the inscriptions on this plan date to the 19th century, but were added by Father Thomas Maguire, the Ursulines' chaplain, who titled the illustration: "Plan changing the Northeast part of the Grande Allé [*sic*] or Rue S^{t} loüis and Moving it several d[egrees] east."

Monastère des Ursulines de Québec; drawing by Rémi Chénier from a copy on file at the Archives Nationales du Québec, Québec

Champigny inspected the site and saw that if construction continued, it would reduce the area of the square. Dumont was therefore summoned and agreed to comply with the order instructing him to follow the alignment of Jean Le Picard's house. On 13 May Dumont was issued an alignment for his house and was required to set back the foundations already built, even though they were within his lot line.[52]

Harbour Administration

Because he had authority over all warships and merchant ships, the governor was involved in harbour administration. Any vessel wishing to leave Québec had to obtain written permission from the governor. He also set sailing dates and dates for delivering furs to the company's warehouse.[53] However, in 1684 a limit was set on his authority over maritime matters when Versailles denied La Barre's right to hear admiralty cases. In the same year, Secretary of State Seignelay refuted the governor's claims and forbade him to seek control over water traffic, shore patrols, and the placing of guards to prevent fraud in the transport of pelts. In 1685 the minister added that the governor could not release ships nor compel the clerks of the tax *fermiers*, who had a monopoly on the fur trade, to provide him with lists of the guards visiting the ships. The governor was reduced to obtaining accounts from ships' captains of their ports of origin and cargos.[54] These instructions remained in effect for subsequent governors and restricted their jurisdiction.[55]

The intendants of Canada were responsible for the administration of the port of Québec to the extent of their overall regulatory powers and in view of the absence of an intendant of Marine. In France the intendant of Marine carried out navy ordinances, managed and inspected stores, and had authority over port officials. He also saw to the safety of vessels, established patrols, and controlled the commissioning and decommissioning of ships.[56]

It is not known whether the intendant carried out all these duties in the colony, but as part of his financial prerogatives he administered the king's stores and the king's shipyards, and enacted certain regulations relating to the unloading of vessels. In April 1683 Demeulle drafted an ordinance requiring all ship's captains and masters to declare, before unloading, the quantity of wine, brandy, and tobacco on board. He also stipulated that unloading, for which he set a time, must take place in the presence of the clerks and guards assigned by the receiver of the king's tax *fermiers*. Offenders were subject to fines of 500 *livres* and their merchandise was liable to confiscation. This measure, to ensure taxes were collected on certain goods, was applied on 21 September: Jacques De Lalande, a merchant, was fined for attempting to smuggle in a bale of tobacco. And seven people caught smuggling furs were fined on 16 October 1683.[57]

Such was the intendant's actual role with respect to maritime law. Except for certain proposals concerning harbour administration, his responsibility was to ensure the collection of duty by the king's *fermiers*. The intendant also faced the contentious issue of creating the office of Québec harbour master. In 1665 Talon suggested that a harbour warden be appointed, considering such a position to be indispensable. In 1666 the agent general of the Compagnie des Indes Occidentales, Le Barroys, made several petitions to the king's representatives. To protect the company's monopoly, he suggested a number of expedients: permits signed by the company clerk to receive pelts on board ships, other permits to board vessels, as well as inspection of vessels by company officials before the ships were unloaded. Le Barroys also called for giving the lieutenant-general of the Prévôté jurisdiction in navigational matters.

Seven years later Frontenac's bylaws prohibited anyone from using boats anchored in the port of Québec without the owners' permission. Enforcement of this measure was to be the responsibility of the harbour master, a position to be created by him or his successors. This official would also be responsible for visiting ships and ensuring that the regulations practised in the ports of France were complied with.

In spite of the port of Québec's apparent need for a harbour master, Intendant Champigny does not appear to have been convinced, for he recommended that the lieutenant-general and the *procureur du roi* take on this responsibility. Champigny made the proposal following Frontenac's 1692 appointment of Sieur de L'Espinay as harbour master. In fact, as early as 1679 Frontenac had similarly appointed Sieur Maheu, who remained in office until 1683. Afterward the position was left vacant. Following inhabitants' complaints, Frontenac provisionally appointed L'Espinay to this function. In the exercise of his duties he was to be responsible for all the functions incumbent upon harbour masters in France. L'Espinay's appointment did not receive royal approval. In November 1702 Callière and Beauharnois explained the reasons for the refusal: the port of Québec was too small and L'Espinay did not have the necessary qualifications.[58]

* * *

The governor and the intendant played essential roles in urban administration not only because of the extent of their powers, but also because of their actions. The various governors' involvement in town affairs depended on the personalities concerned, a desire for precedence over other colonial officials, and sometimes on chance circumstances. Until 1663 the governor dominated the scene; from 1665 on, he had to take into account the intendant's presence. The lack of an intendant explains to some extent Frontenac's feverish activity during his first mandate: concessions, bylaws, alignments, etc.

Nevertheless, the intendant was the main figure in urban administration. His influence on the town flowed from his powers. This may seem obvious, but one must not overlook the realities of his functions as the official responsible for justice, peace, and finance.

The Conseil Souverain

The Conseil Souverain, established in Québec in 1663, was essentially a court of law and as such was given broad powers by Louis XIV "to deal with all civil and criminal cases, having ultimate sovereign authority according to the laws of the realm, and to do so expeditiously, keeping as far as possible to the forms and procedures used in our court and parlement of Paris."[59]

In addition to the usual powers of sovereign courts — recording and the right of remonstrance — the council combined within itself powers that in France were normally assigned to separate jurisdictions. Thus the Conseil Souverain also played the role of the Chambre des Comptes (recording acts of fealty and homage and patents of nobility), the Chancellerie (letters of restitution, disclaimers, and decrees), and the Chambre des Requêtes (cases involving councillors or their widows personally).[60] These powers were implicit only; the edict establishing the council did not spell them out.

The edict did specifically endow the council with other prerogatives, especially regarding appointments of judges. Although the king retained overall authority over the council and appeals from its decisions were to the Crown, he did empower the council to "appoint in Québec, Montréal, and Trois-Rivières, and in any other place, to whatever extent and in whatever manner they shall deem necessary, officials to render judgement in the first instance [and] to appoint whatever clerks, notaries, scriveners, sergeants and other officers of justice they shall think fit."

The Conseil Souverain also enjoyed powers denied to French courts. By the edict of 1663 it was entrusted with financial management, control of commerce, and maintenance of law, in all of which it was the successor of the Conseil de traite, 1659 incarnation.

These functions were to undergo changes and a tendency developed to confine the Conseil Souverain within its duties as a sovereign court. That tendency was chiefly attributable to the appointment of an intendant and the establishment of the Compagnie des Indes Occidentales. After 1665 the council had to yield control of the colony's finances, and briefly the appointment of judges, to the intendant. The company took from the council the management of fees levied on furs, the rent of the Tadoussac trading area, and all its commercial authority. After the dissolution of the Compagnie des Indes Occidentales, the council did not get back all its erstwhile authority; the king withdrew the extensive powers it had been granted.

During its existence the Conseil Souverain seems to have gone through two distinct phases: one that ran from 1663 to 1665 when it was at the peak of its power and another beginning in 1665 when its powers began to be whittled away, especially with the appointment of an intendant and, later, the return of the colony to direct rule by the Crown.

At first the council was made up of the governor, the bishop, a *procureur général*, a *greffier*, and five councillors appointed for renewable one-year terms who acted as *rapporteurs* and, during the suspension of the lieutenant-general of of the Prévôté in 1676, took turns looking after the particular administration of the town of Québec. In 1675 their number was increased to seven, the king reserving the right to appoint them. At the same time he made official the intendant's membership in the council, which had, however, been the practice since Talon's time.[61]

Like the governor and the intendant, the Conseil Souverain played an important role in town administration, especially in the areas of roads and harbour administration. However, its chief influence on town life lay in its power to enact bylaws.

The roads activity of the council began in 1664. On 2 August it passed an ordinance providing that landowners on Grande Allée were to keep the thoroughfare passable. On 3 September, at the behest of the *procureur général*, who complained that the ordinance was being flouted, the council provided that offenders would be fined 20 *sols* per *arpent* of frontage on Grande Allée and repeated its order that the road be made passable before winter.

The council acted again on 13 May 1665 with a bylaw providing that fences adjoining the St. Lawrence must be built two *perches* (36 *pieds*) above high water. Its purpose was to ensure easy passage "both for cattle and carts" and it applied to new and old fences alike. It also permitted anyone to demolish fences that did not comply with the new rule. Then, on 29 May of the same year, in response to requests from the *procureur général* and the Ursulines, the council made it illegal to open new roads or to pass over seeded land except by way of established roads.

The council's activity regarding roads extended to planning their routes. In 1667 the inhabitants of côte Sainte-Geneviève and route Saint-Michel applied for repair of the roads leading to Québec. They also wanted the width of these roads to be fixed at 18 *pieds* and stakes planted along the roads to stop cattle from doing damage. Following that request the council appointed the *procureur général*, Jean Bourdon, and a councillor to determine how wide roads should be, to look into the necessary repairs, and to decide where roads should be built. Their report was submitted on 13 July 1667 and the council implemented it by ordering a road to be built from Québec to the seigneury of Sillery, construction being entrusted to Bourdon. The council fixed the road's width at 18 *pieds* and enjoined the habitants to help in its construction and upkeep.

The council also concerned itself with streets. By 1665 it had already set at five *pieds* the width of a lane behind Claude Charron's house at the corner of Sous-le-Fort and Notre-Dame streets. Charron, a merchant, was ordered to maintain the lane, but was permitted to use part of it in rebuilding his house. In 1670 one of Charron's neighbours, Charles Roger Descoulombiers, was obliged to move a fence back on his property and so keep clear the lane leading from the côte de la Montagne to rue Sous-le-Fort.[62]

In spite of these cases of direct intervention, it appears that the council's main mode of action was the legislation it enacted. In January 1674 it ordered surveyors to hand in their compasses and instruments to Martin Boutet de Saint-Martin, a professor of mathematics and navigation, so that he could calibrate them. No surveyor was allowed to practise until his instruments were calibrated by Boutet to match those of the other surveyors. The same regulation provided that four markers were to be installed at the four points of the compass in the Lower Town square and were to be used for the alignments laid out for Crown grants, although seigneurs were not prevented from laying out whatever alignments they liked on their own fiefs.[63]

When it came to alignments, those done in Québec were the council's responsibility, as a decision[64] of the colonial power dated 17 May 1674 makes clear: "as regards the alignments laid out for those who build within the Town, this is a general administrative matter that must be dealt with by the conseil Souverain." The council itself admitted that its function was legislative and not that of an enforcer or a maker of alignments, and indeed in 1689 passed a bylaw recognizing the jurisdiction of the *grand voyer*. The bylaw did contain a provision stating that stairs and stoops must not encroach upon the street and prohibiting anyone from building without first obtaining an alignment, but that in no way eliminated the functions of Robinau de Bécancour, who was obliged to provide only "fair And reasonable alignments."[65]

As well, the council concerned itself with street paving. Under section 5 of the bylaw of 27 January 1687, this concern extended only to Lower Town: within two years all landowners were to pave the street frontage of their properties. The same provision was repeated in 1689, but this time if an owner declined to do the work, it would be done for him at his expense, his goods being seized for the purpose if necessary. In 1690 it was enacted that experts would establish the street level in the presence of the lieutenant-general and the *grand voyer*. In the case of tenants, paving work was to be paid for out of their rent.

In roads administration the Conseil Souverain did do a great deal between 1664 and 1667, but that was because the *grand voyer*, René Robinau de Bécancour, had not yet taken up his duties. After he did so in 1668, the council's functions were limited to two: by virtue of its responsibility for general administration, it enacted bylaws for the town and the colony, and it acted as a tribunal for roads cases.[66] It did not replace the *grand voyer*.

Regarding harbour administration, the council's role began on 25 June 1664, when it enacted a regulation prohibiting anyone from leaving planks or foodstuffs on the quays for more than 48 hours. At the same time the council prohibited unloading stones on the waterfront or the shore and particularly on the Cul-de-Sac, where the stores and public square were. On 27 August of that year, acting on orders from France, the council legislated the sailing permits that could be given to the ships that were to come to Québec in 1665. Those who hoped to get permits would have to meet certain conditions: allow searches of their vessels for hides and furs, give free passage to the colony to one workman for every ten registered tons, and load two tons of salt, iron, and charcoal for an equivalent tonnage of other cargo. In 1667 the council appointed commissioners — two of its members — to enquire into shipboard fraud involving beaver pelts.[67]

The last two bylaws involved shipping traffic. There were also laws relating to harbour administration: in the enactment of 11 May 1676 was an attempt to protect private property, as it prohibited anyone from using rowboats or other watercraft without the owners' permissions; offenders were liable to 50-*livre* fines. Then, in 1687, the council ordered harbours to be cleaned and set the share of the cost to be paid by vessel owners. In addition, stone carters were forbidden to unload their cargo on the lot between the houses of Jacques Lebert, on rue Saint-Pierre, and Louis Levasseur, on rue De Meulles. The same bylaw was re-enacted in 1689 and appropriate measures were taken to clean up the waterfront at the foot of the Cul-de-Sac and just in front of the Lebert house.[68]

Bylaws

Bylaws were required by France, or the colonial authorities decided on them on their own in response to problems associated with the town's growth.

From 1663 to 1673 the Conseil Souverain enacted the main bylaws for Québec. In March 1673 Frontenac wrote a series of bylaws for the town, most of which were reused by the council when it drew up 42 bylaws for the town in May 1676. In addition to the subjects Frontenac had already covered, the council dealt with morals, land, Indians, and Huguenots. The 1676 bylaws constituted a real municipal code; they were annually reprinted, in parts, from 1686 to 1689. In these updates the council modified certain sections dealing, among other matters, with fire safety, and brought in new ones having to do with the use of shingles and digging wells.

If we are to point up the Conseil Souverain's role within municipal administration and get to know the town and its problems better, we must look carefully at the bylaws. However, neither roads nor harbour administration ordinances will be considered because they are amply covered elsewhere in this chapter. Bylaws on land and the Indians will not be considered either, because they have no bearing on urban problems. This analysis deals only with bylaws the council enacted from 1663 to 1690, to the exclusion of Frontenac's ordinances and those issued by governors and intendants between 1660 and 1690.[69]

The chronological distribution of Québec bylaws was very uneven (Graph 1). Ninety bylaws were spread over 28 years, an average of over three a year.

The Conseil Souverain's regulatory activity fluctuated at first, peaking in 1663–65, 1667–70, and 1675–77, but was sustained after 1686. As soon as it was created, the council enacted two bylaws, and the highest number of provisions for any year until 1676 were passed in 1664. It is clear from Graph 1 that 1676 marked a turning point in the council's regulatory activity not just because of the large number of bylaws, but also because of the variety of subjects covered.

There were nine years when no bylaws were passed, or almost half the period between 1663 and 1690. It is hard to explain these slack periods.

Graph 1
Frequency of Bylaws by Year
1663–1690

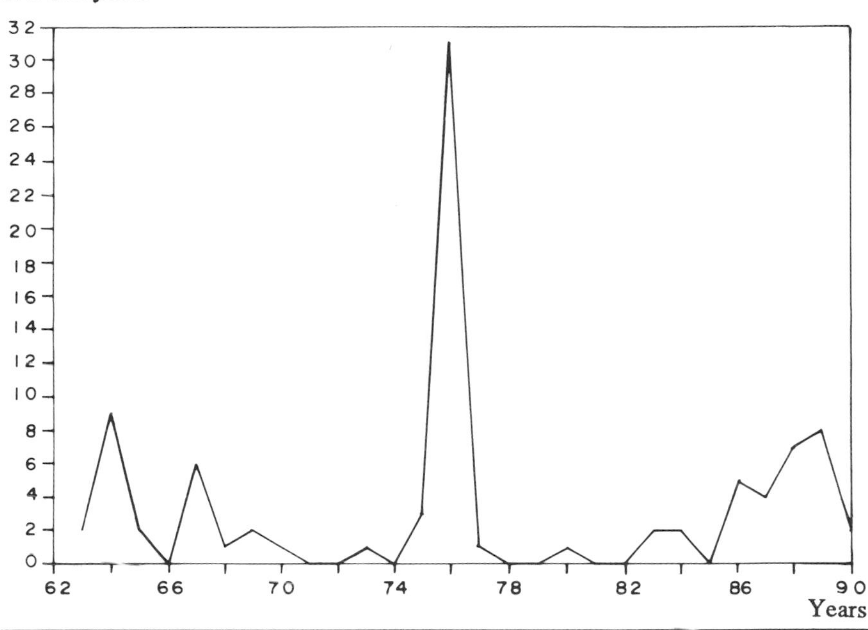

For the years around 1673 we may suppose that, as Frontenac regretfully noted, there was little interest in administration, as if the Conseil Souverain thought it unnecessary to supplement his bylaws with its own. The importance and diversity of those enacted in 1676 make it easier to understand how few and far between the bylaws were until 1686, in which year the majority of the ordinances were just repetitions of what had been adopted in 1676. Too, Frontenac and the council were at loggerheads during these years over various matters: the trial of Fénelon and the governor of Montréal in 1674, the imprisonment of some members of the council in 1678–79, the differences of opinion over the fur trade in Montréal in 1680, and the quarrel between Frontenac and Intendant Duchesneau, which led to the jailing of Duchesneau's son and one of his valets in 1681. These various incidents must have greatly harmed the council's legislative endeavours and taken up much of its time.[70] On the whole, the year-by-year fluctuation of the number of bylaws shows a changing situation: Québec was becoming better adminis-

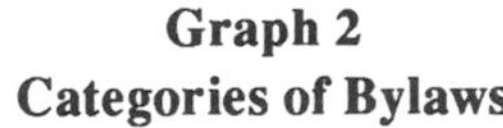

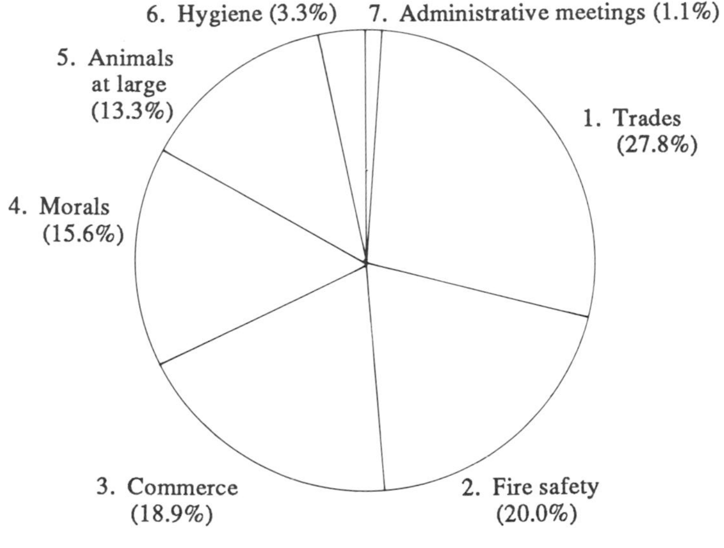

tered, despite the shortcomings, and after 1686 the concern for good administration became constant.

For purposes of analysis the bylaws can be divided into seven categories, and Graph 2 shows the aspects of urban life affected by regulation. Between 1663 and 1690, trades were most often the subjects of bylaws; subsequently the authorities became more concerned with fire, commerce, and morals. The importance attached to bylaws concerning animals at large shows how far Québec remained an agricultural community. Hygiene was rather far down the list of the council's concerns, no doubt a sign of the times. Only one provision dealt with administrative meetings.

In the 1676 bylaws the Conseil Souverain decided that semi-annual administrative meetings would be convened every 15 April and 15 November by the lieutenant-general of the Prévôté, and there the principal citizens of Québec would discuss the price to be set for bread. The meetings were also to consider ways of enlarging and enriching the colony. If it thought fit, the council would appoint two councillors to preside over the meetings, and the results would be submitted to it for possible action.

Grouping the bylaws in subcategories more clearly reveals their thrust and content (Table 1). The trades category shows the greatest diversity

Table 1
Breakdown of Bylaws by Subcategory

Category	Subcategory	No. of Bylaws	%
Trades	Millers	6	24.00
	Domestic servants	5	20.00
	Tavernkeepers	5	20.00
	Butchers	4	16.00
	Bakers	2	8.00
	Construction workers	2	8.00
	Guildmasters	1	4.00
		25	
Fire safety	Combustible materials	6	33.33
	Chimneys	5	27.78
	Houses	4	22.22
	Residents' roles	3	16.67
		18	
Commerce	Supply of Québec	5	29.41
	Merchants' status	4	23.53
	Weights and measures	4	23.53
	Price setting	3	17.65
	Markets	1	5.88
		17	
Morals	Prostitution	5	35.71
	Begging	3	21.43
	Vagrancy	2	14.29
	Poverty	2	14.29
	Blasphemy	1	7.14
	Huguenots	1	7.14
		14	
Animals at large	Pigs	7	58.33
	Cattle	5	41.67
		12	
Hygiene	Streets	2	66.67
	Latrines	1	33.33
		3	

in the bylaws, since the council dealt with seven sectors of the labour market. Distribution of articles within this category is a little surprising. Millers got the most attention from the legislators and were closely followed by domestic servants and tavernkeepers, while very few provisions are found for bakers, construction workers, and guildmasters.

The high incidence of bylaws relating to millers is explained by the fact that the Conseil Souverain's concern was chiefly the marking of weights and measures. On 20 June 1667 it set milling fees at one-fourteenth of the amount milled, ordered the lieutenant-general of the Prévôté to inspect mills' weights and measures, and decreed that habitants were to have their wheat and flour weighed. In January 1687 the council decided that weights and balances for weighing wheat would be examined and "made correct, as will measures for milling." It appears there was some difficulty in applying this bylaw, which was again promulgated in 1689, for on 19 December of that year the council ordered judges to visit the mills, inspect the weights for accuracy, and report back to the *procureur général.*

Other bylaws were brought about by external events. On 28 March 1667, because of habitants' complaints, the council ordered millers who had given short weight to compensate owners at their own expense, and on 21 October 1686, complying with an order from the king's Conseil d'État, it enjoined seigneurs to build communal mills on their fiefs within the year; after that time anyone could build such mills and enjoy the advantages attached to their "banalité" (a charge levied by a seigneur for a service provided).

Supervision of domestic servants constituted one of the authorities' major concerns. The council's first ordinances forbade any person from enticing valets or domestic servants away from their masters' service, and in 1664 the order was extended to indentured servants. Between 1663 and 1676 the bylaws pertaining to servants hardly varied; only the penalties changed. At first, offenders and those harbouring them risked various fines, but in 1673, even while keeping the fines in force, the council ordered that corporal punishments be meted out to truant servants, who were to be "pilloried for the first offence; for the second, they shall be caned and branded with a fleur-de-lis."

Bylaws governing innkeepers show how vigilant the council was toward them. Through its ordinances the council regulated the sale of wine and spirits, and attempted to stem the abuses that might breed in taverns.

As early as 1665 a decree of the Conseil Souverain set the price of wine at 15 *sols* a *pot*. The council passed an act in 1668 to encourage beer production in Canada: under the act, those who wanted to sell wine and spirits had to obtain permits. In 1676 the council prohibited tavernkeepers from extending credit to soldiers or servants, or serving liquor after nine o'clock at night. Drunkenness was forbidden, either in taverns or elsewhere; offenders might be sentenced to fines of any amount or imprisonment. Tavernkeepers were required to report those who broke the ordinances to the lieutenant-general of the Prévôté and to the *procureur du roi*.

In 1688, tavernkeepers were ordered not to buy any of the tools and clothing given to the poor by the Bureau des pauvres. Two years later a bylaw limited the sale of wine with meals (certain tavernkeepers sold wine "au pot" and others, with meals) and limited permission to put up winesellers' signs to persons who had obtained written approval from the king's magistrates. Such persons were also subject to inspection by the lieutenant-general of the Prévôté or his deputies. Tavernkeepers were also protected by numerous other bylaws, particularly those forbidding wine wholesalers to sell liquor at retail.

The bylaws seem to have been particularly strict for two of the food trades. By the 1676 bylaw butchers could display their meats only in the stalls, which the town rented to them, in the market.[71] When slaughtering animals they were ordered, for reasons of health, to dump the blood and offal in the river. Butchers were permitted to cut up meat only on market days, and in 1687 the council ruled that butchering must take place only on the outskirts of town. The following year it ordered that weights and scales used for weighing meat not have capacities of more than ten *livres*.

Bakers were obliged to keep enough bread on hand to satisfy the public. They were subject to special control in the form of town meetings, in theory held every year, where the price and weight of a loaf of bread were decided, as well as the amount of white and brown bread needed and how many bakers might do business in the town, inhabitants being preferred to non-residents.

Such meetings were in fact held intermittently starting in 1677, the lieutenant-general of the Prévôté tasting the bread in the course of the proceedings. The lieutenant-general was also required to frequently inspect the bakeries to see that the bylaws were being followed. Until 1690, bakers had a monopoly on baking bread within the town; after that, countryfolk were permitted to bring their bread to market.

Only three bylaws affected the construction industry. In 1676 a bylaw was passed forbidding tavernkeepers to serve food or drink to masons, carpenters, and other workmen without their employers' consent. If such workmen did leave a worksite without the contractor's permission, they risked "being made to pay the salaries of the labourers under them, as well as a fine of three *livres* to the proprietors." In 1689 the council added that contractors were obliged to fulfil their contracts. The 1676 bylaws also specify that guildmasters must take oaths before the lieutenant-general of the Prévôté and the *procureur du roi*, who invested them with the same powers Paris guildmasters enjoyed. Except in the case of surgeon-barbers, these bylaws do not seem to have been enforced; instead, the custom was to ask experts and arbitrators to settle disputes.

The authorities' second concern was to protect the town from fire (Table 1). To that end the council passed an act regarding combustible materials, chimneys, houses, and the role townspeople were to play in case of fire.

The Conseil Souverain's efforts to counter the threat of fire were hindered by the bad habits of a great part of Québec residents. On 26 April 1664 it ordered Lower Town residents to clear the streets of straw and dried dung, which could cause fires. In 1676 it forbade people to keep fodder in their houses, especially in Lower Town, or feed animals over the winter. The council announced plans to establish firewood depots and forbade residents to keep firewood in the street or in vacant lots between houses. A square *arpent* was set aside near Talon's brewery for firewood in 1689. Lastly, the council forbade taking tobacco and carrying flames in town streets. These measures, particularly those concerning tobacco, must have been difficult to enforce, as they were reiterated in 1689.

Residents were required to have their chimneys swept every two months in the presence of witnesses and to certify to the lieutenant-general of the Prévôté or the *procureur du roi*, in writing, that the work had been done. Thc lieutenant-general of the Prévôté was required to visit houses to ensure that the bylaw had been obeyed. After a judgment handed down in 1688, he was also required to report on chimney conditions, so that they met council's standards. Fireplaces had to be so designed that iron or brick stoves could be installed in them, these not being permitted elsewhere in the house.

Housing bylaws concerned the installation of ladders and the use of shingles. In 1676, householders were obliged to install ladders on their roofs so that in case of fire, the roof timbers would be accessible and could be axed if necessary. Following the Lower Town fire in 1682, the council recognized that the measure was insufficient and ordered ladders installed on every chimney and along house walls. In 1688 and 1689 the council forbade the use of shingles for roofing except for gables; however, these ordinances did not stop the people of Québec from shingling their houses.[72]

The few clauses on people's role in case of fire were simple ones. At the first alarm bell they were to go to the fire with buckets or pails full of water. Those refusing to do so were subject to punishment, and in 1689 the council ordered all carpenters to go to fires "with axe in hand and be ready to use it."[73]

Commercial regulations were concerned, in order of importance, with supplies for the town, with the status of merchants, with weights and measures, with prices, and with the town market.

Supply regulations for Québec governed the distribution of goods within the colony. As early as 1664 the Conseil Souverain forbade merchants to wholesale more than ten per cent of their merchandise, all of which they were to display only in the town for a month; after that they were allowed to send a quarter of the unsold goods to Trois-Rivières and as much again to Montréal. The remainder of the goods had to stay in Québec. It was also in 1664 that the council forbade merchants to take their stock to Montréal, and obliged Montréalers, as well as Trois-Rivières residents, to declare the goods they wished to take out of the town.

In resupplying the town, certain goods were subject to special regulations. In 1676 the council obliged lumbermen, under threat of fines and dismissal, to stack cordwood only in cords eight *pieds* long and four *pieds* high. In 1677, fearing that Québec bakers would buy up all the wheat for speculative purposes, the council ruled that the bakers could not buy wheat in the town or within six *lieues* of it. (This ban was lifted in 1689.) In 1686 the council required a Lévis tanner to supply skins to Québec shoemakers.

Legislation on the status of merchants distinguished between inhabitants and non-residents, and sought to protect habitants' privileges. The term "habitant" had then a very exact meaning: "no non-resident can claim the privileges enjoyed by the habitants of this country unless, Having been married in france, he brings with him his wife And family, or owns a dwelling valued at two thousand *Livres* at least, And in Either Case has lived in the country at least two years, or he has married a local girl."[74]

In 1664, outside merchants — those not permanent residents of the colony — were forbidden to sell garments or have them "manufactured." In March 1676, following habitants' requests, the council refused outside merchants permission to sell liquor at retail or sell tobacco of more than a *livre* weight; they were also forbidden to take part in the fur trade on pain of confiscation of their goods and 500-*livre* fines. After April 1676 they were no longer allowed to sell goods either wholesale or retail during the period when the Ottawa Indians came down. Another regulation, passed in 1683, forbade outside merchants to sell retail from August to October of every year.

In its attempt to standardize weights and measures, the council delegated the stamping of them to the clerk of the Québec Prévôté in 1676. They were to bear the king's mark only, affixed in the presence of the lieutenant-general of the Prévôté; the revenue generated was to be fairly shared between the clerk and the town. In 1687, because the 1676 enactment was so little observed, the council ordered that weights and measures be stamped anew in the presence of the *procureur du roi* and the lieutenant-general of the Prévôté. This ordinance, first applied in Québec, was extended to Montréal and Trois-Rivières in 1688. The council then obliged the various courts of first instance (in the Prévôtés of Québec and Trois-Rivières and the *bailliage* of Montréal) and the seigneurial courts to keep standard weights and measures in their respective registries. This provision was repeated in the 1689 regulations.

The practice of setting prices, the goods "tariff," made its appearance early on. It arose from the idea that merchants' profit margins could be established. The council decided as early as January 1664, on the basis of prices charged in France, that these margins should be limited to 65 per cent. On 30 June 1664 it allowed merchants a profit of 55 per cent on their dry goods, 100 per cent on "more valuable liquids," and 120 per cent on goods whose prices "did not exceed the sum of One Hundred *livres* per tun." To enforce this arrangement the council assigned two counsellors as deputies. This "tariff" continued, with minor changes, until 1676, at which time the council decided that a scale of prices for all goods would be drawn up annually, hoping that merchants' activities could thus be monitored and controlled.

Certain measures were passed to ensure that these regulations were followed. Merchants were required to submit their books to the council-appointed commissioners, who checked whether the merchants had charged the going rates. The commissioners also inspected the merchants' shops, assessed their goods, and set prices. They also were responsible for looking into violations of the tariff, a copy of which was posted in all commercial premises. Merchants were obliged, on pain of 500-*livre* fines, to report the whole of their stock to the council.

Only one business bylaw dealt with the town market. In May 1676 the council, in a decision in keeping with the spirit of Frontenac's regulations, provided for a site to be set aside in Upper or Lower Town where markets would be held every Tuesday and Friday. The council did not want the habitants, whether town or country dwellers, to sell their produce door to door before having displayed their wares in the market until 11 o'clock. Finally, to allow householders time to do their shopping, the council did not permit tavernkeepers and other merchants to buy supplies before certain times of day.[75]

There were 14 bylaws on morals, more than a third of them dealing with prostitution; beggars, vagrants, and the poor were the subject of 7 bylaws, while just 2 dealt with blasphemers and Huguenots.

Except for a few isolated instances, most cases of prostitution are recorded for 1675. That August the council appointed one of its members, the Sieur Dupont, as commissioner of inquiry into prostitution arising from the arrival of ships from France, which had attracted women of ill repute to the town. In a judgment handed down on 19 August 1675 the council sentenced two women to banishment, their customers being fined ten *livres*. It also ordered all shameless and loose-living women to leave the town within the week or face whipping.

Seventeenth-century Québec's most famous case of prostitution was that of Anne Bauge, wife of Guillaume Corruble. She was jailed on 26 August 1675, charged with prostitution with sailors on shore leave. She was freed by the lieutenant-general of the Prévôté of Québec, who for that reason was relieved of his duties by the council in August 1676. Anne Bauge was banished from the town for three years and jailed once more in 1678 for violating her ban; however, the council relented at her husband's earnest appeal and because both were shortly to embark for France.

The year 1675 saw so many prostitutes' trials that it is not surprising that clause 32 of the council's bylaws, dated 11 May 1676, addressed the problem. It forbade all citizens to harbour women or girls of loose habits, as well as pimps or madams, on pain of the penalties prescribed by ordinance. All who engaged in prostitution would be punished to the limit of criminal law.[76]

Québec had another problem: poverty, begging, and vagrancy, which sometimes took on alarming proportions. In the 17th century the terms "vagrants," "beggars," and "poor" were quite distinct. In the eyes of justice and the authorities, vagrants were masterless men having no legal existence; in New France the groups who mainly came under this category were coureurs de bois, discharged soldiers, deserters, and counterfeiters. By a Conseil Souverain regulation of 13 April 1676, such men were forbidden to engage in the fur trade in either Montréal or Trois-Rivières or to work for outside merchants; offenders were liable to confiscation of trade goods, corporal punishment, and fines of any amount. A month later the council decreed that vagabonds might not live within the town of Québec and its *banlieue* unless they reported the reason for their stay to the lieutenant-general of the Prévôté and the *procureur du roi*. They had to obtain permission to settle in the town or nearby, otherwise they could be expelled and fined any sum the court saw fit.

Beggars, too, were homeless men, but were layabouts who preferred begging to working. Begging was not tolerated in the colony, as it was a burden and a sore on society. On 11 May 1676 the council forbade anyone claiming to be poor and needy to beg in the town or *banlieue* of Québec without a certificate of poverty. The certificate, which gave the applicant's residence, had to be signed by a magistrate or *curé* and submitted to the lieutenant-general of the Prévôté and the *procureur du roi*; failure to do so would result in corporal punishment.

This first regulation had very little effect. According to the *procureur du roi*, begging first appeared in Québec in 1673, introduced by some local women. Since then the situation had deteriorated because people were attracted to this easy life and householders had been generous to door-to-door beggars. In the summer of 1676 the council appointed a commissioner to look into the matter; he determined that there were 300 beggars in the town, an unruly lot who might rob the great houses. Council then decreed that no able-bodied beggar might ply his trade in Québec and that all must quit the town within the week, going back to their lands and cultivating them. It also discouraged townspeople from giving to beggars.

In 1682 Governor LaBarre claimed that there were few beggars in Canada, but in April 1683 the council noted with regret that the beggars expelled from the town in 1676 had returned. They were a burden on the public, they brought up their children in idleness, and they had ringed the town with shanties where disorder and debauchery flourished. The council therefore renewed its order of 1676, but this time punishments were harsher: first offenders would be pilloried and recidivists lashed.

The state took a different view of truly needy cases, the "shamefaced poor who remained on the family land" and who were not "depraved," as well as the aged and the disabled. In its war on poverty and begging, the council's greatest achievement was the introduction of Bureaux des pauvres in the colony's towns and parishes. Recognizing that its previous ordinances had failed, the council on 8 April 1688 founded Bureaux des pauvres in Québec, Trois-Rivières, and Montréal "to give the poor the means of subsistence."

Each *bureau* or office was staffed by the *curé* and three administrators. The *curé* was to identify the poor, who then applied for alms to the director of the Bureau des pauvres; the latter made sure applicants were indeed poor, and he also looked for work for the able-bodied and set their wages. Another administrator acted as treasurer and looked after monies donated during public collections or deposited in church poor-boxes. The third administrator was the secretary, who recorded the office's proceeding and kept exact records of which poor people had received alms.

The Bureau des pauvres met every month. Its administrators supplied the poor with money, tools, or food as they thought fit; they could sentence ne'er-do-wells to terms in prison or a dungeon on bread and water, or punish them by withholding food. Administrators were not to give alms to layabouts and might not accept any poor person who had not resided in the area for at least three months. Their permission was necessary if special collections were to be made to aid indigent families. The administrators could oblige the poor to work and press into service the children of large families who asked for charity.

Blasphemy and Protestantism were also offences against morality that the Conseil Souverain was concerned with. In May 1676 it outlawed swearing and blasphemy; offenders were liable to fines of varying amounts. A fifth offence brought the offender to the pillory, and for a sixth he also had his lower lip cut. Those guilty of blasphemy for a seventh time had their tongues cut out. Offenders who could not pay fines were imprisoned for a month on bread and water. Recidivists were listed in a special registry of those caught and convicted a second time. The council required anyone who overheard blaspheming to report the culprit to the local magistrates within 24 hours; those who did not made themselves liable to fines of 60 *sols*.

As in France, the council forbade Huguenots to assemble to practise their religion. At first, Protestants were not allowed to winter in New France without permission; when this was granted, they were not to practise their religion publicly and were obliged to live like Catholics, not setting an "evil example." All other offences against morality, especially such crimes as murder and theft, were not covered by special bylaws; these were matters for the courts.

Regulations on animals at large were intended to protect seed and grain, and were closely bound up with health and fire safety. Two regulations will illustrate the legislation dealing with pigs. On 4 February 1686 the council ordered that pigs be kept penned in Upper and Lower Town both. First offenders were liable to fines of three *livres*, to go to the Hôtel-Dieu, the fines being doubled or trebled for subsequent offences. During his visits of inspection the lieutenant-general of the Prévôté collected the fines and turned half of them over to those, if any, who had laid information.

This regulation turned out to be difficult to enforce. On 19 August 1686 the lieutenant-general of the Prévôté complained to the council that the townspeople were allowing their pigs to wander through town and that though he had made his inspections, he had been unable to levy

Table 2
Date Ranges of Bylaws by Subcategory

Subcategory	First Bylaw	Last Bylaw
Millers	1667	1689
Domestic servants	1663	1676
Innkeepers	1665	1690
Butchers	1676	1688
Bakers	1676	1690
Construction workers	1676	1689
Guildmasters	1676	—
Combustibles	1664	1689
Chimneys	1676	1689
Houses	1676	1689
Residents' roles	1676	1689
Supply of Québec	1664	1676
Merchants' status	1664	1686
Weights and measures	1676	1689
Price setting	1664	1676
Markets	1676	—
Prostitution	1667	1676
Begging	1676	1683
Vagrancy	1676	1676
Poverty	1663	1688
Blasphemy	1676	—
Huguenots	1676	—
Pigs	1664	1688
Cattle	1664	1680
Streets	1676	1686
Latrines	1676	—
Town meetings	1676	—

any fines because no one would acknowledge ownership of the free-roaming pigs. The council renewed the ordinance and instructed all the bailiffs and law-enforcement officers to kill pigs found at large in the town when the lieutenant-general of the Prévôté gave the order during his inspection tours. The animals killed were to be confiscated and given to the nuns of the Hôtel-Dieu and their poor. In January 1688 the council forbade residents of Lower Town to keep more than one pig,

Table 3
Penalties Prescribed by Bylaws

Category and No. of Bylaws	No. of Penalties Prescribed	% of Sections in Bylaw	% of Total Penalties
Morals (14)	10	71.43	28.57
Trades (25)	8	32.00	22.86
Animals at large (12)	7	58.33	20.00
Commerce (17)	6	35.29	17.14
Fire safety (18)	3	16.67	8.57
Hygiene (3)	1	33.33	2.86
Town meetings (1)	0	—	—
Total penalties	35	38.89	100.00

which had to be washed daily so it would not inconvenience the neighbours.

Legislation regarding cattle, though passed and posted within the town, also applied to the surrounding countryside and to the colony as a whole. Essentially it stipulated that all cattle were to be watched on commons or on individual lots from spring thaw until the harvest was in, at which time the local magistrates would give permission to discontinue the watch. In Québec itself the authorities sought to prevent cattle from being stabled in Lower Town during winter. Feed stored in houses constituted fire hazards, and manure in the streets inconvenienced the public and might cause infections.

Apart from the specific statements on animals at large, the legislators did not add much to the health measures already passed. True to the spirit of Frontenac's bylaws, the council required that landlords and tenants whose houses had no latrines clean their house fronts every morning. Council ordered sewage to be taken to a place where it would not inconvenience the public; disposal of sewage in the streets was prohibited and violators were liable to fines of any amount.

Such was the essence of the various bylaws enacted by the town of Québec from 1663 to 1690. To bring some balance to the impressions that may be left by Table 1 and to attempt to define the council's changing regulatory thrust, we must look at the subjects of the bylaws year by year.

Five of the bylaws passed in 1664 pertained to trade, while all of those passed in 1675 dealt with prostitution. In 1689 three-fifths of the bylaws were concerned with fire prevention. In 1676 the bylaws fell into four broad categories: trades, morals, fire safety, and commerce. It

Table 4
Cases of Compliance or Violation Mentioned in Bylaws

	Compliance		Violations	
Category	No.	%	No.	%
Morals	1	1.11	5	5.56
Animals at large	0	—	4	4.44
Trades	6	6.67	3	3.33
Fire safety	0	—	1	1.11
Commerce	1	1.11	1	1.11
Hygiene	0	—	0	—
Town meetings	1	1.11	0	—
Total	9	10.00	14	15.55

was in 1676 that the council first legislated in the fields of hygiene, beggars and vagrants, butchers and bakers, weights and measures, and — except regarding inflammable materials — fire safety (Table 2). That year also saw the elimination of the bylaws dealing, among others, with supplies for Québec, price setting, domestic servants, prostitution, and vagrancy.

Certain urban problems were quite temporary while others held the council's attention almost continuously, like the bylaws on the various trades and on animals at large. After 1676, apart from the bylaws on weights and measures and the status of merchants, commercial bylaws were displaced by those dealing with fire safety. Only two morals bylaws were passed after that year.

Such variations in the purview of the bylaws show that the council's role was limited once an intendant had been appointed. In addition, they show that ad hoc solutions were sought to various urban problems and that the town's servant population was dwindling (*see* Chapter IV). They may also be a result of the Lower Town fire of 1682, which led the authorities to take more thought for fire safety. Finally, the changing bylaws indicate the importance of Frontenac's 1673 regulations and their influence on those the council passed in 1676.

How coercive were these bylaws? On examination, 39 per cent of them provided penalties for infractions. Judging by the number of sections in the bylaws in each of the six categories listed in Table 1, four main areas are affected by penalties: morals, animals at large, commerce, and trades (Table 3).

The morals category contains a very high percentage of penalties to total number of sections. It also has the highest percentage of the total penalties recorded, closely followed by the trades category, in which the bylaws relating to domestic servants all call for fines and other penalties for delinquents, to the tune of five-eighths of all such penalties provided under trades bylaws. Only three bylaws on fire safety mention punishments, and that regarding town meetings mentions none at all. The small amount of information gathered on hygiene does not allow any useful extrapolation.

Penalties were of two kinds: first, financial penalties, then corporal punishments. Financial penalties might consist of fines alone or might also include corporal punishments; they varied from 2½ to 500 *livres*. The most common fine was 10 *livres*, and frequent reference was made to "fines of any amount" and to confiscation of goods in bylaws relating to commerce. Apart from domestic servants, merchants were sentenced to the heaviest fines.

Financial penalties were attached to all bylaw categories and made up more than 74 per cent of all penalties prescribed. Corporal punishment was reserved for morals offences, for domestic servants, and for certain offences related to fire safety; it could include the pillory, prison terms, whippings and mutilations. Analysis of the penalties points up the council's attitude toward various problems and various strata of the town's population; it also casts light on the council's priorities and concerns.

It is difficult to gauge how far the bylaws were complied with (Table 4 [percentages are based on the total number of bylaws, i.e., 90]). The data on the instances of compliance with the ordinances do not support any more definite conclusion than that the trade bylaws were better enforced than the rest, probably because of the supervisory role allotted to the lieutenant-general of the Prévôté of Québec. The instances of violation cited are more extensive; they appear in more than 15 per cent of the bylaws. There again, the most common offences relate to morals and to animals at large. That would appear to justify the bylaws' penalties for these two kinds of offences.

Repeated promulgation of the bylaws is another indicator of how difficult they were to enforce. Between 1663 and 1690, fifteen bylaws were thus renewed, or 16.67 per cent of the total. More than a third of these bylaws related to animals at large, while 26 per cent had to do with fire safety. The few other cases of repeated promulgation were of bylaws on domestic servants, millers, and weights and measures.

Analysis of municipal bylaws allows us to determine whether France's directives on bylaws were followed. It points up the various actors' roles in town management and sheds light on the authorities' thinking. France had delegated the drafting of bylaws to the Conseil Souverain, which had to obtain the cooperation of the governor and intendant. In exceptional cases either of these two administrators could himself draw up bylaws. The policing of the town of Québec was a prerogative of the lieutenant-general of the Prévôté. In fact, the council at first enjoyed supremacy in policing, both general and particular, but it later became a responsibility shared by the governor, the intendant, and the council. For his part, the lieutenant-general of the Prévôté seems to have been entrusted only with applying the bylaws within the town and its own jurisdiction.

In most cases, then, colonial authorities deferred to France; moreover, bylaws were often copied directly from French municipal legislation. The colony's legislation compounded, since the Conseil Souverain referred often in its general ordinances to earlier regulations, either its own or those promulgated by governors.

The variety of bylaws is evident, but it seems surprising how apt they were and how similar to modern bylaws, especially those on fire safety and — for all its failings — on hygiene. They reflected the main concerns of the council, and of its principal members (the governor, the intendant, and the bishop), and they show these men's determination to exert control, especially over commerce and the trades, and to enforce conformity, particularly moral, on all citizens of the colony. The penalties accompanying the bylaws show us an authoritarian state that in some cases wanted citizens to inform on offenders. That first impression must nonetheless be tempered, since the constant renewal of certain bylaws shows how hard they were to enforce, and there is also evidence of the authorities' tolerance of non-compliance, as in the use of shingles.

Through analysis of the bylaws we can also get a clearer idea of what daily life was like in Québec during the last half of the 17th century and describe certain behaviours in an urban environment. The problems noted in the bylaws are indicative of the situation that prevailed in Québec; they show us a typical 17th-century town, not just by its outer appearance and its agricultural flavour, but also by its people's customs. Their laxness, their negligence, and their resistance to the ordinances are so many indications of their outlook on life and of their occupations, all reflecting something of their mentality. Town life itself causes a certain number of problems due to the density and mixing of the population. The town's attraction for people of the surrounding countryside and the presence of a large transient population aggravates the situation.

The *Grand Voyer*

By examining the roads administration and the role of the *grand voyer* we can better appreciate the complexity of Robinau de Bécancour's jurisdiction, which he shared with the senior officials and the Conseil Souverain. Though the *grand voyer* could issue orders for beautifying the town, the actual alignments were laid out by his clerk, and they most affected the urban landscape.

What did the *grand voyer* do and what was the *voirie*, the roads department? In his jurisprudence directory Guyot stated:

> *The law on public thoroughfares relates, generally speaking, to the power to pass ordinances & bylaws governing the alignment & regularity of buildings, & the paving & cleaning of streets and public places, so that thoroughfares are kept in good condition, convenient and unimpeded by such dangers as may arise there, to prevent any construction & undertaking that might mar the town's appearance, hinder commerce & impair citizens' safety & convenience.*[77]

This definition implies a judicial power to do what Guyot referred to as "policing the thoroughfares," but that power was not limited to just streets; the *grand voyer* regulated house construction and town beautification. The definition does not, however, draw the administrative distinction between public thoroughfares and high roads. High roads, main streets, and paving of thoroughfares in town and country both came under the treasurers of France after 1626. Public thoroughfares dealt with awnings, signs, gutters, and projections.[78] In towns where there was no treasurer of France nor any magistrate dealing particularly with thoroughfares, these were considered administrative matters and assigned to the *procureur du roi* or another officer of justice.[79]

Such was, in theory, how thoroughfares were administered in France until 1693. In reality, as French historian Jean-Louis Harouel has noted, they were not under a unified administration; also involved were municipal councils, seigneurs *hauts justiciers* (dispensing "high justice"), the director of the king's buildings, and masters of the hunt.[80]

Legislation on the subject came mainly from the Crown, and ever since the 16th century, policy on thoroughfares had been consistent. Thus the Ordinance of Blois (1579), like that passed in August 1669 and the king's order-in-council of 1686, ordered that the breadth of the high roads and public thoroughfares be kept clear, obliged those whose properties bordered the road to dig ditches and raise embankments to facilitate drainage, and stipulated that they clean the ditches annually. After letters patent the king granted in July 1638, seigneurs claiming the right to administer justice and public thoroughfares could no longer close or alter any of the high roads. After the adoption of the king's council regulations of November 1666 no one could build or rebuild along any of the king's highways without an alignment. There were many other regulations, including one passed in 1686 ordering the planting of trees along highways; however, the chief law on the subject remained Henri IV's 1607 edict, which ordered that streets be straightened, widened, and beautified. He also stipulated that the width of the king's highways should be increased to 24 *pieds*, and for the first time, ordered that alignments be obtained before any building went ahead. Together these ordinances formed a kind of highway code that the responsible officers referred to.[81]

In New France the situation was slightly different, especially since the current *grand voyer* was responsible for both main roads and smaller thoroughfares. René Robinau de Bécancour had been appointed to those functions in 1657 by the Compagnie des Cents-Associés, and his appointment was confirmed by the Compagnie des Indes Occidentales on 29 March 1667;[82] the latter's confirmatory letter ordered him to perform his office in accordance with the Coutume des Paris and "to comply therewith in the honours, *authorities* and *prerogatives* of the said office." In other words, Bécancour was to obey the laws of the realm in discharging his duties.

This resemblance to French practice was the first of many, particularly in the area of shared responsibilities. In addition to the governor, intendant, and Conseil Souverain, whose roles have already been described, the *Prévôté* and certain seigneurs took part in administering thoroughfares in Québec. Relevant cases were dealt with initially by the Prévôté and if necessary, appealed to the Conseil Souverain. The Prévôté acted upon cases concerned with alignments within its jurisdiction and with country roads, and was competent to order the demolition of walls encroaching on town streets; it also dealt more generally with prosecuting violators of the thoroughfare bylaws.[83]

For example, on 5 September 1682 Robinau de Bécancour ordered the demolition of the chimney of a certain Rochon on rue De Meulles because it was ruinous and encroaching on the street. Unless Rochon complied, his chimney would be demolished at his expense. However, the *grand voyer* was said to have exceeded his authority in that instance; he should instead have had the fellow brought up before the lieutenant-general in a case of non-compliance. Subsequently, on 9 July 1689 at the request of François Genaple, the mason Pierre Guénet was hauled before the Prévôté to be fined for having undertaken construction of a house foundation for Jean-François Bourdon de Dombourg on rue du

Cul-de-Sac without having an alignment done by the *grand voyer*'s clerk.[84]

I have found only one case in which seigneurs influenced decisions relating to thoroughfares. In 1683 the widow Couillard, holder of a fief in Upper Town, laid out a road 20 *pieds* wide from the seminary to the côte du Palais.[85] This is an instance, probably not unique, of a fiefholder being able to lay out roads in town and country both. Identical rights were enjoyed by seigneurs in France.

Thoroughfares nevertheless continued to be chiefly the responsibility of the *grand voyer*, whose role was like that of roads agents in France. First, he had to look after alignments, which were defined by three criteria. First, according to Furetière, there was the plan laid down by architects and road agents for house fronts; the plan had to be followed in building on pain of demolition.[86] Therefore the survey document was by and large equivalent to a building permit. Except under the administration of Frontenac, who in 1673 allowed municipal magistrates to set up shops in Lower Town and in 1675 approved Denys de Vitré's construction of a house in Upper Town, there is no evidence that such permits were ever required in Québec.[87]

Moreover, Guyot stated that the alignment was the plan drawn up by experts or owners for construction or repair of houses or buildings. As such, it was a private act requiring the authorities' endorsement. He added that before beginning construction or repair work, landlords and masons were required to survey the property in the presence of a magistrate and the *procureur du roi*, failing which the building might be demolished and the offenders fined.[88]

Another element to this type of survey was that there had to be a legal demarcation between the public thoroughfare and the private spaces adjoining it. Jean-Louis Harouel pointed out that in the absence of an official town plan, the alignment itself created the plan: the very act of surveying creates the legal demarcation between the public thoroughfare and the lot adjoining it. If there was such a plan, however, the line marked on it determined the boundary of the public thoroughfare.[89]

Such plans did exist in Québec under the French régime. From 1660 to 1690 there were no overall plans showing the alignments to be observed, only individual layouts to which reference was made when necessary. The following are cases in point: the Ursulines' plan of 1674 (Fig. 18), the Place Royale plan of 1683 (Fig. 15), the alignment of rue De Meulles in 1689 (Fig. 21), and the 1681 plan for the Récollets' grounds (Fig. 26). Since the surveys covered not only streets and houses, but also courtyards, walls, and fences, they also showed the

Table 5
Alignments Registered in Québec
1681–1690

Year	No. of Alignments
1681	1
1682	0
1683	0
1684	0
1685	3
1686	2
1687	6
1688	3
1689	18
1690	0

Table 6
Location of Alignments
1681–1689

Street	No. of Alignments
Buade	2
Côte de la Montagne	2
Côte de la Fabrique	1
Des Jardins	2
Place d'Armes	1
Saint-Louis	2
Sainte-Anne	2
Total, Upper Town	12
Côte de la Montagne	1
Cul-de-Sac	1
De l'Escalier	1
De Meulles	6
Notre-Dame	2
Saint-Pierre	6
Sault-au-Matelot	3
Sous-le-Fort	1
Total, Lower Town	21

Table 7
Street and Alley Widths shown in Alignment Registrations, 1681–1689

Street	Width in *Pieds*
Côte de la Fabrique	24.00
Côte de la Montagne	21.00
Cul-de-Sac	24.00
De l'Escalier	12.00
De Meulles	16.00
Des Jardins	22.75
Du Porche	12.00
Street from rue Saint-Pierre to the shore	13.50
Saint-Louis	36.00
Sault-au-Matelot	24.00
An alley perpendicular to rue De Meulles	12.00
Another alley perpendicular to rue De Meulles	16.00
An alley perpendicular to rue Sous-le-Fort	3.50

boundaries of private lots. Accordingly, they were required not just for construction, repair, or rebuilding, but also for demolition.[90]

The registry of the *grands voyers* shows the real impact of these officials' activities on the fabric of Québec, especially regarding alignments. As of 1690 the registry contained 46 documents. The first, dating from 1667, is the commission given to René Robinau and registered with the Conseil Souverain in 1668. The registry also contained his son's commission, from 1689, and its registration in 1690. There were also seven ordinances in the registry, a survey report, a permit for building a portico, and 33 alignments.

These alignments were laid out between 1681 and 1689. Although six were registered in 1687, the highest number (18) were registered in 1689 (Table 5). The many registered in those two years reflects the number of houses constructed and lots granted. The absence of such registrations for four years and for the years prior to 1681 may be attributed to the loss or destruction of documents if in theory an alignment was to be registered for each construction project. Construction contracts do exist for the years for which no alignments were registered (*see* Chapter III).

Statistics on the location of alignments (Table 6) also reflect housing construction activity and the granting of lots. Twelve alignments were given in Upper Town and 21 in Lower Town. The 1682 fire in Lower

Town and subsequent reconstruction projects explain the volume of alignments there. Six were laid out on rue De Meulles and six on rue Saint-Pierre. We know that Québec's physical expansion was to be channelled toward the part of town near rue De Meulles, and a number of lots on rue Saint-Pierre were granted at the end of the 17th century by governors and intendants.

The *grand voyer* laid out only four alignments; the rest were the work of his clerk, François Genaple, who after 1685, under the terms of his commission, was primarily responsible for them.[91] At times he was aided by a surveyor: Jean Le Rouge assisted in drafting seven of them. However, surveyors were not authorized to lay out alignments alone. In June 1687 François Pachot had to remove the foundations he had begun on rue Saint-Pierre for failing to recognize the authority of the *grand voyer*'s clerk and using an alignment laid out by the surveyor Boisbuisson.[92]

Only two alignments delineated streets. On 30 October 1681, at the request of Philippe Gaultier de Comporté and the bishop's *grand-vicaire* Henri de Bernières, René Robinau de Bécancour had a line laid out for the côte de la Fabrique. He had surveyor Jean Le Rouge place two markers and set the street width at 36 *pieds*.[93] An alignment for another street, rue du Sault-au-Matelot, was laid out in 1685. At the request of the bishop's *grand-vicaire* and to facilitate granting lots in that area, de Bécancour had Le Rouge extend rue du Sault-au-Matelot past Pointe-aux-Roches (Fig. 28) to the lands below the Hôtel-Dieu. The *grand voyer* set the street's width at 24 *pieds* and authorized construction toward the northeast, on the river side; he also ordered affected landowners to respect the street width and have house alignments done.[94]

For house or lot alignments the *grand voyer* or his clerk set street and alley widths (Table 7). Some streets, such as rue Saint-Louis, whose width was set at 36 *pieds* in 1689, reflected military considerations and resembled the avenues planners and engineers recommended.[95] These streets formed military routes that, if necessary, could provide easy access to the ramparts or to the main square. Other streets corresponded at least to some extent to the width Henri IV prescribed (24 *pieds*): in 1687 côte de la Montagne was 21 *pieds* wide; in 1689 rue des Jardins was said to be 22 *pieds*, 8 *pouces* wide, and rue du Cul-de-Sac, 24 *pieds* wide. By Governor Davaugour's time, rue Saint-Pierre was 24 *pieds* wide. Some streets were little more than alleys: rue De Meulles was only 16 *pieds* wide; rue de l'Escalier and rue du Porche, 12 *pieds*; and the street leading from rue Saint-Pierre to the shore, 13.5 *pieds*. Thus there was considerable diversity in street widths, depending on their use (military use, for example) and location (as in the case of rue De Meulles, situated below Cap-aux-Diamants; Fig. 20).

Most alignments registered (18 of the 33) were for houses, 8 were for lots and courtyards, and 5 were for various structures, including porches, additions, archways, shops, and stables. As a result, 69.7 per cent of roads officials' work was construction-related (not counting dual-purpose projects combining, for example, housing and courtyard walls). House alignments were laid out to conform with existing street alignments; for example, in 1685 Adrien Le Comte's house had to conform to the alignment of rue du Sault-au-Matelot. On the other hand, where no street alignments had been set, house alignments gradually created and delineated the street. These processes also extended urban arteries and created a subsidiary network of alleys (Table 7).

Alignments affected public road easements, including rights of way, and conveniences such as stairs, balconies, steps, and porches. This situation gave the *grand voyer* the opportunity to legislate. On 5 September 1682, right after the fire that summer, de Bécancour visited Lower Town. House reconstruction had begun. He saw that the residents were building the first floors of their houses too high, so that stairs and stoops would be required. The *grand voyer* grew concerned about traffic, fire prevention, and public health: the stairs and stoops would be hindrances to draymen and fire hazards, and people would dump all sorts of garbage under them.

That day de Bécancour merely wrote a report. On 8 September he drafted an ordinance to correct the situation, expressing his desire for reform. His objectives in rebuilding Lower Town were public convenience and city beautification. Citing the same reasons as in his September 5th report, he forbade all residents to build stoops and other extensions on their house fronts unless absolutely necessary, and then only with his permission. He did allow stairs of no more than four steps. Porches and archways were banned outright: if built, they would be torn down.

His ordinance applied to Upper Town as well as Lower Town. It was first enforced on 28 April 1683, when Mme. Beaulieu was authorized to rebuild a porch in Lower Town, but forbidden to add any balconies to the house she was rebuilding. On 13 October 1683 de Bécancour granted André de Chaune, a master tailor on côte de la Montagne, permission to construct a *tambour* (a temporary shelter) in front of his house to protect it from winter damage and the risk of fire. Authorization was granted only after the *grand voyer* had visited the premises in person and was satisfied that the addition would not constitute a nuisance. However, he

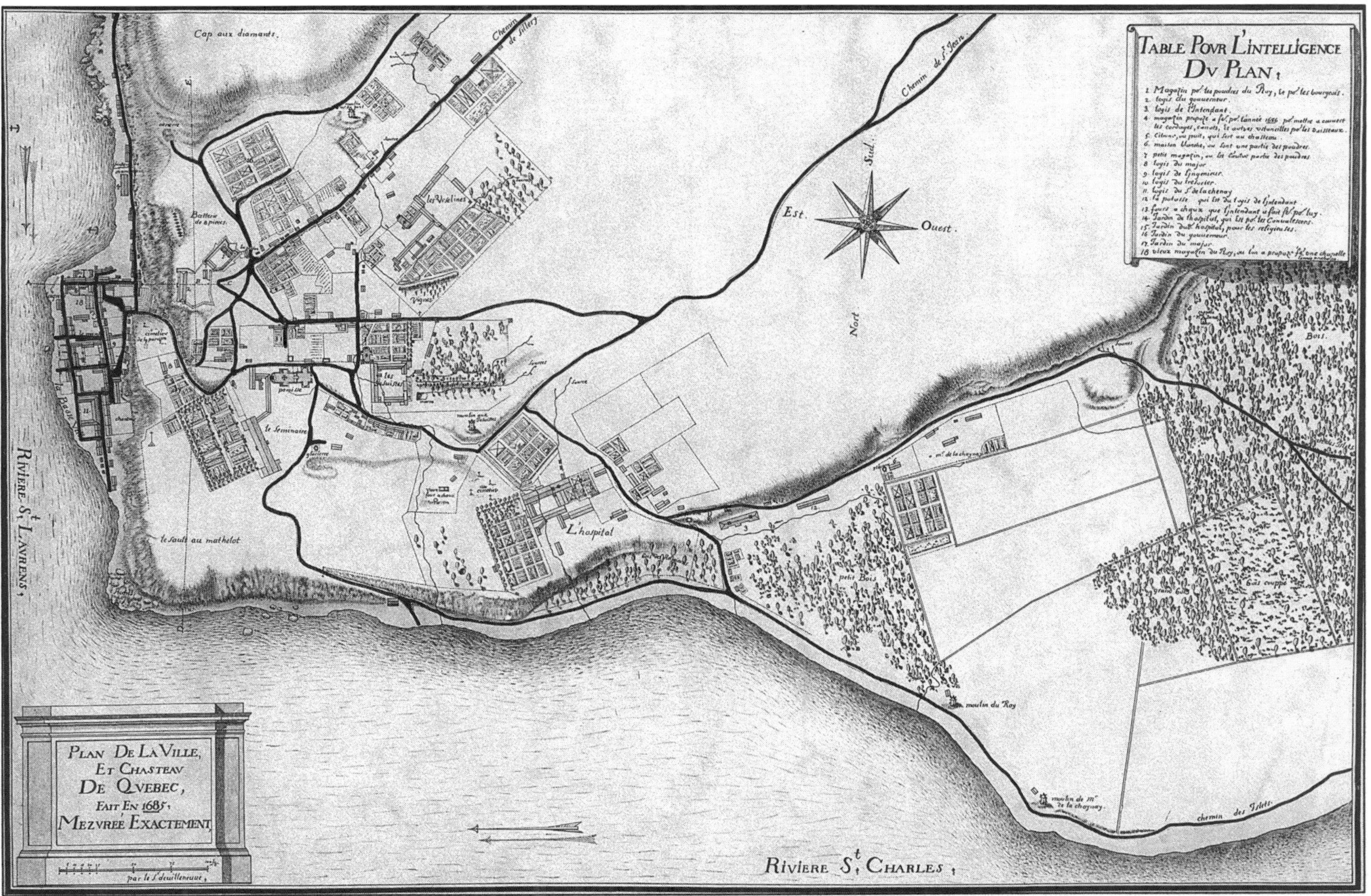
TABLE POVR L'INTELLIGENCE
DV PLAN,
1 Magazin po. les poudres du Roy, le po. les bourgeois.
2. logis du gouuerneur.
3 logis de l'Intendant.
4 magazin propozé a fe. po. l'année 1686 po. mettre a couuert les cordages, canots, le autres ustancilles po. les vaisseaux.
5. Citerne, ou puits, qui sert au chasteau.
6. maison blanche, ou sont une partie des poudres.
7 petit magazin, ou est l'autre partie des poudres
8 logis du major
9. logis de l'ingenieur.
10. logis du tresorier.
11. logis du S. de la chenay
12 la potasse qui est du logis de l'intendant
13. fours a chaux que l'intendant a fait fe. po. luy.
14. Jardin de l'hospital, qui est po. les Conualescens.
15. Jardin dud. hospital, pour les religieuses.
16 Jardin du gouuerneur.
17. Jardin du major.
18 vieux magazin du Roy, ou l'on a propozé fe. une chapelle
Cap aux diamants.
Chemin de Sillery
Chemin de S. Jean
Batterie de 8 pieces.
les Ursulines
Vignes
les Jesuistes
le Seminaire
le sault au mathelot
L'hospital
petit Bois
Bois
moulin du Roy
moulin de Mr de la chesnay
chemin des Islets
Est.
Sud.
Ouest.
Nort
Riviere St Lavrens,
Riviere St Charles,
PLAN DE LA VILLE,
ET CHASTEAV
DE QVEBEC,
FAIT EN 1685,
MEZVREE EXACTEMENT
par le S. deuilleneuue,

20 Québec streets in 1685

The urban network of both Upper Town and the sector below the Hôtel-Dieu has developed since 1670. This drawing shows that Québec streets were not laid out on a rectilineal grid, except perhaps in Lower Town, but are intertwined.

Drawing by Robert Gagnon

specified that this encroachment on a public road could be demolished if necessary.

De Chaune was not granted the land for his *tambour* until 4 April 1689. As well as granting him the land specified in the 1683 authorization, Governor Denonville and Intendant Champigny assigned him another parcel of land and imposed certain obligations on him. To facilitate downhill cart traffic, part of his *tambour* at the turn in the road was to be cut; in addition, de Chaune was required to keep the area surrounding his addition tidy.

The *grand voyer*'s jurisdiction over public squares, particularly the one in Lower Town, appears to have been broader. In 1685 he opposed the construction of buildings that had been undertaken on that square by Regnault *dit* Baillif and some others. To preserve the space — used as a drill square, market, and place of safety in the event of fire — in the interest of the Crown and the public, de Bécancour authorized the demolition of any buildings put up on the Place Royale.[96] Although as a result of representations by Governor La Barre and Intendant Demeulle, his ordinance, dated June 6, was not proclaimed, it is evidence of the *grand voyer*'s influence and his concern for urban planning.

To what extent were alignments respected — or arbitrary? Most often (in all but four cases, in fact) and as required by law, they were laid out at the request of landowners who wished to build. In three-quarters of the cases where no requests had been made, the landowners were caught red-handed by Genaple, who made them remove the foundations they had begun without authorization. Furthermore, in nine instances Genaple, while laying out new alignments, discovered individuals who had not respected existing ones. One widow refused to remove the foundations of her house, and one landowner on rue Sous-le-Fort refused to sign the official's report. Several residents ignored one alignment: in 1689 de Bécancour was obliged to redo the alignment for rue De Meulles, laid out by Genaple the previous year, because residents did not respect it. The *grand voyer* took this opportunity to straighten the street and have a bakehouse in the middle of it demolished (Fig. 21).

Twenty-seven of the 33 registered alignments imposed unilateral or reciprocal obligations on landowners. Most common was the obligation to respect the alignment; in eight violations, roads officials authorized the demolition of walls and foundations encroaching on streets. Only one alignment, for côte de la Fabrique, included a paving requirement for the benefit of residents along the route. Five registrations ordered the actual removal of foundations already laid, and one required a landowner to demolish the part of a building infringing on a street.

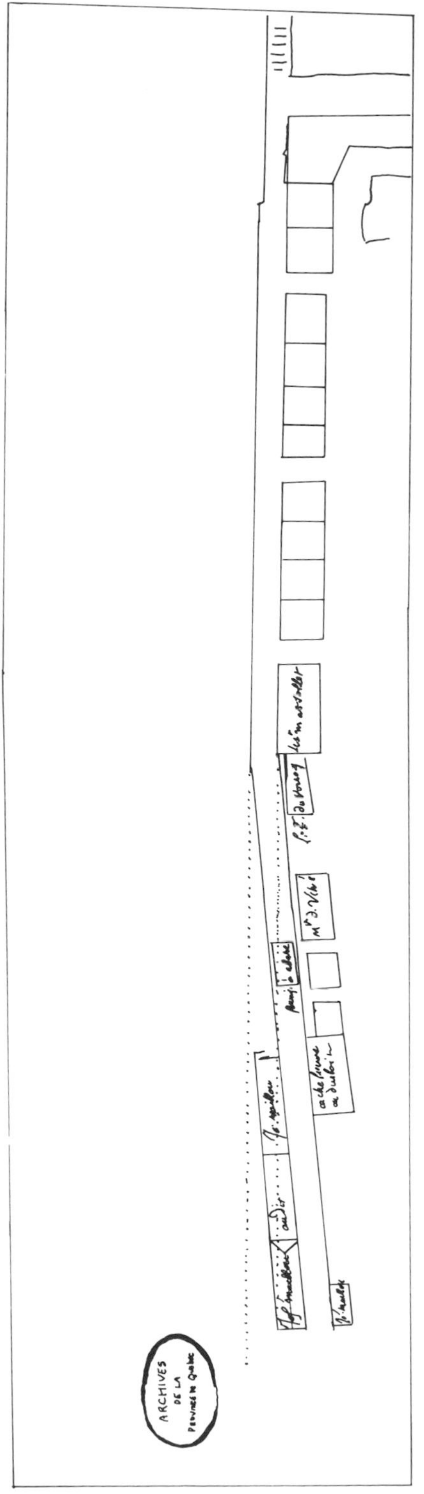

21 Proposed alignment of rue De Meulles, *circa* 1689, anonymous

This diagram is taken from the *grands voyers'* records. It concerns straightening the south section of rue De Meulles (dotted lines).

Archives Nationales du Québec, Québec; drawing by Rémi Chénier

The demands of the public road system sometimes imposed other obligations. Documents mention that two houses and an addition had to be moved in order to straighten streets. In two cases of alignments for road easements, the landowners agreed to observe height restrictions on porches and archways. Guillaume Pagets *dit* Carcy was obliged to cut a six-*pied* section off the corner of his house nearest a curve in côte de la Montagne in order to facilitate the passage of vehicles.

Overall, if we consider not only the statistics but also the people who issued these alignments and orders, we can see a desire for rational urban organization largely inherited from France. We can also compare Québec's history with that of other towns in the colony. In Montréal especially, the concern for wide, symmetrical streets first appeared in the work of Dollier de Casson, who started reorganizing the town on Coteau Saint-Louis beyond the Saint-Pierre River in 1672.[97] According to historian Peter N. Moogk, alignments were the responsibility of the bailiff, who neglected his duties.[98] Although Champigny set street width at 30 *pieds* in 1688, the standard was not applied; their actual widths varied from 18 to 24 *pieds*. At Trois-Rivières, street width was not set until 1735.

In this area of urban planning neither Québec nor New France is unique. In Charleston and Philadelphia, streets were laid out before houses were built. Around 1635 Boston appointed four "Surveyors of ye Highways." Newport soon followed suit and appointed surveyors as early as 1639 "[who] laid out the lane which ran to the harbour." In New Amsterdam not until 1666 were officials appointed whose duties corresponded to those of New France's *grands voyers*. Responsibility for public roads varied from one city to another. In Charleston it came under the jurisdiction of the South Carolina provincial parliament and in Philadelphia, under that of the provincial council. Interestingly, from 1665 on, most New York streets were 30 feet wide, and that city had the same street-cleaning and paving problems as did Québec.[99]

In many ways the organization of Québec's public roads and the various officials' activities reflected the structure in France. Indeed, the same laws were in force. An intriguing case is that of the *grand voyer* charged by Intendant Duchesneau in 1680 with failing to carry out his duties.[100] This indictment was undoubtedly justified in part, since de Bécancour had many business interests and often lived in Trois-Rivières.[101] As well, he was repeatedly out of the country, at which times his clerk acted for him. However, as early as 1682 de Bécancour showed at least some interest in beautifying the town and straightening its streets. It is also difficult to evaluate roads legislation and its application. Cases of removal and demolition are described, but so are many criticisms of lack of respect for the regulations. Infringements must be attributed to administrators' tolerance, though alignments, along with the various authorizations required, most often had the desired effect. The extreme rarity of documents (Chapter III lists 184 masonry and framing contracts from 1663 to 1690 for which alignments should theoretically exist) does not allow us to draw further conclusions.

A Separate Municipal Administration

The trading companies first introduced a separate municipal government for the town of Québec. The lieutenant-general of the Prévôté and the *procureur du roi* apparently had direct responsibility for municipal administration. The purpose of any legislation they originated was more effective enforcement of the edicts issued by the intendant or the Conseil Souverain and, in carrying out their duties, these officials acted simply as agents. In the course of the 17th century a short-lived aldermanic system was introduced in Québec, and at one time a syndic also represented the citizenry.

The Québec Prévôté and its Officials

Jean-Baptiste Gareau, Pierre-Georges Roy, and John Alexander Dickinson have fully described the history of the Québec Prévôté,[102] but except for Dickinson, few writers have examined that institution's influence on the city.

When the Cents-Associés gave up their monopoly of New France in 1663, the Sénéschaussée, the town's court of first instance, disappeared. Under the administrative reorganization that took place that year, the Conseil Souverain assumed responsibility for cases formerly heard by the Sénéschaussée. With the rise of the Compagnie des Indes Occidentales, the council in Québec did not hear any cases at that level for over a year.[103]

On 1 May 1666 the Compagnie des Indes Occidentales invoked its judicial powers to re-establish a court of first instance in Québec, appointing Louis-Théandre Chartier de Lotbinière lieutenant-general for civil and criminal matters. On the same date it created the office of *procureur fiscal* and entrusted it to Jean-Baptiste Peuvret Demesnu; four days later Gilles Rageot became clerk of the Prévôté.[104] The terms of

Lotbinière's appointment were not registered with the Conseil Souverain until 10 January 1667; that date marks the official beginning of the Prévôté even though it had been active since 1666.[105]

When the edict revoking the charter of the Compagnie des Indes Occidentales was issued in 1674, the king abolished the Prévôté and made the Conseil Souverain responsible for administering justice of the first instance. The Prévôté was reinstated in May 1677 in order to conduct trials more expeditiously and "to make orders concerning real property, seizures & other matters that the Conseil Souverain cannot deal with in the first Instance." Once again it was composed of a lieutenant-general, a *procureur du roi*, a clerk, and bailiffs. Its abolition in 1674, although official, was nonetheless in theory only. As Gareau noted, the Prévôté's activity was uninterrupted between 1674 and 1677, as is shown by the existence of registers for these years. Another indication is the fact that in 1675 Lotbinière received a royal commission as lieutenant-general. Thus it appears that this court operated continuously; it would do so until the fall of New France.[106]

When the Prévôté was established in 1666 it was made responsible for "all matters, both civil and criminal, of justice, administration, trade and navigation" in accordance with the laws of the realm and the Coutume de Paris.[107] That year the company's agent general asked that the Prévôté be empowered to hear appeals from the seigneurial courts under the government of Québec.[108] Thus the Prévôté not only dispensed justice within the town of Québec, but was also authorized to hear appeals, although this function was shared with the intendant and Conseil Souverain.

During Talon's first term the Prévôté was already subordinate to the intendant; under Intendant Boutroue there was competition between the two offices, since Boutroue heard cases of the first instance between 1668 and 1670.[109] Although the council could hear cases on appeal from the Prévôté, its jurisdiction extended to cases in the first instance as well. Only in 1679, under a royal edict confirming the 1667 ordinance, were cases of the first instance as well as appeals from the seigneurial courts placed under the Prévôté's exclusive jurisdiction.[110] It was also responsible for litigation, protecting minors' possessions, registering various official documents, and keeping records of births, marriages, and deaths.[111] These functions, despite occasional adjustments, would remain unchanged.[112]

A study of Prévôté officials, particularly the lieutenant-general, is the best way to determine its influence on the town of Québec. Louis-Théandre Chartier de Lotbinière, the first lieutenant-general to be appointed, held that office — except for several months' hiatus in 1676 —

from May 1666 until 25 October 1677, when he resigned in favour of his son, René-Louis, who held the position until 1703.[113]

The lieutenant-general of the Prévôté was primarily a judge, the most senior judge of this court, and was responsible for the administration of justice of the first instance. However, he was also an administrator, as is seen from the authority granted him over trade and navigation. During the term of Lotbinière *père* this mandate was disputed and was recognized only after some time.

The controversy began in 1666 when Agent General Le Barroys requested that, in the absence of the intendant or as his delegate, Lotbinière be given authority over administrative matters and navigation, which was as much as saying that the lieutenant-general's administrative responsibilities were assigned at the intendant's pleasure. Then, in 1673, Frontenac tried to strip Lotbinière of this responsibility by setting up an aldermanic system. In so doing — since aldermen's appointments would be subject to his ratification — Frontenac hoped to achieve greater control over the enforcement of bylaws. Lotbinière objected to this limitation of his authority, and Colbert's reply to Frontenac was not long in coming: "Administration is rightly the responsibility of the senior Judge established by the Company, and you could not remove part of His jurisdiction, which he holds from the King under the authority His Majesty has bestowed on the Company, and give it to another Judge you have established without authority."[114]

The king renewed his official sanction in 1675. As well as recommending that Frontenac leave responsibility for the administration of the town of Québec with the lieutenant-general, Louis XIV defined Lotbinière's duties in that area, making him responsible for enforcing bylaws. Similar directives were given to Duchesneau when he was appointed intendant: "enact with the conseil souverain all the bylaws you deem necessary for the general administration of the said country, for fairs and markets together, for sale, purchase and trade in all goods and foodstuffs, which general bylaws you will have applied by the subordinate judges charged with enforcing local regulations within their own jurisdictions." In addition, when the council established bylaws, the lieutenant-general of the Prévôté was invited to give his opinion; however, he was not allowed to participate in the council's deliberations and had to withdraw after making his statement. Ordinances were sent to the Prévôté to be read, proclaimed, and registered with the clerk of that court.[115]

As the official responsible for enforcing bylaws, the lieutenant-general had a number of duties. He called administration meetings for the town, held at the Prévôté and on which he reported to the council.[116]

His required tours of inspection in the town included duties in the areas of fire prevention, verifying weights and measures, supervising taverns, and granting certificates of poverty, as well as enforcing other bylaws.

We do not know whether the lieutenant-general carried out all these duties, but we do know that citizens' meetings took place and that Lotbinière *père* and *fils* did take responsibility for fire prevention and tavern regulations. In 1682, at Procureur du Roi Pierre Duquet's request, René-Louis wrote a report on the fire in Lower Town. On that occasion the lieutenant-general, like the intendant, rallied residents to fight the blaze and ordered carpenters to pull down houses to stop its progress. In 1677 Louis-Théandre issued an ordinance setting the price of wine, an order upheld by the council despite representations from tavern owners. Supervision of taverns was one of the lieutenant-general's main duties; in particular he had to ensure that no drinks were served while Sunday Mass was being said.[117]

The lieutenant-general was still empowered to legislate. Historian André Vachon noted the existence of 16 ordinances issued by the Prévôté en 1667 and 1668 alone.[118] They dealt with topics as varied as domestic animals, public roads, volunteers, and domestic help. These ordinances applied only to the town of Québec and seigneuries located within the Prévôté's jurisdiction. More importantly, they appear to set out in detail, for the town, the bylaws enacted by the council; legislation proclaimed by the lieutenant-general was simply a means of enforcing the general bylaws.[119]

Under the Compagnie des Indes Occidentales, the lieutenant-general of the Prévôté ensured that grantees received their lots and set the lot boundaries.[120] He also saw to it that *papiers terriers* were compiled for the town. From 1667 to 1668 Lotbinière received *aveux et dénombrements* (lists of the landholdings within a seigneury, including the buildings, cleared land, livestock, and dues charged) for the *censive* of Québec and seigneuries in its jurisdiction, and in accordance with an order issued by Tracy, Talon, and Courcelle, drew up the first land registration.[121]

Two areas appear to fall in part under the lieutenant-general's jurisdiction: harbour administration and alignments. The extent of his responsibility for harbour administration remains unclear. In 1684, in a *mémoire* from La Barre and Demeulle to Seignelay, the governor asked whether admiralty cases fell under the lieutenant-general's jurisdiction or the governor's. The king ruled that neither the lieutenant-general nor the governor could hear these cases or direct officials who did have such jurisdiction. In other words, the lieutenant-general had nothing to do with harbour administration. Yet in 1691, following Frontenac's appointment of a harbour master, Intendant Champigny, who considered the position inessential, recommended that the lieutenant-general and *procureur du roi* be made responsible for harbour administration and for preventing the filling in of the port adjoining rue du Cul-de-Sac with landfill and stones. One explanation is that under the commission giving him jurisdiction over navigation and in the absence of an admiralty at Québec, the lieutenant-general did in fact take on responsibility for harbour administration. And, of course, starting in 1686 if not earlier, admiralty cases were tried before the Prévôté.[122]

It appears that the lieutenant-general's involvement with alignments originated with an order by Intendant Demeulle concerning the street leading to the Champlain Fountain. On 13 April 1685 the intendant ordered landowners to respect the alignments on both the hill and river sides of that street; he also decided to lay out an alley between the cliff and the shore, and stipulated that retaining walls were to be built.[123] He ordered Lotbinière first to have the ordinance registered with the clerk of the Prévôté and then to enforce its provisions for the construction of retaining walls and the observance of alignments.

At first glance it seems that the lieutenant-general was competing with the *grand voyer* and, with the intendant's blessing, challenging his jurisdiction. However, closer examination shows that he intervened only in exceptional circumstances or as the intendant's deputy. For example, on 26 June 1687, on Champigny's orders, he laid out an alley 12 *pieds* wide between rue De Meulles and the river. Two days later he was asked by François Genaple, clerk of the *grand voyer*, to set the height of a porch and give the alignment for Sieur Beaulieu's house. His presence was requested on that occasion because the alignment affected two streets, du Porche and Saint-Pierre, and because the porch was not to inconvenience the public. On 3 July 1687 the lieutenant-general was asked to lay out alignments for rue du Sault-au-Matelot because they would realign the street and Genaple did not dare act alone. Another extraordinary situation occurred in 1689 when Lotbinière, acting as the intendant's deputy, set the height of an archway that L'Espinay wanted to have built on rue Sous-le-Fort.[124]

Such were the lieutenant-general's main duties despite the fact that in 1683 Demeulle considered this position extraneous and wished to take over special administration himself and have first-instance cases heard by a councillor. In carrying out his duties as a subordinate judge, the lieutenant-general was assisted by a *procureur du roi* who helped draft land registrations, accompanied the lieutenant-general on his inspection tours, was involved in fire prevention, and ensured that tavern regulations were observed. Under Intendant Champigny's recommendations the *procureur du roi* was also responsible for harbour administration. Generally, while the jurisdiction of the *procureur du roi* corresponded to that of the lieutenant-general, he was still accountable to him as chief magistrate of the Prévôté and acted as the deputy of the *procureur général* in that court. The *procureur du roi* was thus responsible for registering, proclaiming, and posting ordinances and bylaws. The public part of his duties consisted in prosecuting those who failed to observe them.[125]

The lieutenant-general was also assisted by a clerk and bailiffs. The clerk took charge of the legal archives, keeping registers of hearings, writing up sentences and proceedings minutes, receiving documents for registration, and providing copies of notaries' documents deposited in the archives after the notaries died. The bailiffs were responsible for serving notices of sentence and seizure, and for auctions preceeding judicial sales and leases. They also served writs, assisted with inventories, and made inspections. They were the lowest rank of officials to apply bylaws.[126]

These, then, were the operations, main officials, and responsibilities of the Québec Prévôté. As a court it was similar in many ways to the courts of first instance in France. However, where administration was concerned, it developed differently in Québec than in France: the office of justice of the peace (*juge de police*) was retained by the lieutenant-general and there was no separate administrative lieutenant-generalship after 1667.[127] Existing officials were probably capable of assuming these responsibilities, as the much later creation in 1695 of the position of *lieutenant particulier* indicated.

Public Participation in Urban Administration

The extent of public participation in local government depended on the tolerance of the authorities, who held all real power over Québec affairs despite the sporadic presence of a syndic and aldermen.

The position of syndic was established in 1647. The duties of the first incumbent, Jean Bourdon, were simply to represent the people on issues involving trade. When the Conseil de traite was reshuffled for the first time in 1648, seats were given to two councillors chosen among the habitants and elected for three-year terms by the council and the syndics of Québec, Montréal, and Trois-Rivières. When the council was reshuffled for the second time, in 1657, the number of councillors was raised to four: two from Québec, one from Montréal, and one from Trois-Rivières. The syndics, who had always reported to government authorities, saw their positions abolished by Governor Davaugour in 1662.

On 10 October 1663 Jean-Baptiste Legardeur de Repentigny and Jean Madry were sworn in by the Conseil Souverain as mayor of Québec and alderman respectively. The council later summoned Claude Charron de la Barre to be sworn in as an alderman. On 14 November the council's *procureur général* reported that Repentigny, Madry, and Charron were not performing their duties. The council therefore revoked their appointments and ordered that an election be held for the position of syndic.

The order did not come into effect immediately, for the mayor and aldermen of Québec had still not left their posts on 9 April 1664. As "deputez de Quebecq" they submitted a request to the council, from which they had received instructions to post a decree on tithes in both Québec and Trois-Rivières. As the residents of Trois-Rivières had refused to read out, publish, or post the decree, the council ordered officials to see to its publication.[128]

It appears that the aldermanic system was abolished shortly thereafter, for on 28 July 1664 the Conseil Souverain again called for the election of a syndic by majority vote to be held during a meeting in the council chamber. On 3 August, 23 habitants — for the most part seigneurs, merchants, and craftsmen — chose Claude Charron de la Barre. Charron, a *bourgeois* from Québec, was elected *in absentia* and was subsequently sworn in by the council.

Charron spent very little time in office. In September 1664 the council objected to Charron's election in the context of a power struggle between Bishop Laval and Governor Mézy. Not only had Charron been elected by only a few habitants, but also the election had involved him in a conflict of interest. The council received requests that the syndic be relieved of his duties because, being a merchant, he could not enforce the goods tariff and protect habitants' rights. Consequently the council issued a letter to Mézy requesting Charron's resignation.

Another meeting was called to elect a new syndic, but too few people showed up for the election to take place. Mézy then sent messages to about 60 habitants asking them to appoint a syndic; they chose Jean Lemire. But the *procureur général* and two councillors opposed the nomination. During a stormy council meeting on 19 September, Lemire was sworn in as syndic by the governor. Claiming it was time to change the councillors, Mézy dismissed La Ferté, d'Auteuil, Villeray, and Procureur Général Bourdon. When Bourdon refused to accept his dismissal, Mézy became so angry that he began to insult and hit Bourdon.[129]

Despite this infamous incident in the council's history, Jean Lemire was kept on as syndic. During the early part of his term he seems to have spoken for all habitants in the colony, as he was referred to as "procureur syndic des habitants" or "syndic des habitants" until December 1664. Some time between 3 November 1664 and 29 April 1665 the council authorized the residents of Trois-Rivières to elect their own syndic so that their rights would be protected.

The office of syndic may have fallen into disuse for a short time, for there are no references to it from April 1665 to January 1667. On 24 January 1667 the habitants complained that merchants' profits on sales of various goods were too high. They sought permission to hold a meeting and elect a syndic, and asked the council to appoint commissioners to enforce the goods tariff. The council agreed and ordered an election by all habitants before the lieutenant-general of the Prévôté. However, candidates for syndic had to be residents of Québec or its *banlieue*. The council also appointed two commissioners, then instructed the councillors and *procureur général* to hear all complaints filed against the merchants.

On 20 March 1667 the residents of Québec and its *banlieue* elected Lemire for a second term. However, by July 1667 it appears that Lemire was speaking for all habitants; in 1672 he even acted on behalf of the Communauté des Habitants in a claim requesting payment of its debts.[130]

Charron never really had the time to adequately perform his duties. His name appears only in regard to an ordinance of 6 August 1664 wherein the council requested the syndic's opinion before enforcing a decree of the king's Conseil d'État on the inclusion of uncleared lands in the king's domain. Lemire, on the other hand, was very active during his two terms. Between 1664 and 1672 he made 24 complaints, written and verbal, and remonstrances to the council.

Most of the Conseil Souverain's orders — setting goods tariffs, limiting merchants' profit margins, and requiring them to keep books and ledgers — are described in the pages on trade regulations. The syndic was responsible for the regulations enacted by the council, to whom he addressed his grievances. Lemire's primary duty was to control trade and enforce the goods tariff. As early as October 1664 the syndic could, with a councillor's help, investigate cases of abuse committed by merchants. In December Lemire tried to obtain a *monitoire* against merchants who were cornering the colonial market in certain goods and creating artificial shortages that hampered retail sales. On 31 December 1664 Bishop Laval refused to grant it despite the fact that the council had approved such action. Then, on 30 July 1667, in the face of an unwarranted increase in prices, the syndic asked the council to force the merchants to produce invoices for the goods they had purchased in France.[131]

Lemire was also concerned about the ten-per-cent tax collected on all goods imported into the colony. The tax had been instituted in 1660 to absorb debts incurred by the Communauté des Habitants. According to a 1662 estimate of the Communauté's indebtedness since the fur trade monopoly was accepted in 1645, it owed some 170,000 *livres* to creditors in France and Canada. Commissioners, some of whom were members of the Conseil Souverain, were appointed to recover the amount owed.

In June 1664, acting on habitants' complaints that traders were using this tax to raise the prices of their goods, the council decided to limit the tax exclusively to wine and spirits. The council's decision did not receive royal assent; however, in 1670 Louis XIV agreed to reduce the tax by half following further representations by the syndic and the council. That year the colony saw a return to the situation of 1664 following further remonstrances by Lemire. The ten-per-cent tax was collected at 10 *livres* per barrel of wine, 25 *livres* per barrel of spirits, and 5 *sols* per pound of tobacco.

According to historian Thomas Chapais, the king assumed the debts of the former Communauté des Habitants in 1674 and began to collect the tax for his own coffers. Louis XIV ordered Talon to pay off the Canadian creditors and ordered Councillor Pussort, Colbert's uncle, to pay off those in France. By 1665 the Communauté's debt had been reduced to 45,000 *livres*; by 1676 it had been completely repaid except for 24,000 *livres* owing to Aubert de la Chesnaye. French historian Émile Salone argued that the ten-per-cent tax was still being collected in the same manner as late as 1738. After the initial debt had been absorbed, income from the ten-per-cent tax was simply added to the colony's other revenues.[132]

In the course of his duties the syndic kept a watchful eye on sales of wine and spirits, as well as on the prices tavernkeepers charged. Many of the council's ordinances on sales of these goods were enacted on the basis of complaints by the syndic, who instituted legal proceedings against tavernkeepers who had exceeded set prices on wine and spirits.

The syndic also protected the habitants' interests. In October 1664 he asked council to order Jean-Baptiste Peuvret Demesnu to hand over the council's books and minutes to the new council clerk as their absence was detrimental to the public good. On 28 April 1670 Lemire had a council regulation on the care of livestock and hogs amended. Two years later he presented Talon with a petition, signed by 20 habitants, on the reporting of pelts. He informed the intendant that habitants did not want their houses searched and that they would file their reports at the company warehouse. Still in 1672, Lemire submitted a request to the council regarding pelt freightage and fees charged habitants for passage to France. The council set freightage at 10 *livres* per hundredweight of beaver pelts and 12 *sols* per moosehide in French currency, or the usual Canadian equivalent in pelts. Passage was set at 40 *livres* in Canadian currency for passengers eating at the seamen's mess.[133]

The authorities often consulted the syndic on matters of trade. In 1668 the council sought his opinion on establishing breweries in the colony and on the price it should set for beaver pelts; in 1669 the council asked his advice and that of the leading merchants in regard to an order on the payment of debts in wheat. The syndic's opinion was also sought in 1670 regarding fur prices.[134]

Lemire also took part in requesting free trade for the colony. In 1665 Talon obtained permission for the habitants to import foodstuffs for their own use despite the Compagnie des Indes Occidentales monopoly on imports; however, the intendant did not stop there and demanded free trade. His efforts paid off in 1666, when trade and commerce were freed of tax for one year, but the concession was rescinded the following year. The habitants' reaction was swift. In 1668 the syndic asked council to write to Colbert to request reinstatement of free trade. Talon supported the syndic's action and the council complied. At the intendant's suggestion, Lemire recommended that the colony set up its own company if free trade were denied.

Versailles acceded to the habitants' request and free trade was granted in 1669. Things seem to have stayed the same until 1674, when the charter of the Compagnie des Indes Occidentales was revoked and the principle of free trade ratified. Louis XIV granted all of his subjects in New France permission to trade as they were doing in the other possessions of the French empire.[135]

Although there is no record of the fact, the syndic of Québec appears to have been relieved of his duties when Frontenac appointed aldermen in March 1673. Moreover, on 13 June 1673 Colbert ordered Frontenac to phase out the position of syndic and forbade him to call a meeting of the États Généraux for Canada, the reason being that the king distrusted popular representation and did not want the colony to develop its own government; he believed that each person should speak for himself and no one should speak for all. Despite these instructions, the Montréal syndic was only relieved of his duties in 1674, at the time of the notorious case involving Abbé Fénelon.[136]

Curiously enough, Louis XIV did not abolish the aldermanic system in Québec. However, he did reprimand Frontenac on 17 May 1674, accusing him of exceeding his authority by drafting bylaws and appointing aldermen. The governor replied to the king's charges in November, stating that when he drafted the bylaws he had consulted Québec's leading citizens, who had been delegated by the population at large, and that the majority of council members had been designated as commissioners to review the regulations. He also pointed out that the aldermen, the first of whom was to be justice of the peace (*juge de police*) were appointed on an interim basis only, pending royal assent. When Louis XIV refused to grant that, Frontenac turned the particular administration of the town of Québec over to the lieutenant-general of the Prévôté.[137]

According to bylaws drafted in March 1673, aldermen were to be elected by majority vote by town residents and the election had to be approved by the governor. The first year three aldermen were elected, with one of the three to be replaced each year thereafter. The maximum term in office was set at three years and the maximum number of terms at two. These provisions were followed. In 1673 Claude Charron de la Barre was elected as *premier* alderman, holding that position until 1675 and being replaced, probably the following year, by Charles Roger Descoulombiers. Assisting Charron were aldermen Jean Juchereau de La Ferté and Thierry Delestre Duvallon, who remained in office until 1677.[138]

On 15 April 1673 the aldermen asked Frontenac for permission to built a covered market along the walls of the Vieux Magasin in Lower Town. They offered to pay the cost of building the shops and stalls if allowed to collect rents for them so as to fill the town's coffers and enable them to carry out their duties "with some sort of dignity." The governor granted their request on condition they follow the alignment he had set so as not to detract from the Place Royale.

The experience pitted the aldermen against the butchers several times. On 17 March 1677 the council ordered three butchers to pay rent on their stalls in Lower Town. A fourth butcher, Pierre Parent, received a similar sentence, but was not required to pay because Davaugour had granted him a concession in 1662. The case dragged on and was finally settled in July 1677. Parent was made to pay 80 *livres*, representing two years' rent on a stall, and the council upheld the concession title granted to the aldermen in 1673.[139]

Charron acted as *juge de police* for Québec until the position was abolished. On 21 August 1673 three habitants appeared before the council for drinking and fighting during a religious service. The three men were fined and ordered to make amends for having resisted Charron's authority at the time of their arrest. Like the syndic before them, the aldermen were charged with protecting the habitants' business interests.

On 25 September 1674 the council, with the governor's approval, ordered the *premier* alderman to call a meeting of the habitants to seek their opinion on setting a goods tariff. In June 1675 Charron remanded a La Rochelle merchant to appear before council in a matter involving trade with the Indians. The aldermen also acted as judges for the council. Between 1673 and 1675 they were called upon three times to hear criminal cases and swear in a new councillor.[140]

In 1677 the king again ordered Frontenac to abolish syndics "généraux et particuliers." Consequently, on 23 March Frontenac issued an order that not only abolished the syndics, but also forbade all meetings not expressly authorized by the governor. The ordinance also suppressed the Québec aldermanic system, of which there is no further mention.

Thereafter, public participation in government took the form of habitants' meetings, the result of the governor's habit of calling upon the habitants to deal with issues concerning the colony's welfare: war, peace, and prosperity. Between 1672 and 1680 at least 17 public meetings were held in Québec, but they were in no way representative of the general population as they were attended only by leading citizens. In Québec's case, as we have seen, such meetings were followed by smaller meetings on city administration matters.[141]

Conclusion

We have now reviewed the colony's various levels of government as represented by officers such as the intendant or by organizations such as the Conseil Souverain. By outlining their powers and duties we could determine their influence on the town's administration. There are two reasons for this approach: the colonial government of New France largely supplanted that of the town at various times, and the fact that the various government bodies were located in the capital made this approach the only logical choice.

At the top of a simplified organizational chart of the municipal government is the intendant, next is the Conseil Souverain, and lastly, the Prévôté. Justice played a major role in municipal government; also, Versailles sought to divide duties and responsibilities. The continuity in the instructions and guidelines France issued bespoke an overall plan for the town. During the 17th century Colbert was the prime mover in the kind of state intervention that prevailed in France. Of course, certain changes were made to adapt the model to the colonial context, but there were many more similarities than differences between France and Canada. In

Québec the system of government resembled the one in France with its provincial governors, intendant, etc. Even the legislative and administrative systems were the same. But the town provided an opportunity to make major changes, such as the short-lived aldermanic system.

The administrative role of the town of Québec seems to have been a dynamic one, not only because of the town planning carried out by the governors and the intendants, but also because of various expansion projects put forth by these administrators. The bylaws passed and the attitude shown by the officials and citizens are indicative of the Québec's urban problems, whereas the solutions adopted indicate a certain mindset and a desire for conformism.

In its system of government Québec was not only a typically French 17th-century town, but also the capital of a North American colony.

Chapter III
THE URBAN LANDSCAPE AN EVOLVING TOWN

The site and geographical location of Québec make it unique because there the St. Lawrence River is only about 1000 metres wide and becomes an estuary. The narrowness of the river means that the town exerts an influence on both sides of the river and on the surrounding countryside because of the many access routes, such as the Chaudière River.[1]

The importance of Québec's location is enhanced by its port and defence facilities. Of the various features that combine to make it a natural harbour for even large vessels, the most notable are the depth of the river, between 48.7 and 51.8 metres, and the presence of a narrow tract of land at the bottom of a promontory that in places is 91.5 metres high. The promontory is a natural fortress that is difficult to attack on two sides though the area to the west, which opens onto the plains, is more vulnerable.

These physical features, plus the fact that in winter shipping is impossible for four to six months, have profoundly affected the town's history.

The site was transformed by intense phases of lot distribution and the pattern of land use. Between 1608 and 1663 the city began to take shape: a network of streets was set up and most of the land was granted as concessions. More than a quarter of the town's area was owned by various religious communities (Jesuits, Ursulines, and Hôtel-Dieu), as well as the Notre-Dame *fabrique*. After 1663 the Récollets and the Québec seminary also occupied sizeable portions of the urban landscape.

From 1663 until 1690 there were fewer concessions of land, and the lots were smaller than those granted at the town's founding. Lots were distributed more in some parts than others: in Upper Town most development was on rue Saint-Louis and côte de la Fabrique, while in Lower Town it was on rue De Meulles and rue du Sault-au-Matelot.

Studying Québec's physical evolution in the second half of the 17th century illustrates man's impact on his environment. This is particularly evident in the people's day-to-day lives as revealed through the study of their dwellings. By looking at the external components of the houses (materials, roofs, dimensions, and number of floors), we can not only describe the structures that so strongly influenced the urban landscape, but also trace the development of a major industry, housing construction.

Land Tenure and Lot Distribution

The Legacy of the Trading Post (1608–1663)

In 1608 Champlain built the Québec Habitation, which was repaired in 1616 and 1620, and rebuilt beginning in 1623. Also from this period is the warehouse with two turrets in Lower Town (Fig. 22). There were very few buildings in Québec in those early days. The Récollets' residence and chapel were added to Champlain's Habitation in 1615, and two years later Louis Hébert settled in Upper Town. In 1620 Champlain built the first Upper Town fort, but he demolished it in 1626 and replaced it with another building completed in 1629.

On the eve of the Kirkes' occupation, Québec amounted to very little: "in Lower Town, [there were] the Habitation, the homes of the locksmith and baker outside the walls, a chapel and a residence built for the [Récollets], a mill, built in 1628, with its building to shelter it, and perhaps a few small cabins." In addition to the residence of Sieur Juchereau, the few buildings in Upper Town included Champlain's fort, the homes of Louis Hébert and Guillaume Couillard, "with their outbuildings, mills, brewery, well, and perhaps a house for the Pierre Desportes family."[2]

In 1632 Québec became a French possession again, and until 1663 the town saw remarkable expansion marked by the arrival of various religious communities and efforts to populate it.

Phases of land occupation paralleled the arrival of immigrants. Historian Marcel Trudel points to a number of key years: 1637 marked the beginning of the distribution of lots. In that year alone, the Cents-Associés granted a total of 792¼ *arpents* of land to commoners (that is, not to seigneurs), in Québec and its immediate surroundings. In 1647 there was a systematic distribution of lots. Although there were many land grants in 1649, the peak in Upper Town was reached in 1655, when 22,743 *toises* were distributed. In Lower Town three years saw particularly intense activity: 1655, 1656, and 1658, when 79 per cent of Lower Town was divided into building lots. However, the largest single year was 1655, during which 4755 *toises* were distributed. As of June 1663, a total of 151 lots had been granted in Québec. In Upper Town the average size was 2.5 *arpents*, while in Lower Town it was 0.105 *arpents*.[3]

Some of the individuals who received these lots deserve particular mention. As of 1623 the Hébert-Couillard family owned a large part of Sault-au-Matelot, most of which was distributed in 1627, when Guillaume Couillard received 100 *arpents* in Upper Town. Some parts of the fief were later severed, most going to the Hôtel-Dieu. Nevertheless, the family's properties remained impressive at some 16,200 *toises*. One of Couillard's properties was a piece of land that looked out on what later became the côte du Palais, while another was located behind the Jesuits' lot. When Couillard died these properties went to his widow, Guillemette Hébert (Figs. 8 and 22).[4]

The various religious communities settled in Upper Town because of the protection the fort provided and because more land was available there than in Lower Town.[5] In January 1637, through Jean de Beauvais, 12 *arpents* were set aside in Upper Town for a convent school for girls. The Ursulines arrived in 1639 and managed to get only six of the *arpents* initially granted. In February 1640 they took possession of the site, bounded on the northeast by the Jesuits and on the southeast by a street that ran parallel to rue Saint-Louis (Figs. 1 and 22). As a result of several additions of land over the years, these six *arpents* increased to 9.1 *arpents* by 1663. In 1650 Mme. de La Peltrie gave two *arpents* to the Ursulines, who also received an extra *perche* "along the side of their yard, and two *perches* on its length." Beginning in 1651 the Ursulines also gained possession of the three-*toise* strip that separated their land from rue Saint-Louis. In 1655 Père Guillaume Vignal gave them half an *arpent* located outside of their yard on rue Saint-Louis. The same year the Ursulines bought from Robert Caron a lot 36 *pieds* wide by 90 *pieds* deep at the corner of rue du Parloir and the three-*toise* strip.[6] (The order also possesses land in Lower Town.) By 1663 the Ursulines owned 9.7 *arpents* in Québec.[7]

Like the Ursulines, the Hospitalières got a concession of 12 *arpents* in Upper Town in March 1637. However, by the time the nuns took possession of the land in 1640, the area had been reduced to 7.5 *arpents*. In the same year, Guillaume Couillard gave them 25 *perches* of land so that a laundry could be built. Later, in 1644, he sold the Hôtel-Dieu an *arpent* and a half of land that fronted on the Saint-Charles River. Eleven

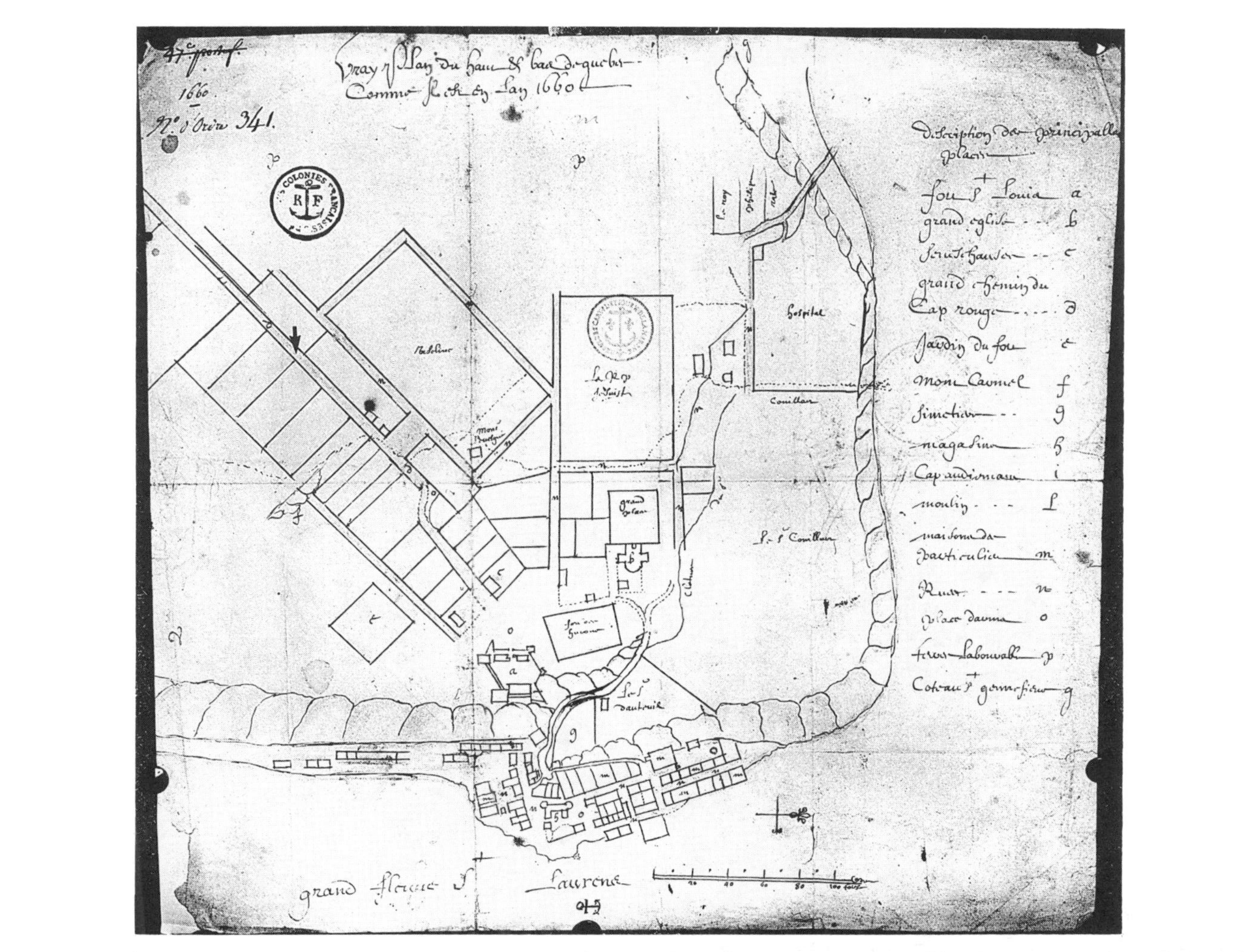
1660
N° d'ordre 341.
COLONIES FRANCAISES
RF
Description des principalles places
fort St Louis a
grand eglise b
grand semin du Cap rouge d
jardin du fort e
mont Carmel f
magasins h
moulin L
Hospital
grand fleuve St Laurens

22 "Vray Plan du haut & bas de quebec Comme Il est En Lan 1660," Jean Bourdon

This plan reflects the difference in land distribution between Upper and Lower Town. In Upper Town, large lots had been granted to religious orders and to a few families, while in Lower Town the land was parcelled into much smaller lots. Bourdon also showed streets and roads; however, only rue Saint-Louis is given a name: "grand chemin du Cap rouge" (*see* arrow). For modern street names, *see* Figure 1.

Archives Nationales, France; copy on file, National Archives of Canada, C-15801

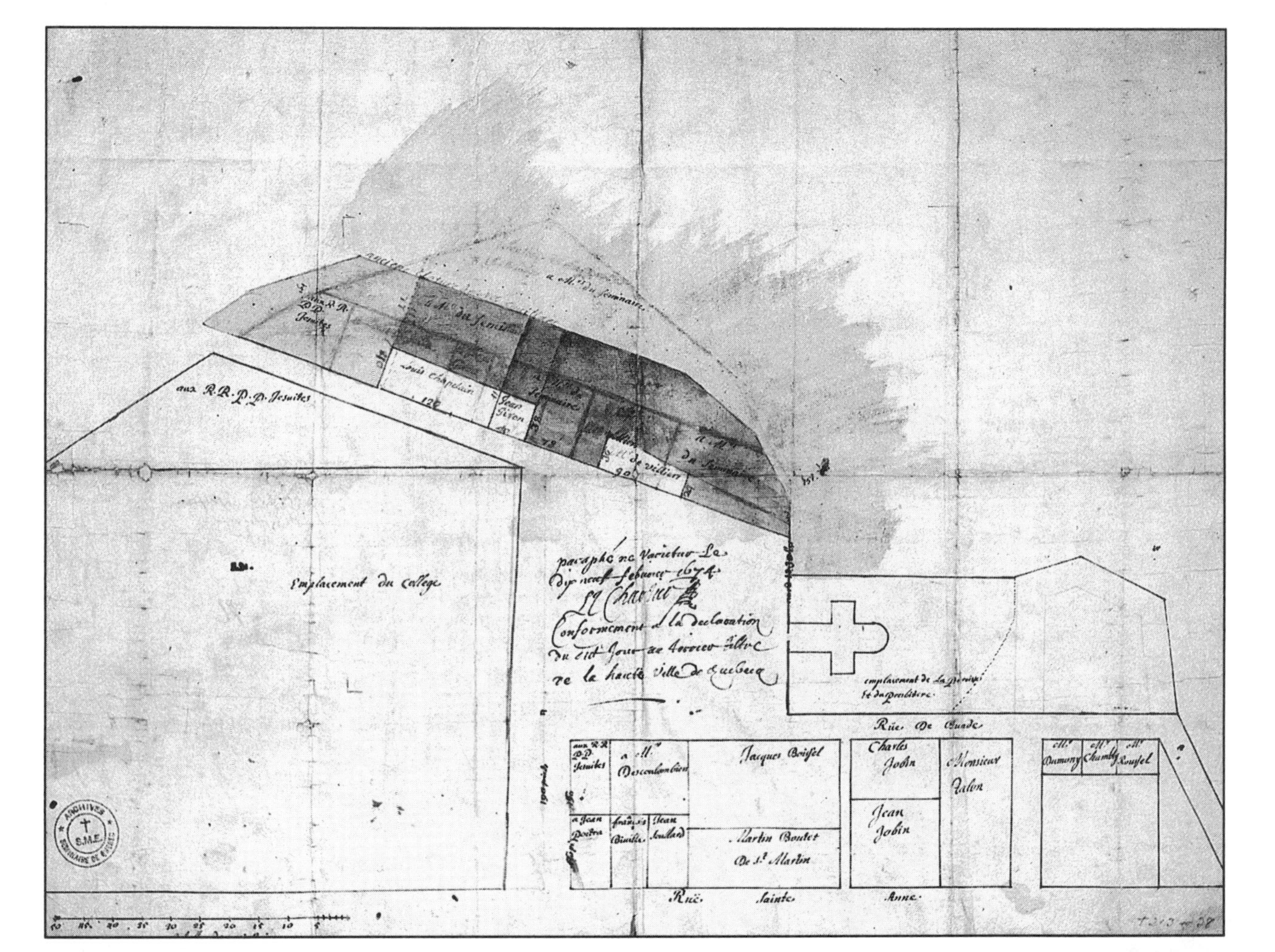
aux R.R. P.P. Jesuites
Emplacement du College
Louis Chapelain
Jean Piron
Rüe De Buade
Jacques Boisel
Martin Boutet De St Martin
Charles Jobin
Jean Jobin
Monsieur Talon
Rüe Sainte Anne

23 Plan of the fief of the Notre-Dame *fabrique*, 19 February 1674, anonymous

Signed by Chartier de Lotbinière, lieutenant-general of the Prévôté, This plan shows lot allocations and the layout of certain streets: Buade, Sainte-Anne, and côte de la Fabrique.

Archives du Séminaire de Québec

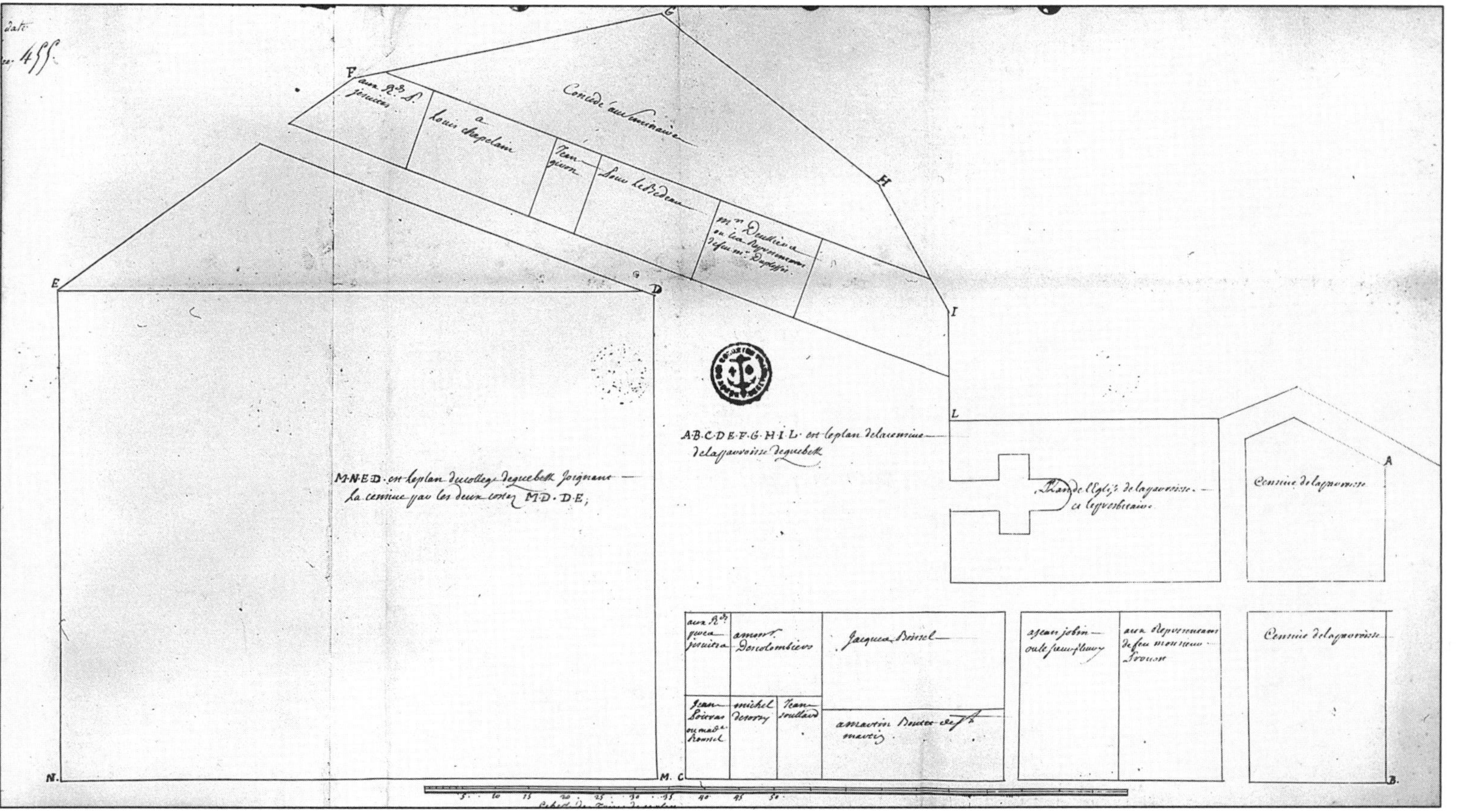
455
A
B
C
D
E
F
G
H
I
L
M
N
Concédé au Seminaire
Louis Chapelain
Louis le Bedeau
M.N.E.D. est le plan du college de quebek
5
10
15
20
25
30
35
40
45
50

24 Plan of the fief of the Notre-Dame *fabrique*, [after 1 June 1702], anonymous

This plan differs somewhat from Figure 23: the lot in the lower right-hand corner is not subdivided, a few lots have changed ownership, and the overall configuration is clearer.

Archives Nationales, France; copy on file, National Archives of Canada, C-15802

years later he gave the Hospitalières a small parcel of land "to help in the building of a new Infirmary, Chapel, and an Enclosure around the hospital." Couillard also donated to the Hôtel-Dieu the land for a cemetery in 1661. By June 1663 the Hospitalières' property had increased to 9.33 *arpents*, or 8397.2 square *toises*. Other lots were added to the property after 1663. In 1665 the widow of Nicolas Maquart sold a six-*arpent* lot to the community. In 1666 the gardener at the Hôtel-Dieu, Denis Dieudonné, transferred to them ten *arpents* that fronted on what is now côte du Palais.

The Jesuits also got a grant of 12 *arpents* in 1637, but it, too, was reduced, to 6 *arpents*, 42 *perches*. In 1663 their college site was enlarged by the purchase of two *arpents* from Guillaume Couillard. The Jesuits were also granted two other lots outside their main location; these lots looked onto the square on which Notre-Dame church was built and adjoined the Ursulines' land. In 1661 the Notre-Dame *fabrique* granted them 70 *perches*, in a triangular lot, between their location and côte de la Fabrique. On the north side of the street the *fabrique* also gave them 28 *perches* in January 1663.[8] Including the land they held in Lower Town, the Jesuits had a total 8686.6 square *toises* in Québec, similar to those of the Ursulines.[9]

The Notre-Dame *fabrique* was set up in 1645, and the gift of a lot 80 *pieds* by 38 *pieds* from Guillaume Couillard meant that a parish church could be built. Seven years later Couillard gave 80 *perches* to the *fabrique*. These two initial lots combined to form the so-called fief of the *fabrique*. In June 1651 the *fabrique* got a concession of 38.5 *perches* and another of one *arpent*, which was bounded by the streets that are now Buade, des Jardins, Sainte-Anne, and du Trésor (Figs. 23 and 24). In May 1652 the holdings were increased by 140 *perches* and later by 12.5 *perches* in 1654–55. The latter lot was severed from the land that Governor d'Ailleboust had set aside for himself on rue Buade. The *fabrique*'s fief totalled some 9.75 *arpents* in 1656. Before 1663 the *fabrique* also owned the land on which the cemetery was built on côte de la Montagne (now Montmorency-Laval park). Beginning in 1655 the *fabrique* acquired eight *arpents* located behind the château garden (Fig. 28).[10]

By 1663 the three religious communities mentioned above and the *fabrique* owned about 27 per cent of the land in Québec. This affected the town's development, particularly in Upper Town.[11]

On the religious communities' arrival or return, Governor Montmagny reduced the initial concessions granted to them in order to leave room for other residents to build their houses. His attempts to rationalize Québec's development and to establish a plan for it ran into difficulties because of the existing concessions.

The land the religious communities occupied greatly hampered his plan. Drawings of Québec in 1660 and 1664 show that the land held by the Ursulines changed the layout of the streets and made it impossible for Montmagny to carry out his plan for concentric streets (Figs. 2 and 22). Moreover, the Ursuline land reduced the area available to other residents. The Ursulines did not distribute their land in an orderly fashion until the second half of the 17th century, in accordance with a plan approved by Frontenac (Figs. 18 and 19). Similarly, the Hôtel-Dieu properties affected the distribution of land in the côte du Palais area. The Jesuits' centrally located land in Upper Town greatly impeded any development according to principles of town planning popular at the time (Figs. 27 and 28). The *fabrique*'s fief, for its part, did not really have any harmful effect on Upper Town development. A plan by Deslandes in 1674 shows 22 lots already in that area, which had "developed very early, doubtless because of its central location, between the Place du Marché and the Place d'Armes, at the entrance to Upper Town; but also because of its proximity to the Château" (Fig. 23).[12]

Let us now look at the number of houses in the town. In 1636 Marie de l'Incarnation estimated there were five or six buildings, and in 1653 Marguerite Bourgeoys confirmed this. Three years later Père Ragueneau said that there were about 30 houses in Québec. Later, in 1666, Mère Juchereau de Saint-Ignace referred to 70 houses. A quick count of the structures (houses, mills, chapels, presbytery) identified in Marcel Trudel's register of properties (*terrier*) gives a total of 108. For his part, Marc Lafrance, working from Bourdon's 1660 map, estimated 16 houses in Upper Town and 76 in Lower Town.[13] The 1663 map gives similar information: 25 buildings in Upper Town and 61 in Lower Town (Fig. 25). By 1663 there were probably about 100 houses in Québec, with most of the people living in Lower Town, and residents of Upper Town living mainly on rue Saint-Louis (Fig. 25).

Concessions between 1663 and 1690

In the second half of the 17th century the seminary and the Récollets also occupied large tracts of land in Québec. In 1666 Veuve Couillard sold part of Sault-au-Matelot to Bishop Laval. The land was bounded by the land of the parish church, a lot belonging to Sieur d'Auteuil, and the properties of the Hôtel-Dieu and Veuve Couillard. It also extended to the St. Lawrence and Saint-Charles rivers. In 1680 Laval gave this land

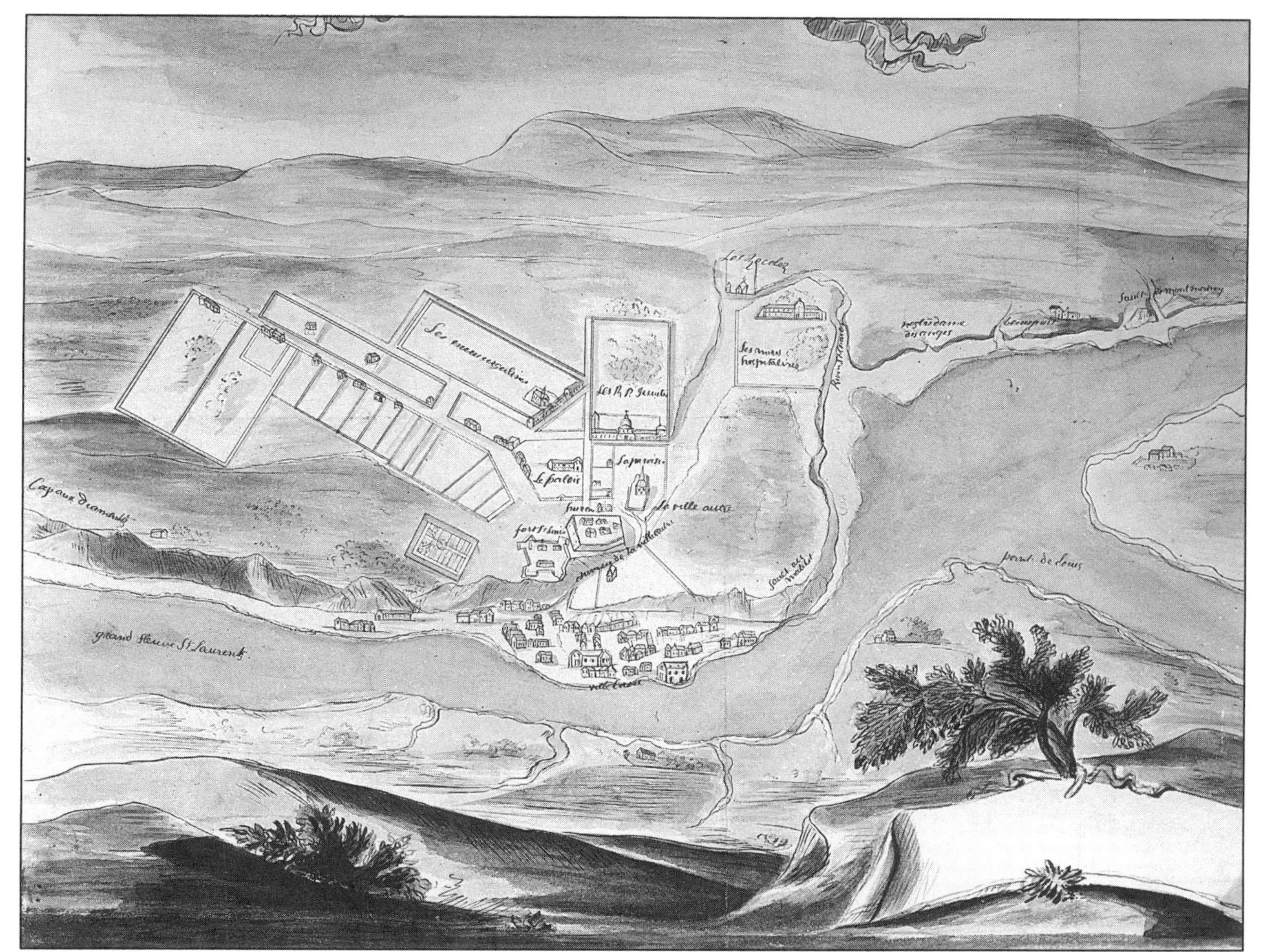

Les meres ursulines
Les R. P. Jesuites
Le palais
La ville haute
fort St Louis
ville basse
grand fleuve St Laurent
Les meres hospitalières

25 "Le Veritable plan de quebec fait en 1663," Jean Bourdon

This plan adds a third dimension to the 1660 version (Fig. 22) by giving a perspective of the streets, houses, and buildings. It clearly shows the radial layout of avenues in Upper Town. Furthermore, most of the houses front on the streets. It contains a few errors: the Récollet convent is located too close to the Hôtel Dieu and the orientation Bourdon gave to the palace (or Sénéschaussée) does not correspond to that shown on Figure 26. Lower Town is a jumble that certainly cannot be described as a grid. Also noteworthy is the width of rue Saint-Louis where it meets the Place d'Armes.

Service historique de la Marine, Vincennes, France, portefeuille 127, division 7, pièce 3

Table 8
Concessions in Québec, 1687–1690

Year	Upper Town	Lower Town	Unspecified Location
1687	—	11	—
1688	1	—	—
1689	2	5	—
1690	—	—	1
Total	3	16	1

to the seminary, and in 1687 the governor and the intendant added the riverbank area the whole length of the fief.[14] As a result, the seminary owned not only part of Upper Town, but also a section of Lower Town.

In 1681 the king gave the land belonging to the Sénéschaussée to the Récollets, since it was "a place not Useful to his Service," so that they could have a hospice in Upper Town.[15] From the beginning there was a quarrel about what type of building should be constructed: the Récollets wanted to build a convent with a bell tower, while Bishop Saint-Vallier wished to restrict them to a hospice. There were, however, some attempts to repossess the Sénéschaussée land, a prime Upper Town site, since it ran along rue Saint-Louis and the Place d'Armes. In 1686 Governor Denonville suggested that Secretary of State Seignelay repossess it and build the intendant's palace there. His intention was to relocate the Récollets to the building that had been Talon's brewery. Denonville seems to have been willing to concentrate public buildings in Upper Town, around the Place d'Armes, where the château was located, which would facilitate dealings between the various administrative levels and would give the Place d'Armes another monument. In 1687 Louis XIV allowed the governor "to have the Récolects do what Would be appropriate [granting the Sénéschaussée land] for the good of His Service." The Récollets seem to have kept the land: a 12 May 1689 description of the boundaries was the same as those Intendant Duchesneau set in 1681 (Fig. 26).[16]

The period from 1663 to 1690 was very different from the previous one regarding concessions to individuals. Most of the city was occupied; there was very little vacant space. During that time the most intensive period for land grants was between 1687 and 1690, when 20 lots were distributed (Table 8).[17]

The figures in Table 8 are only indicative of the concessions granted between 1663 and 1690; however, we can make some extrapolations

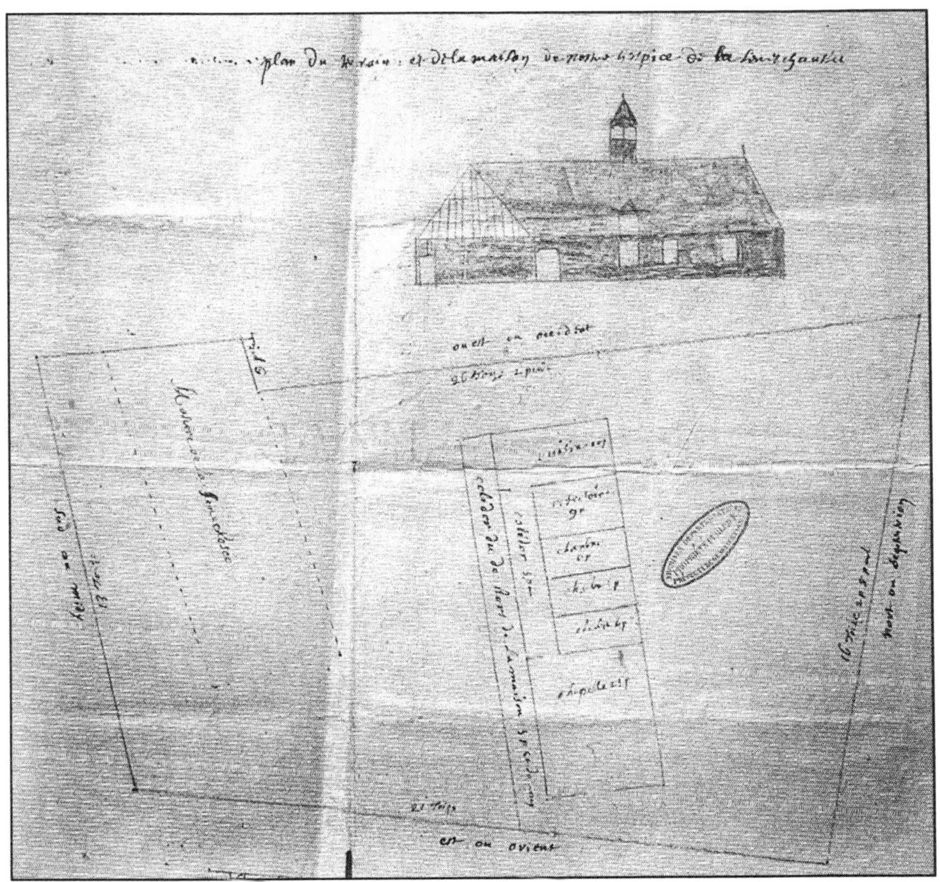

26 Plan of the Récollets' lands in Upper Town, [October 1681], anonymous

This drawing shows the Récollet hospice and the boundaries of their land in Upper Town.

Archives Yvelines, Seine-et-Oise, Grandes Ecuries, Versailles; photo by Jean Bélisle

from them. For example, most of the concessions were made in Lower Town, particularly on rue Saint-Pierre. In 1687 alone, nine lots fronting on that street were granted to some important landowners: Pachot, Lebert, Lachenaye, d'Auteuil, and others. With the exception of rue De Meulles and the extreme northeastern part of rue Saint-Pierre, the concession contracts were rarely for large pieces of land. In most cases, space was set aside for courtyards or additions (staircases, balconies, and porches). The time of sizeable concessions had passed; the city *intra muros* had largely taken on its final form.

If we compare the 1663, 1670, and 1685 maps (Figs. 25, 27, and 28) we can determine whether the town's growth occurred in certain areas and we can assess the changes in the number of houses in Québec after 1663. The maps of 1670 and 1685 show some similarities with that of 1663. However, the haphazard street layout is more evident in the later maps except in Lower Town. In addition, some of the structures shown (such as the Huron fort) disappeared whereas others (the seminary, for example) have been added. Curiously, the houses east of the Ursulines' land, close to rue des Jardins, are no longer visible.

The anonymous map dating from 1670 suggests that the town was expanding in three areas: rue Saint-Louis and rue Sainte-Anne in Upper Town, and rue Sous-le-Fort in Lower Town. This map shows an increase in the number of buildings: approximately 70 in Upper Town and 85 in Lower Town. From some 100 houses before 1663, the number in 1670 had increased to 155.

The map drawn by Villeneuve in 1685 reveals that rue Saint-Louis, côte de la Fabrique, and the area near the intendant's palace had become more settled. It also illustrates changes in the main buildings: Château Saint-Louis, the Ursulines' convent, the seminary, the cathedral, and so forth. In Lower Town it is clear that in addition to rue Saint-Pierre, development occurred to the south, on rue De Meulles, and in the northeast, on rue du Sault-au-Matelot. The map depicts 213 structures (houses, sheds, and other buildings): 105 in Upper Town and 108 in Lower Town, an increase of 58 buildings as compared to the 1670 map and showing that Upper Town offered more opportunities for expansion and land use.

These maps show the development of the urban landscape up to 1690. By then Québec had 200 buildings at most. Upper Town and Lower Town projected very different images: one was the centre of commerce, while the other was a place of steeples.

The Urban House

In 1644 Marie de l'Incarnation mentioned several types of building materials used in Québec: "there are houses built of stone, wood, and bark. Ours is entirely made of stone.... The fort is made of stone, as are its outbuildings. Also of stone are the homes of the Reverend Fathers, of Madame our Founder, of the Mères Hospitalières, and the Indians living in the town. The habitants' houses are half-timbered, with stone fill between the timbers; 2 or 3 being also entirely of stone."[18] This would indicate that stone was used only for public and religious buildings, while the townspeople's houses were mainly half-timbered (*colombage pierroté*). In 1664 Pierre Boucher described the dwellings in the colony as a whole: "Some [houses] Are made entirely of stone, & roofed with pine or other boards; others Are half-timbered or wood frame, & masonry between them; others Are built entirely of wood; &, as was said, all the above-mentioned houses Are roofed with boards."[19] Twenty years later Lahontan described the capital, making particular mention of the presence in Lower Town of "very handsome, three-storey houses, [built] of a stone as hard as marble."[20]

How accurate are these descriptions? A study of 229 contracts listed in the "Inventaire des marchés de construction des Archives Nationales à Québec, XVIIe et XVIIIe siècles" reveals a portrait of the standard type of home in Québec in the second half of the 17th century and also allows us to check the accuracy of the reports quoted above.[21] The contracts provide an excellent sample of house-building activity in Québec between 1660 and 1690 (*see* Appendix B). These records give information about annual fluctuations, types of contract, construction materials, roofing materials, the size of the houses, and the number of floors. They also indicate in which parts of the town most of the construction was occurring.

Housing Construction Activity by Year

"Activity" refers simply to the total number of contracts for each year. Three types of contract (for masonry, framing, and roofing; *see* Appendix B) were examined.

Table 9 shows the total annual activity for the town of Québec as a whole.[22] No figures are available before 1663. An apparent lack of house-building activity in 1664, 1665, and 1670 seems improbable, even given the type of contracts considered here, and documents are probably missing or lost, or the contracts were not properly reported.

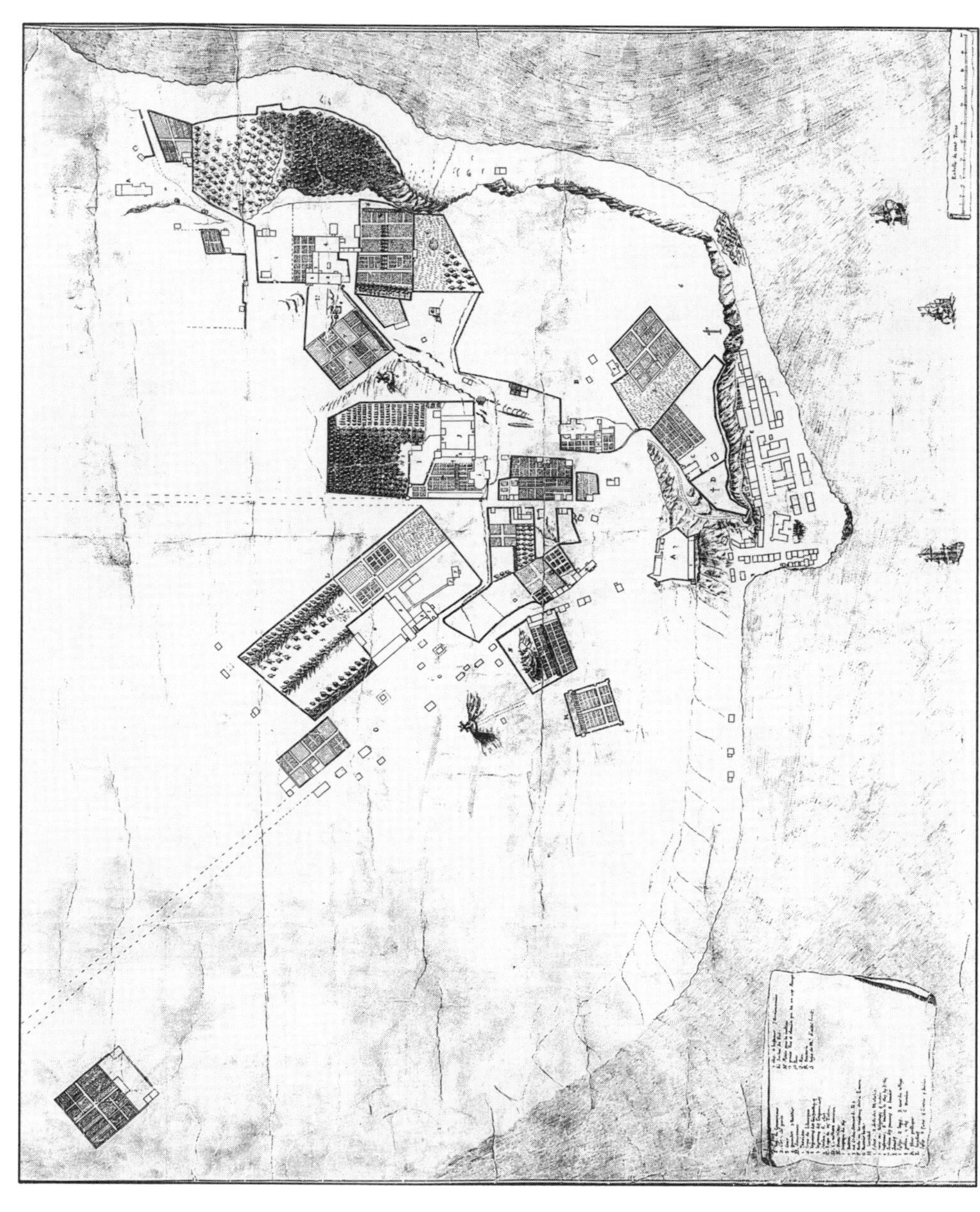

27 La Ville Haute et Basse de Quebek en la Nouvelle France 1670," anonymous

Lower Town is laid out on a more regular grid. This plan provides an excellent picture of the town of Québec with its public and religious buildings. Note, in comparison to Figure 1, the appearance of rue Saint-Jean, the extension of Buade, and the outline of rue du Trésor.

Archives Nationales, France; copy on file, National Archives of Canada, NMC-11088

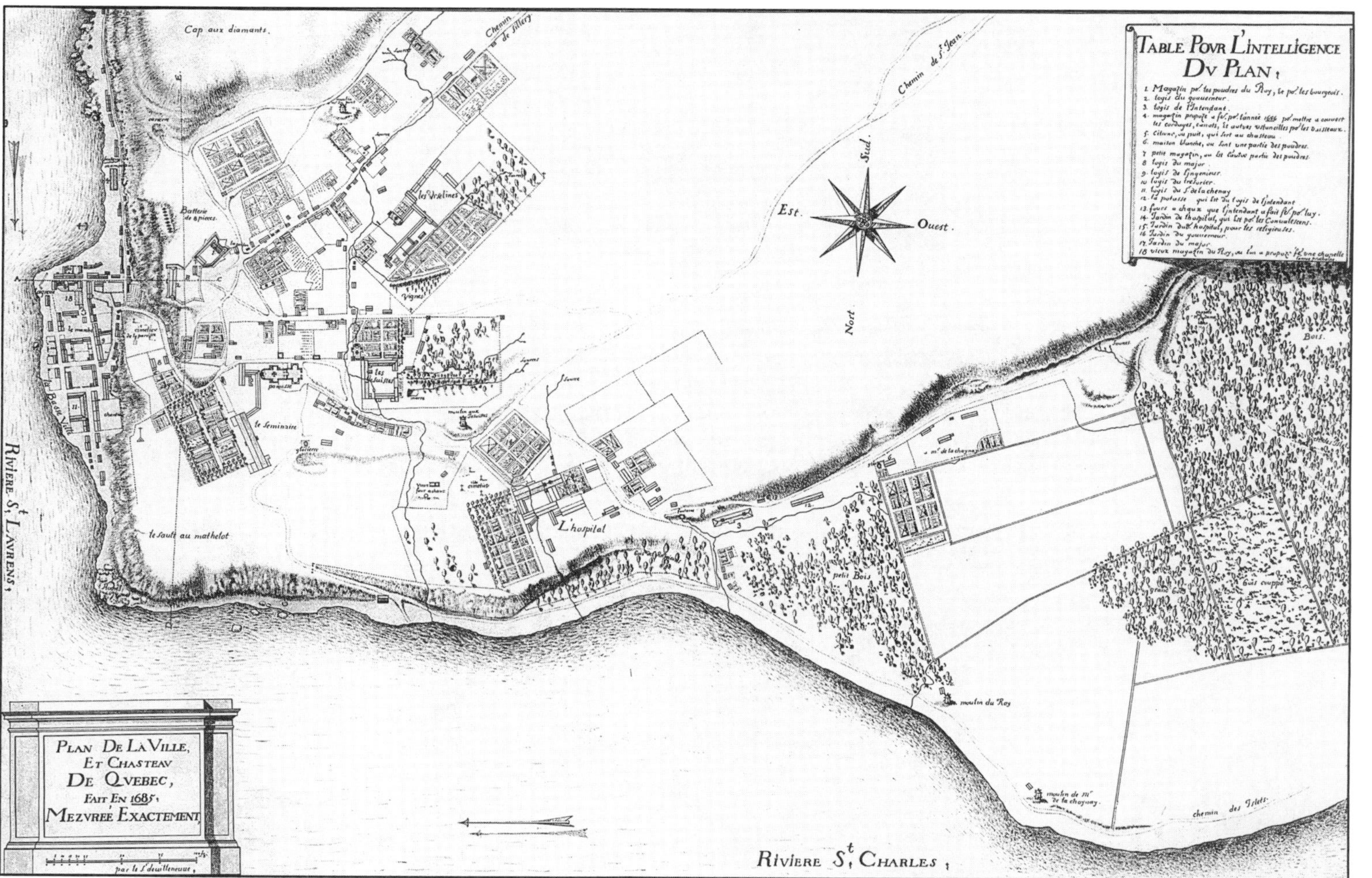

TABLE POVR L'INTELLIGENCE DV PLAN,
1 Magazin po. les poudres du Roy, le po. les bourgeois.
2. logis du gouverneur.
3. logis de l'Intendant.
4. magazin propozé a fe. po. l'année 1686 po. mettre a couvert les cordages, canots, et autres ustencilles po. les vaisseaux.
5. Citerne, ou puit, qui sert au chasteau
6. maison blanche, ou sont une partie des poudres.
7 petit magazin, ou est l'autre partie des poudres.
8 logis du major.
9. logis de l'ingenieur.
10 logis du tresorier.
11. logis du S. de la chenay
12 la potasse qui est du logis de l'intendant
13. fours a chaux que l'intendant a fait fe. po. luy.
14. Jardin de l'hospital, qui est po. les Convalescens.
15. Jardin dud. hospital, pour les religieuses.
16 Jardin du gouverneur.
17. Jardin du major.
18 vieux magazin du Roy, ou l'on a propozé fe. une chapelle
Cap aux diamants.
Chemin de Sillery
Chemin de S.t Jean
Batterie de 8 pieces.
les Vrselines
Vignes
les Jesuistes
le Seminaire
paroisse
L'hospital
petit Bois
Bois
Bois couppé
m.r de la chesnay
moulin du Roy
moulin de M.r de la chesnay
chemin des Islets
te sault au mathelot
la Basse Ville
Est.
Ouest.
Sud.
Nort.
PLAN DE LA VILLE, ET CHASTEAV DE QVEBEC, FAIT EN 1685, MEZVREÉ EXACTEMENT,
par le S. devilleneuve,
RIVIERE S.t LAVRENS,
RIVIERE S.t CHARLES,

28 "Plan De La Ville, Et Chasteau De Quebec," 1685, Robert de Villeneuve

Villeneuve's survey is probably the best made in the 17th century; not only the concessions but also the houses are clearly delineated. Comparing this plan with the one (Fig. 27) in 1670 gives a good idea of the town's growth. The plan also vividly illustrates Upper Town's agrarian nature.

Archives Nationales, France; copy on file, National Archives of Canada. C-15797

Table 9
Construction Contracts in Québec, 1663–1690

Year	Côte de la Montagne	Québec	Lower Town	Upper Town	Total No. of Contracts
1663	—	—	1	—	1
1664	—	—	—	—	—
1665	—	—	—	—	—
1666	—	—	2	—	2
1667	—	—	2	1	3
1668	—	—	2	—	2
1669	—	—	—	1	1
1670	—	—	—	—	—
1671	—	—	4	—	4
1672	1	1	2	1	5
1673	—	2	3	—	5
1674	—	—	2	2	4
1675	—	—	2	2	4
1676	1	2	2	1	6
1677	1	1	2	2	6
1678	—	—	2	1	3
1679	—	—	16	1	17
1680	4	—	7	2	13
1681	1	1	4	1	7
1682	1	1	18	6	26
1683	2	2	25	2	31
1684	1	2	11	3	17
1685	—	1	11	4	16
1686	—	1	8	2	11
1687	—	2	10	1	13
1688	1	—	8	3	12
1689	1	1	5	4	11
1690	—	1	4	4	9
Total	14	18	153	44	229

In some years there were large increases in the number of homes being built: 1679, 1680, and 1682 to 1690. Table 9 shows to what extent contracts were concentrated between 1682 and 1685. There were 90 contracts in those years, or 39 per cent of the total. Lower Town, with 153 contracts, accounts for 66.8 per cent of the total while Upper Town, with only 44 contracts, represents 19.2 per cent of the total. The number of contracts not specified as being in either of these locations is minimal and amounts to around 7 per cent of the total, in the case of houses on côte de la Montagne and those for which the specific location was not available.

Graph 3
Québec Construction Contracts
1663–1690

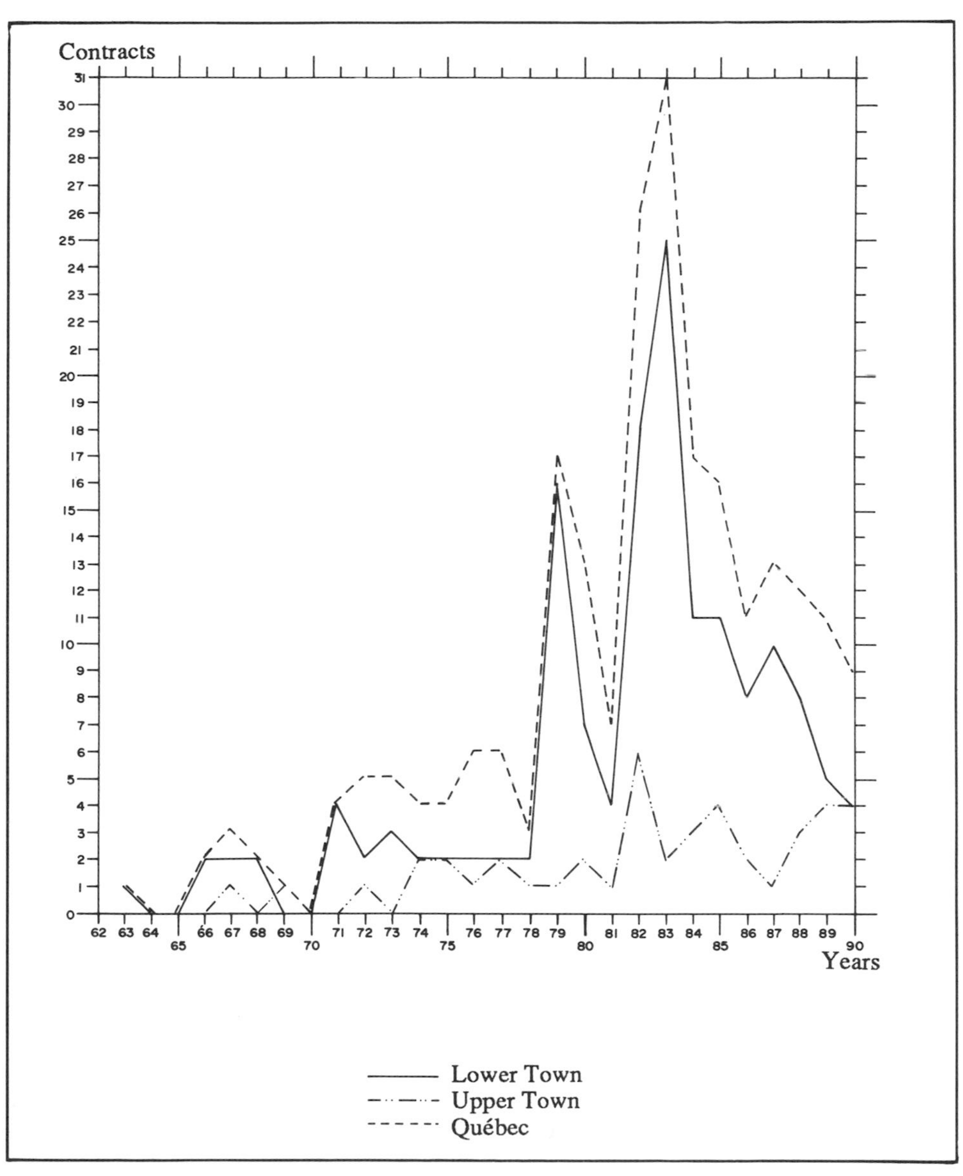

These trends can be seen on Graph 3, where the line for Québec represents the total of 229 contracts listed in Table 9. There are no real peaks in the line except during the key years mentioned above. Before 1679 there were minor peaks in 1672 and 1677, followed by a marked increase in 1679. In 1682 and 1683 there was a spectacular increase in house building. After 1683, although the numbers remained large, they gradually fell off, with the exception of a slight rise in 1687 that subsequently tapered off to a total of nine contracts in 1690.

To understand the peaks and valleys on this line we must look more closely at Lower Town. It strongly influenced the figures for the town of Québec as a whole. Table 10 shows that the trend noted for the town of Québec occurred in Lower Town as well, particularly in years with the greatest building activity. Most contracts were given out in 1679 and 1680, and from 1682 to 1690. Furthermore, 42 per cent of all construction contracts in Lower Town were awarded between 1682 and 1685.

Table 10 breaks down construction contracts in Lower Town by street and gives us some information that did not appear in the figures (Table 9) for the town as a whole.[23] In 1679 the increase in contracts was due to a large extent to house-building activity on rue De Meulles and rue du Sault-au-Matelot. The figures for the years from 1682 to 1690 largely reflect construction activity on two streets: Saint-Pierre and Notre-Dame. Between 1663 and 1690 these two streets represented a high percentage of all Lower Town contracts. Rue Saint-Pierre accounted for 22.2 per cent of all construction contracts in Lower Town, while rue Notre-Dame was responsible for 19.6 per cent, and both streets had very high figures for individual years as well. There were eight contracts for rue Saint-Pierre in 1682 and a significant number in 1686 and 1687 as well. The year 1683 was an outstanding one on rue Notre-Dame, when ten contracts, one-third of the total, were for houses on that street.

Graph 4 shows the annual variation in the number of contracts for these two streets and for all of the 153 construction contracts recorded for Lower Town (Table 10). Clearly the major increases occurred after 1679. The lines for Notre-Dame and Saint-Pierre influence those for Lower Town as a whole, and they, in turn, follow the line for Québec shown in Graph 3.

The increase in the number of contracts in 1679 and 1680 was attributable to houses built by two men. The six contracts for rue du Sault-au-Matelot in 1679 were for the huge house that Charles Aubert de Lachenaye had built that year. About the same time, Pierre Normand Labrière, a maker of edge-tools, built a second home on rue De Meulles and it involved many construction contracts.

Table 10
Construction Contracts in Lower Town, 1663–1690

Year	Lower Town	Notre-Dame	Saint-Pierre	Sault-au-Matelot	De Meulles	Sous-le-Fort	Total No. of Contracts
1663	—	—	—	1	—	—	1
1664	—	—	—	—	—	—	—
1665	—	—	—	—	—	—	—
1666	—	1	—	—	1	—	2
1667	—	—	—	—	1	1	2
1668	—	1	—	—	—	1	2
1669	—	—	—	—	—	—	—
1670	—	—	—	—	—	—	—
1671	—	3	1	—	—	—	4
1672	—	1	1	—	—	—	2
1673	1	—	—	—	2	—	3
1674	—	—	—	—	2	—	2
1675	2	—	—	—	—	—	2
1676	2	—	—	—	—	—	2
1677	—	—	—	—	2	—	2
1678	—	—	—	—	—	2	2
1679	—	1	2	6	4	3	16
1680	2	4	—	—	1	—	7
1681	2	—	—	2	—	—	4
1682	5	2	8	1	—	2	18
1683	6	10	3	1	2	3	25
1684	1	2	2	3	1	2	11
1685	2	1	4	1	2	1	11
1686	1	—	5	2	—	—	8
1687	—	3	5	1	—	1	10
1688	—	1	2	2	1	2	8
1689	—	—	—	2	2	1	5
1690	—	—	1	2	1	—	4
Total	24	30	34	24	22	19	153

The reasons for the increase in contracts between 1682 and 1690 help us understand the concentrations (1682–85 and 1687) mentioned above. The most important factor was the 1682 fire, which destroyed 55 homes in Lower Town, half or two-thirds of all dwellings in that part of Québec.[24] The fire was the main reason many contracts were signed beginning in 1682: 18 for Lower Town in that year, 25 in 1683, 11 in 1684, and 11 in 1685. In addition, the Lower Town battery was moved about this time, which encouraged construction activity around the Place Royale in 1683 and 1684. The slight recovery in 1687 resulted from the

Graph 4
Construction Contracts for Lower Town
1663–1690

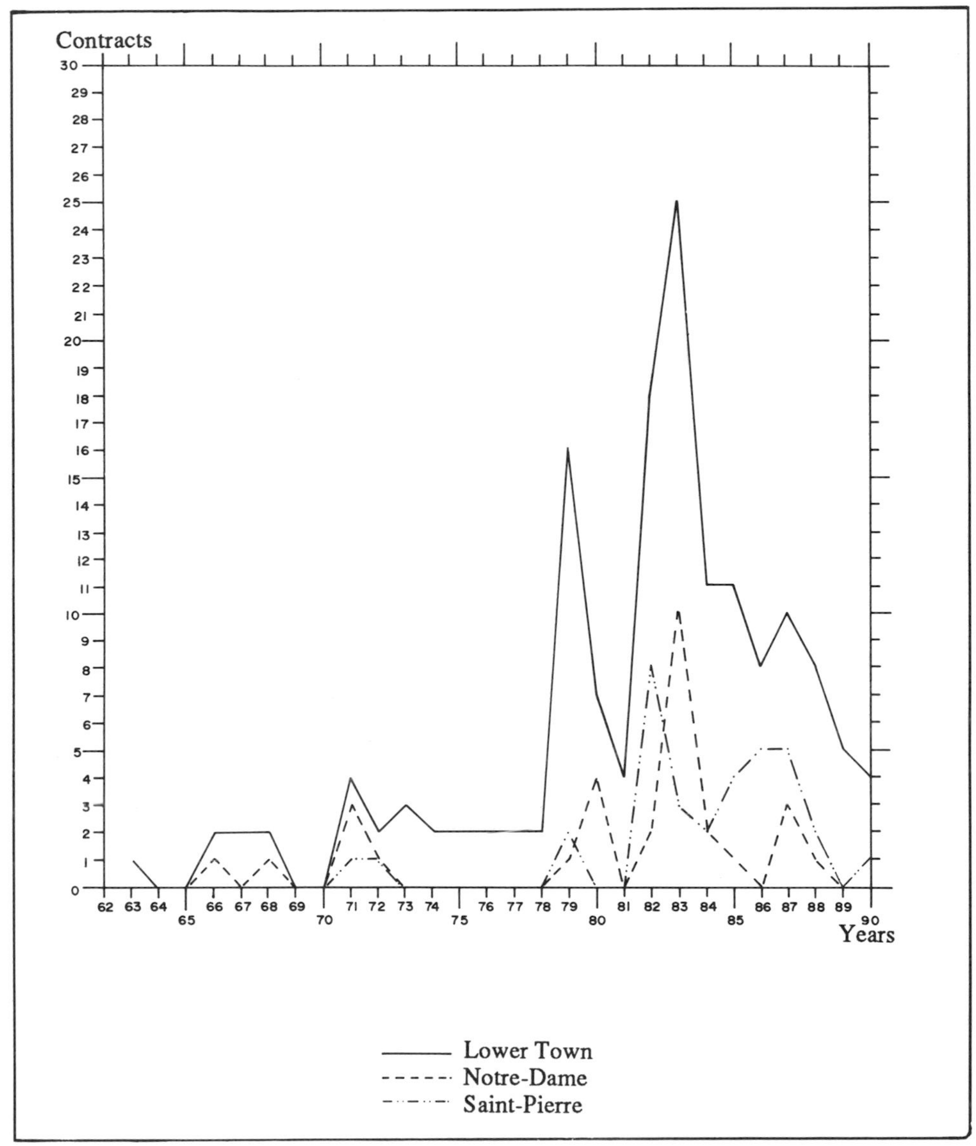

Table 11
Breakdown of Construction Contracts By Type of Contract
1663–1690

Location	Masonry	Framing	Roofing	Framing & Roofing*	Others**
Côte de la Montagne	4	6	4	—	—
Upper Town	21	20	3	4	—
Québec, unspecified location	7	7	4	3	—
Lower Town in general	8	11	5	1	—
Notre-Dame	7	12	10	3	1
Saint-Pierre	11	14	6	2	2
Sault-au-Matelot	9	10	3	2	2
De Meulles	12	9	1	2	1
Sous-le-Fort	8	8	2	3	1
Total	87	97	38	20	7
Percentage	37.9	42.4	16.6	21.0	3.1

* Contracts for both framing and roofing are already included among framing contracts.
** Contracts for unknown services and a few transport contracts.

many parcels of land granted on rue Saint-Pierre that year. Many houses were undoubtedly built after those concessions were made.

External Components of the Urban House

Types of Contracts

Table 11's information on the types of contracts shows the representation of the various trades. Of the 229 contracts, 42.4 per cent were for framing, slightly more than the 37.9 per cent for masonry, while contracts for roofing were far behind, only 16.6 per cent of the total.[25]

The table confirms that Lower Town had the highest number of contracts, as was noted in the analysis of activity by year. The breakdown here shows that more than 60 per cent of all types of contract went to

Lower Town. The figures for Lower Town for the various trades are: 55 contracts for masonry (63.2 per cent), 64 for framing (65.5 per cent), 27 for roofing (71.1 per cent), and 13 of the 20 contracts for both framing and roofing (65 per cent). Upper Town totalled about one-third of the contracts Lower Town had in all categories except roofing contracts, where the figures were 3 out of 27, or one-ninth.

Building Materials

The two main categories of construction and assemblage were the wooden house and the stone house, the main difference being the type of material used: "the shape of the wooden house did not differ from that of a stone house.... Wooden houses did not represent a specific architectural style. The only difference between wooden houses and stone houses was the materials used, and the architectonic arrangement of these materials must therefore become the classification criterion."[26]

Historians and ethnologists have devised various classifications to describe the types of construction used for wooden houses.[27] For our purposes we need only mention some of the generic names that include a number of categories and subcategories relating to various types of assemblage or to the preparation of materials (stakes, posts, beams, and squared timbers).[28] The first construction method, known as "framing," is characterized "by the use of a log roughly squared to make a timber that has different names depending on its position in the wall and its function."[29] The second method of constructing wooden houses was *pièce-sur-pièce*, which some say was the preferred building method in New France.[30] This was a "frequently used procedure in which the timbers were stacked horizontally one on top of the other and attached at the ends with mortise and tenon joints or dovetail joints."[31]

This analysis makes distinction between frame construction and *pièce-sur-pièce*. Nor will it cover dressing or assembling wood, only its general use. As a result of my research I decided to put half-timbered construction (*colombage*) in a different category. Although often included in the category of wooden assemblages,[32] it is a transition between wood and stone and should be looked at separately. Half-timbering refers "more specifically to all of the uprights in a half-timbered wall, and by extension, the whole wall, including the fill between the posts or uprights." Various types of material were used as fill: clay and grass; bricks; and stones, lime mortar, oat flour, and animal hair.[33]

It is not as difficult to classify stone houses. They can be distinguished by the two categories of stones used: field stone, found on site, and quarry stone.

Many types of stone were used in Québec. A black stone from the Cap, a limestone schist, was the most frequently used because it could be obtained locally from quarries in Upper and Lower Town and because it was inexpensive. It was generally used for the bulk of the wall and for interior facings. When it was used as external wall facing it was covered with a coating or a rough-cast covering that provided additional protection from the weather. The stone found in Beauport, of a better quality, was a fine-grained, dark brownish blue limestone. It was used mainly for external facings and as cut stone: piers, framing for bay windows and doors, corners, flue dividers, and fireplace jambs. Sandstone from Île d'Orléans and from the Lauzon area was used, as was stone from Cap Saint-Claude, for wall facings, fireplace masonry, and arch construction.[34]

In a 1940 article Marius Barbeau stated that "most houses in old Québec were half-timbered or stone." The transition from wood to stone occurred around the middle of the 17th century: "as soon as possible, after 1650 or 1675, stone was used instead of wood in the construction of the walls of public buildings, churches, colleges and convents, and even many of the houses in districts that were colonized first."[35] Peter N. Moogk felt that from the beginning of the colony, half-timbered construction predominated: "The earliest, widespread type of domestic house built by the French in Canada was the maison en colombage whose ancestor was the medieval, half-timbered house of northwestern Europe." In Québec the most popular type of half-timbered house was the one in which the spaces were filled in with stone. Moogk saw a gradual transition from half-timbered houses to stone houses, mainly in the 17th century: "at Quebec, half-timbered dwellings slowly disappeared in the eighteenth century. The technique was not abandoned all at once; colombage was retained for a time as a cheap substitute for solid stone in the foundations of a few wooden houses and some later buildings of timber and stone were constructed with colombage gables and partition walls."[36] A.J.H. Richardson saw a similar pattern. He thought that before 1727, almost all the houses in Québec were of half-timbered construction, which gradually gave way to stone construction. According to a listing based on registers of properties belonging to various religious communities, Richardson found that in certain parts of the town between 1737 and 1739, there were 46 stone houses, 29 wooden houses (most in *pièce-sur-pièce* style), and only 8 half-timbered houses.[37]

Table 12
Materials Used in House Construction in Québec
1663–1690

Material	Lower Town	Upper Town	Côte de la Montagne	Unspecified Location	Total
Half-timbered	25	22	1	3	51
Wood	10	3	0	2	15
Stone	27	0	4	1	32
Total*	62	25	5	6	98
No. of contracts**	98	39	10	14	161

* Contracts in which construction material was specified.
** After eliminating duplicates for the same house.

Can we confirm or shed further light on these opinions on house types in the town of Québec in the second half of the 17th century? Of the 161 contracts retained for analysing house materials, only 60.9 per cent contained information on the building materials used (Table 12). At first glance it would seem that there is more information about the construction materials used in Lower Town than in Upper Town; however, further comparison reveals that 63.4 per cent of the contracts kept for the study of Lower Town contained information about building materials, whereas 64.1 per cent of the contracts for Upper Town did the same (Table 12). We actually have about the same amount of information on building materials for houses in Upper Town and in Lower Town.

From the figures for the periods 1663 to 1681 and 1682 to 1690 it is evident that there was more information for both Upper Town and Lower Town after 1681: 69.4 per cent of the information in the case of Lower Town and 72 per cent of the information in the case of Upper Town.

Between 1663 and 1690, half-timbered construction was clearly the predominant style in the town of Québec (Table 12 and Graph 5); there were many more half-timbered houses than wooden or stone ones. By 1681 the proportion of half-timbered houses was 29.4 per cent, that of wooden houses was 26.7 per cent, and that of stone houses was 37.5 per cent (Table 13). These figures merely show that these three types of material were used more often after 1681, which is to be expected since the number of contracts also increased after 1681.

Table 13
Chronological Breakdown of the Use of Building Materials

Material	Lower Town	Upper Town	Côte de la Montagne	Unspecified Location	Total
		1663–1681			
Half-timbered	8	6	1	—	15
Wood	3	1	—	—	4
Stone	8	—	3	1	12
Total*	19	7	4	1	31
		1682–1690			
Half-timbered	17	16	—	3	36
Wood	7	2	—	2	11
Stone	19	0	1	—	20
Total*	43	18	1	5	67

* Contracts in which the building material was specified.

To establish trends in the use of these materials, we have to look at all entries for each period. Until 1681, 48.4 per cent of the houses for which the building materials were identified were half-timbered, 12.9 per cent were wood, and 38.7 per cent were stone. Between 1682 and 1690 the figures for the houses for which the building materials are known were 53.7 per cent, 16.4 per cent, and 29.9 per cent respectively (Table 13). Therefore, the most popular building style in Québec was the half-timbered house, both before and after 1681, and it became even more prominent following the fire in 1682. Stone was the second most popular material, but it was used less frequently beginning in 1682, at least relative to the total number of contracts for which building materials are known. Wood ranked third, but it was used more frequently after 1681 (Graph 5).

To explain the trends in the use of these three materials, we must look more closely at the data for Upper and Lower Towns. Lower Town contracts break down as follows: 40.3 per cent half-timbered houses, 16.1 per cent wooden houses, and 43.6 per cent stone houses (Table 13). Unlike the town of Québec as a whole, Lower Town's dominant building material between 1663 and 1690 was stone. However, as seen in the chronological breakdown, before 1682, half-timbered houses and stone houses were equally common. Both accounted for 42.1 per cent of the

Graph 5
Use of Construction Materials in Québec
1663–1690

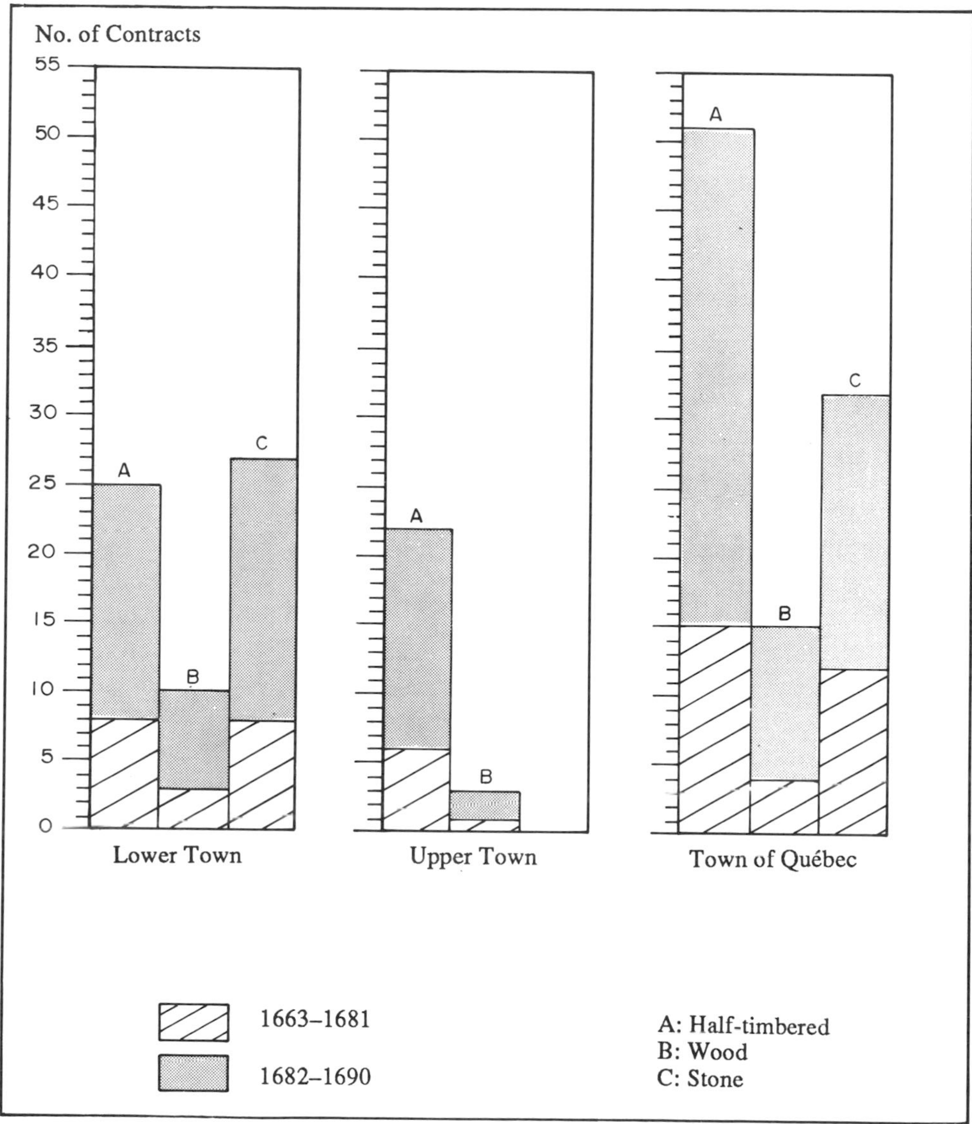

19 houses up to 1681. Wood, only mentioned three times, accounted for only 15.8 per cent of the houses (Graph 5). Between 1682 and 1690, half-timbered houses became slightly less common overall (39.5 per cent), while stone increased to 44.2 per cent. Wooden houses showed only a slight increase, to 16.3 per cent. Almost all of the

wooden houses, five of the seven, were located on rue du Sault-au-Matelot.

The Upper Town breakdown of construction materials was very different. The majority of the known contracts were for houses built after 1681; 88 per cent were for half-timbered houses and 12 per cent were for wooden houses. There were no stone houses (Table 13) in the contracts examined. The preference for half-timbered construction in Upper Town explains the data on that construction method for the town as a whole. The half-timbered house became increasingly common in Upper Town after 1681, whereas it became less so in Lower Town. The percentage representation of half-timbered houses went from 85.7 per cent to 88.9 per cent between 1682 and 1690. Because of the small sample size we cannot talk about a significant increase in wooden houses.

Detailed analysis of the data for Upper and Lower Town does not explain everything, even though these two distinct parts of the town decisively influenced the growth of various house types in Québec. Why did stone houses account for a smaller percentage of dwellings in the capital after 1682, while in Lower Town the representation of that type of house increased during the same period? Table 13 shows a drop in the number of stone houses on côte de la Montagne and in unspecified locations after 1681, affecting the percentage representation of stone houses after 1681.

Half-timbering was the preferred construction method in Québec between 1663 and 1690; however, half-timbered houses accounted for only slightly more than half of the dwellings. Wood and stone were also used; together the number of houses in which these two materials were used compares favourably to the number of half-timbered houses. Furthermore, types of construction differed between Upper and Lower Town: half-timbered houses dominated in one, while stone houses dominated in the other. It is generally accepted as well that the 1682 fire explains to a large extent stone houses' predominance in Lower Town.

This interpretation of building-material trends in Québec house construction is similar, with a few variations, to those of A.J.H. Richardson and Peter N. Moogk. There was, in fact, a move away from half-timbered houses to stone houses, a move that began at the end of the 17th century, but which was limited. Even after 1682, half-timbered construction still dominated. The importance of this method of construction was evident very early. From the time the town was founded, half-timbering was the most popular building method: "stone and clay colombage, in their framed form, were being built in and around Quebec, and ... here at least they were *the commonest important type of timber building at first.*"[38]

The trend in Québec was different from elsewhere in the colony, particularly in Montréal and Trois-Rivières. If we include half-timbered houses with other houses built entirely of wood (the *pièce-sur-pièce* style, for example), we see that wood was the dominant construction material in dwellings in New France in the 17th century. Georges Gauthier-Larouche commented on rural houses:

> *In the 17th century most houses were built of wood. This can readily be explained by the fact that farmers used the material immediately at hand after clearing the land. Before reaching the limestone, even though it did not lie very deep, even before gathering up granite rocks from the ground, farmers had to cut down trees and use them for all sorts of purposes, particularly house building.*[39]

Some authors, such as Robert-Lionel Séguin, actually claimed that "the first rural dwellings were generally built of wood, stone being reserved more for urban houses." It is difficult to know which building method was most common. Séguin thought it was *pièce-sur-pièce*,[40] while Moogk argued it was half-timbered construction, at least at the beginning of the century. Moogk felt that, with the exception of Québec, there was a transition from half-timbered to wooden houses, particularly the *pièce-sur-pièce* style, in New France in the 17th century: "outside of Quebec there was not a simple transference from half-timbering to masonry construction; the trend was towards entirely wood houses.... In the Canadian countryside the *maison en colombage* was superseded by the solid wooden house built in a manner that was distinctive of New France [the *pièce-sur-pièce* style]."[41]

Pièce-sur-pièce was apparently the most popular style in Montréal. A survey by A.J.H. Richardson showed that this method was used in 42 per cent of all dwellings between 1661 and 1700. Richardson also reported that in 1704 the engineer Levasseur de Neré identified 229 *pièce-sur-pièce* houses out of the 282 houses in the town at the time.[42] Only later, in the second quarter of the 18th century, did stone replace wood. Trois-Rivières was always a town of wooden houses, and this did not change in the 18th century.[43]

The use of building materials in Québec and elsewhere in New France raises a number of questions. What accounts for the different trend in Québec, where half-timbering was consistently most popular? Why were houses built entirely of wood not more common there before 1663? Why did their representation remain stable before and after 1681? What explains the popularity of stone houses? What is the significance of the choice of one building material over another?

Answers to most of these questions can be found in the colonists' technical heritage and the fact that they were settling in a new world. The issue of their technical heritage was well summarized by Georges Gauthier-Larouche:

> *There is no doubt that the immigrants from France in the 17th century brought with them to Canada their land system, their architecture, their furniture, their tools, their customs and habits; in short, their entire way of living. There was therefore a continuity between France and Canada, but at the same time, there was a break when they uprooted themselves to come and live in their adopted land.*[44]

Immigrants brought with them a number of techniques that they had to adapt to a new continent. The early immigrants found an abundant supply of wood, a material already scarce in France. Its plentiful supply profoundly affected the history of home building in Canada, particularly along the shores of the St. Lawrence:

> *The great tradition of timber building, which had apparently been in full swing in Europe since prehistoric times, but was now [in the early 17th century] gradually dying there as the forests were depleted, was brought to New France by the first colonists and revived among the Canadian woods, bulking very large in our early construction.*[45]

The first buildings in New France should have been entirely of wood, particularly when we recall that the immigrants had to build shelter quickly. What better material is there than wood for putting up a dwelling quickly? In the early days half-timbering was the preferred construction method, and here again we see the influence of techniques that were familiar to the immigrants. Since wood had become scarce in France, other building techniques, which made a greater use of stone, such as half-timbering, became more common. This method was in fact quite popular in France — in the north, on the west coast, and particularly in Normandy,[46] and many of the immigrants were from these regions. Consequently and not surprisingly, the first colonists built houses similar to the half-timbered style popular in France: not only wood but also stone were readily at hand,[47] and skilled craftsmen were also available because even in the first half of the 17th century, carpenters and masons were in the convoys.[48]

The fact that the immigrants were familiar with half-timbering does not explain everything because other building methods, such as *pièce-sur-pièce*, were also popular in France.[49] Another factor that accounted for half-timbering's popularity was simply that Québec habitants chose to use this method. Peter N. Moogk has said that "the potential of timber in home construction was not fully appreciated by the first generation of immigrants from Europe."[50]

These reasons explain the initial popularity of half-timbered construction in the colony. The same reasons probably account for the fact that it remained popular in Québec in the second half of the 17th century. *Pièce-sur-pièce* was more common elsewhere in New France, particularly in Montréal, because wood was more readily available than stone.[51] Because of building techniques, relatively few houses were built entirely of wood in Québec, where wood was of secondary importance, both before and after 1681. This can perhaps be explained by the fact that it was recent or relatively poor immigrants who built wooden houses. Some of the colonists who arrived between 1663 and 1690 built their first dwellings of wood, as did poor landowners who could not afford half-timbered or stone houses.[52]

The move from half-timbered houses to stone houses reflected not only a change in building materials, but also some aspects of the town's development. The change indicates the residents' level of maturity in construction methods. The transition to stone houses, which began around the end of the 17th century, showed that people were looking for stronger dwellings that would last longer. This was seen first in Québec because it was the oldest settlement in the colony. The move to half-timbered houses was an early indication that people wanted dwellings that were more long-lasting than wooden houses. This movement was accentuated with the popularity of stone houses in the 18th century. Québec was a trend-setter in this regard; Montréal did not follow suit until the 18th century, and Trois-Rivières never did switch to stone houses.

The changing pattern of construction materials in Québec also reveals a fact that is not emphasized enough: its citizens were rich. Québec was first and foremost a town of commerce. Obviously the rich were more likely to build dwellings of stone than the poor. The choice of building material had an economic impact. More labour and more money were required to build half-timbered or stone houses than wooden ones.

Some historians have put forward prices or estimates for domestic construction. Robert-Lionel Séguin found price variations between 40 and 300 *livres* for squaring timber and assembling a house, and he decided that an approximate cost would be 150 *livres*.[53] Moogk estimated the cost of *pièce-sur-pièce* dwellings at less than 250 *livres* in rural areas and around 300 *livres* in urban areas. Stone houses cost between 450 and 2000 *livres* or even more.[54] That estimate seems very conservative, but a full study of 17th-century construction costs in Québec has yet to be made.

Fires greatly influenced home building in Québec. After the Lower Town fire of 1682, many houses were rebuilt in stone. Fire-prevention regulations also had an impact on construction methods.[55]

The choice of any building material had implications and consequences. Much has been written, in particular by Georges Gauthier-Larouche and Peter N. Moogk, about adapting buildings to the climate,[56] but this must have been a secondary consideration in Québec. Otherwise, how could the popularity of half-timbered houses over wooden houses be explained? Wooden houses have better insulating properties and, according to Moogk, the *pièce-sur-pièce* style withstood the wet and intense cold better. Half-timbered construction is said to have had a number of disadvantages. One was that the hard winters caused the masonry to crumble and the wooden frame to sag. In addition, there was a constant danger of fire with half-timbered houses, but that is one characteristic it shared with wooden houses.[57] Stone houses also offered less insulation than wooden houses. Apparently Québec residents decided to trade off their houses' suitability to the climate for greater durability: "stone houses did not replace wooden houses because wooden houses were not warm; the problem with wooden houses was that they were not durable, and that is why more stone houses were built."[58]

Roofing Materials

The roof was one of the most characteristic features of homes in New France in the 17th century. (The roof can take various shapes: gable, mansard, or flat.[59])

The origins of the various roof shapes in New France are well known. The steeply pitched medieval roof was brought from such provinces as Normandy, Brittany, Île-de-France, and Perche to New France, particularly to Québec. The less steeply pitched roof, found particularly in the Montréal area, is thought to have come from provinces in the central western part of France: Saintonge, Anjou, and Angoumois.[60] The transfer of these roof shapes can easily be explained because they were well-suited to the climate. The shapes found in the Québec area had a great deal to do with winter weather: "a steep roof which readily shed rain and snow, was desirable in 'cold regions' because 'if it were too low, the snow would accumulate on it and when it melted, it would form ridges of ice on the eaves; these ridges would cause the water to back up and to leak into the garret or attic.'"[61]

In the 17th century various roofing materials were used for houses and other buildings. On country houses, thatch, bark, and moss were used interchangeably; however, the most common roofing was boards.[62] In towns, boards and shingles were the most common, but some materials were imported as well. Slate was used very little in the 17th century, but became more common in the 18th century, as did tile and tin sheeting. The latter material appeared in the 17th century, but was not really popular or widespread until after 1730, after technical improvements were made to it in France.[63]

Table 14 shows the data on roofing materials in Québec. Of the various types of contracts, 38 were for roofs and 20 were for both the frame and the roof, and with such limited information it would be pointless to try to find pronounced differences between roofing materials used in Upper Town and in Lower Town. One can only note that 22.4 per cent of the contracts were for roofs on rue Notre-Dame, without doubt a result of the fire in 1682.

The contracts show that four types of roofing material were utilized in Québec: shingles, boards, shingles and boards combined, and slate (Table 15). Slate was indeed rare; it was mentioned in one contract only. Roofs combining shingles and boards were not that common either; there were five references to this type of roof, 8.6 per cent of the total. Shingles alone accounted for 34.5 per cent of the contracts, while boards were mentioned in 23 contracts, or 39.7 per cent. These two materials enjoyed similar popularity.

Carpenters and joiners particularly favoured board roofs. Roofers, for their part, specialized in shingles or shingle and board roofs. The data regarding the popularity of both shingle and board roofs in Québec qualify, if not actually contradict, statements made by historians such as Peter N. Moogk, who claimed that "townspeople were not content with the plain board roofs of the countryside and they could not afford tiles or slate for roofing."[64] That was true of tile and slate, but the popularity of board roofs cannot be denied.

Shingles' and boards' inflammability explains the need for fire regulations. The authorities were constantly trying to prevent fires and took various measures to achieve this. In 1688 the Conseil Souverain explicitly prohibited the use of shingles in towns because they were considered highly inflammable. The following year it allowed their use, but only on dormers. It is difficult to determine this law's results because it was passed late in the period under study here. It may have promoted the use of board roofs, which were less inflammable than shingles. Boards also offered other advantages: "board roofs are important because they accentuate the perspective and emphasize horizontal lines, reflecting the string-courses between storeys. Faster to install and manu-

Table 14
Roofing Contracts in Québec, 1663–1690

Location	Roofs	Frames & Roofs
Côte de la Montagne	4	—
Upper Town	3	4
Unspecified locations in Québec	4	3
Unspecified locations in Lower Town	5	1
Notre-Dame	10	3
Saint-Pierre	6	2
Sault-au-Matelot	3	2
De Meulles	1	2
Sous-le-Fort	2	3
Total	38	20

Table 15
Québec Roofs, 1663–1690

Location	Shingle	Board	Shingle & Board	Other*	Total
Côte de la Montagne	2	1	1	—	4
Upper Town	2	4	1	—	7
Unspecified locations in Québec	—	6	—	1	7
Unspecified locations in Lower Town	4	1	1	—	6
Notre-Dame	2	4	1	6	13
Saint-Pierre	5	2	—	1	8
Sault-au-Matelot	2	1	1	1	5
De Meulles	1	1	—	1	3
Sous-le-Fort	2	3	—	—	5
Total	20	23	5	10	58

* Unknown and one slate roof.

facture, and consequently cheaper than shingles, they can be fastened on better."[65]

Roofing materials were also adapted to the available resources and to the climate. Shingles and board roofs predominated because of the abundance of wood, particularly oak and cedar. The weather's influence can be seen in the way the roofs were put together and in the layer of boards placed under the roof: "the latticework used in France to support a roofing material, whether tiles or slates, was no protection against the cold winds and powdery snow of the Canadian winter. An impermeable, primary layer of close-fitting boards under the shingles or overlapping boards took its place."[66]

House Sizes

Historians have paid very little attention to the size of houses in towns. As a result of the work of Gérard Morisset and Marius Barbeau, people often refer to a Québec-style house that is "rectangular, of average depth" and a Montréal-style house that is "a small domestic fortress. Square and solid." These are facile, ill-defined generalizations, just like the assumption that stone houses are more spacious than wooden ones.[67]

Marc Lafrance is one of the authors who have taken particular interest in house size. Without going into statistical analysis, he captured the essential evolution of house sizes in Québec from the 17th to the 18th centuries. Originally houses were small because people needed protection from the cold. That type of dwelling was common until 1682, and it was built side by side with more imposing structures such as Aubert de Lachenaye's residence on rue du Sault-au-Matelot. A typical example of a house from that period was Thierry de Lestre's on rue Notre-Dame: "a house sixteen *pieds* wide, as stated, ... which is his residence, and which consists of a room downstairs, a room upstairs with a fireplace, a cellar, an attic, and behind the house is a bakehouse." After the Lower Town fire in 1682, the new houses were larger. A typical example of the new, larger style is Eustache Lambert Dumont's home: 24 *pieds* by 36 *pieds* (864 square *pieds*).[68]

This is a fairly accurate overview, but it needs a few clarifications, so 161 contracts in the "Inventaire des marchés de construction" were examined to analyse the size of Québec houses between 1663 and 1690. Only 52.8 per cent of the contracts gave any information about house sizes (Table 16).[69]

Between 1663 and 1690, 45.5 per cent of the 85 contracts were for medium-sized houses, while 40 per cent were for small houses. Large

Table 16
Interior Area (in Square *Pieds*) of Québec Houses
1663–1690

	Category						
	Small		Medium		Large		
Location	Area	No.	Area	No.	Area	No.	Total
Québec	342	34	645	39	1305	12	85
1663–1681	342	12	654	13	1375	1	26
1682–1690	342	22	714	26	1298	11	59
Upper Town	359	11	633	7	1056	1	19
1663–1681	363	3	652	4	—	—	7
1682–1690	358	8	609	3	1056	1	12
Lower Town	322	17	720	30	1343	10	57
1663–1681	305	5	680	8	1375	1	14
1682–1690	329	12	735	22	1339	9	43

houses represented only 14.1 per cent of the total (Table 16 and Graph 6). The breakdown by year shows that the small and medium-sized dwellings were more common before 1682. Of the 26 houses built between 1663 and 1681, 46.2 per cent were small, 50 per cent were medium-size, and 3.8 per cent were large. The figures for the period 1682 to 1690 were 37.3 per cent, 44.1 per cent, and 18.6 per cent.

Both before and after 1681, small houses were 342 square *pieds* on average. The average area of medium-sized houses was 645 square *pieds* between 1663 and 1690; however, between 1663 and 1681 their average area was 654 square *pieds*, and between 1682 and 1690 it was 714 square *pieds*. Since there were so few large houses in the information examined, no particular trend can be noted for them other than that for the entire period the average area of these large houses was 1305 square *pieds*, dropping to 1298 square *pieds* after 1682.

Upper Town figures suggest a different pattern. Most of the houses there were small (57.9 per cent of the 19 entries), medium-sized houses were second (36.8 per cent), and there was only one large residence. Small houses increased from 42.9 per cent of the total before 1682 to 66.7 per cent between 1682 and 1690. The opposite trend was noted for medium-sized houses, which went from 57.1 per cent of the total to 25 per cent, an impressive decline. The area of medium-sized houses also dropped after 1682, while small ones remained more or less the same size (Table 16 and Graph 6).

Graph 6
Square Footage of Québec Houses
1663–1690

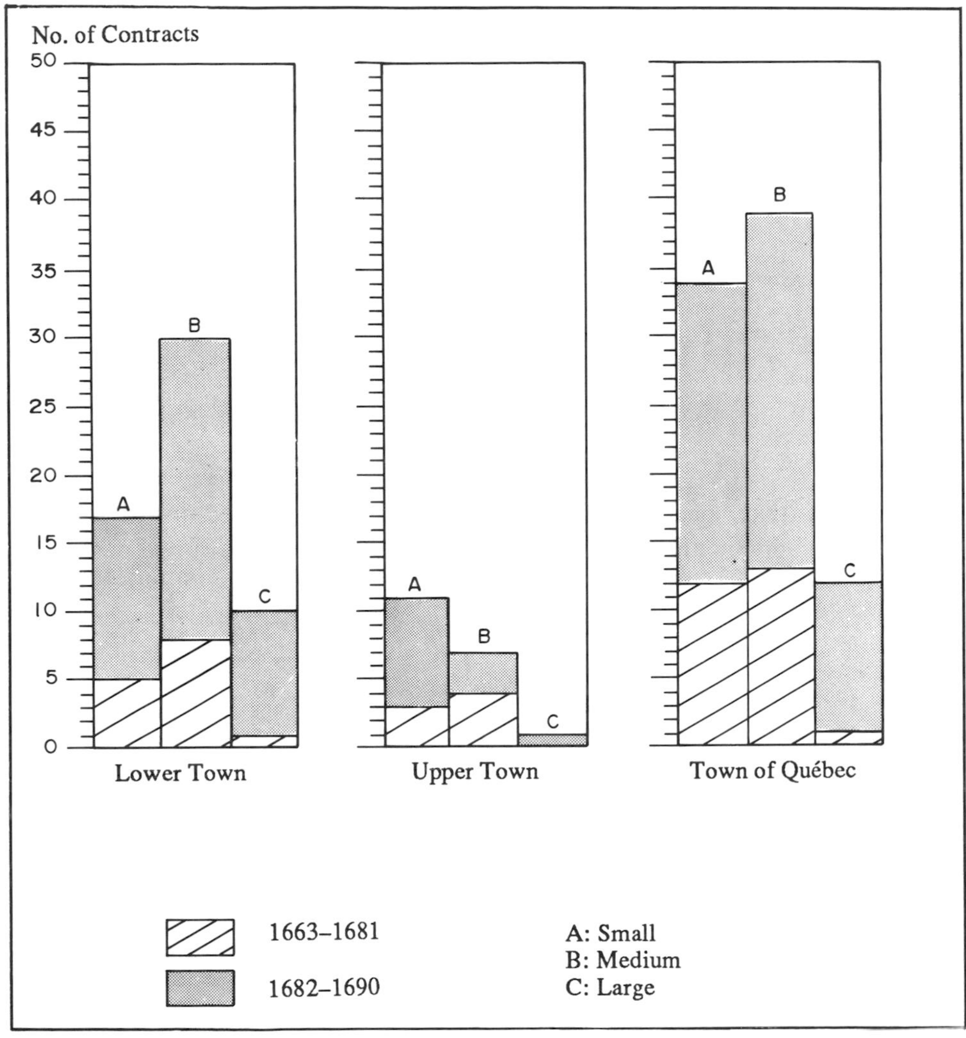

In Lower Town, medium-sized houses were more popular, accounting for 52.6 per cent of the total, while small houses represented only 29.8 per cent of the total between 1663 and 1690. Interestingly, there were far more large dwellings in Lower Town: 10 of the 57 contracts were for such houses, or 17.5 per cent of the total. There was a drop in small houses after 1682 (from 35.7 per cent to 27.9 per cent) and in medium-sized ones (57.1 per cent to 51.2 per cent), due to the increased number of larger houses. Between 1663 and 1681 only 7.1 per cent of the total consisted of large houses, while after 1681, the percentage rose to 20.9. The average area of small and medium-sized residences increased after 1681. The square footage of medium-sized houses and large ones in Lower Town was greater than elsewhere in Québec for the entire period 1663–1690 (Table 16 and Graph 6).

The dominance of medium-sized houses in the second half of the 17th century was obvious, and their numbers increased after the fire in 1682. Both small and medium-sized houses were very popular. Between 1682 and 1690 the number of larger homes increased steadily. There were different patterns in Upper and Lower Town. In Lower Town, medium-sized houses were the most common, and there were many large ones as well. In addition, the size of both types of house increased steadily. However, in Upper Town small houses, rather than medium-sized ones, were very popular.

The reasons that explained the use of various building materials can be applied to explain the pattern in house sizes in Québec as well; however, their significance varies. Having a home that kept out the cold was more important than a person's wealth, for example; comfort was more important than space. As historian Marc Lafrance pointed out, the fire of 1682 undoubtedly had significant consequences and led to increasingly large houses in Québec. Another factor was the larger population and larger families. Census figures suggest that over time, more people were living in each dwelling. In 1685 the average number of people per dwelling was 6.4, whereas it was 6.8 in 1688. These figures are very similar to those for Trois-Rivières for the same dates (*see* Chapter IV).

Number of Storeys

Only 32.9 per cent of the Québec housing construction contracts analysed indicate numbers of storeys. Dwellings were grouped into four categories: one, two, three, or five storeys (Table 17 and Graph 7). Most houses fell into one of the first two categories; others were less common. Of houses constructed in Québec between 1663 and 1690, two-storey buildings accounted for 55 per cent and single-storey ones, 36 per cent. Three-storey houses constituted only 8 per cent of this total, while there was only one five-storey house, that of François Hazeur on rue Notre-Dame.

Chronological analysis of contracts for the entire town is of little interest since until 1681 only seven contracts were drawn up. One- and two-storey houses still predominated after 1681, although some three- and five-storey houses appeared between 1682 and 1690.

Table 17
Number of Storeys in Québec Houses
1663–1690

No. of Storeys	Lower Town	Upper Town	Côte de la Montagne	Unspecified Location	Total
		1663–1681			
One	1	1	—	—	2
Two	5	—	—	—	5
Three	—	—	—	—	—
Five	—	—	—	—	—
Total	6	1	—	—	7
		1682–1690			
One	7	8	—	2	17
Two	22	—	1	1	24
Three	4	—	—	—	4
Five	1	—	—	—	1
Total	34	8	1	3	46

Nine, or 47 per cent, of these one-storey houses were built in Upper Town. Of the 40 houses built in Lower Town between 1663 and 1690 whose registrations indicate the number of storeys, 20 per cent were single-storey, 67.5 per cent two-storey, and 10 per cent three-storey dwellings. Table 17 shows an interesting increase in the proportion of two-storey houses in preferencc to single-storey ones after 1681. From these figures we can conclude that the most popular type of dwelling in Québec, especially after the fire of 1682, was one with two storeys. It also appears that after the fire, houses with more storeys were built. A distinction can be made between rural and urban homes: "[urban houses] have quite a number of storeys, unlike rural houses, whose attics usually rest atop the ground floor."[70]

A Typical Québec House?

The initial goal of analysing construction contracts was qualitative knowledge of Québec's physical development in the latter half of the 17th century. From the search for an accurate portrayal of dwellings there, the image of a typical Québec house has emerged: a two-storey half-timbered construction with stone fill between the timbers and hav-

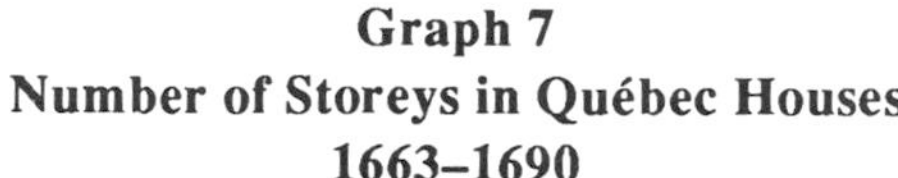

Graph 7
Number of Storeys in Québec Houses
1663–1690

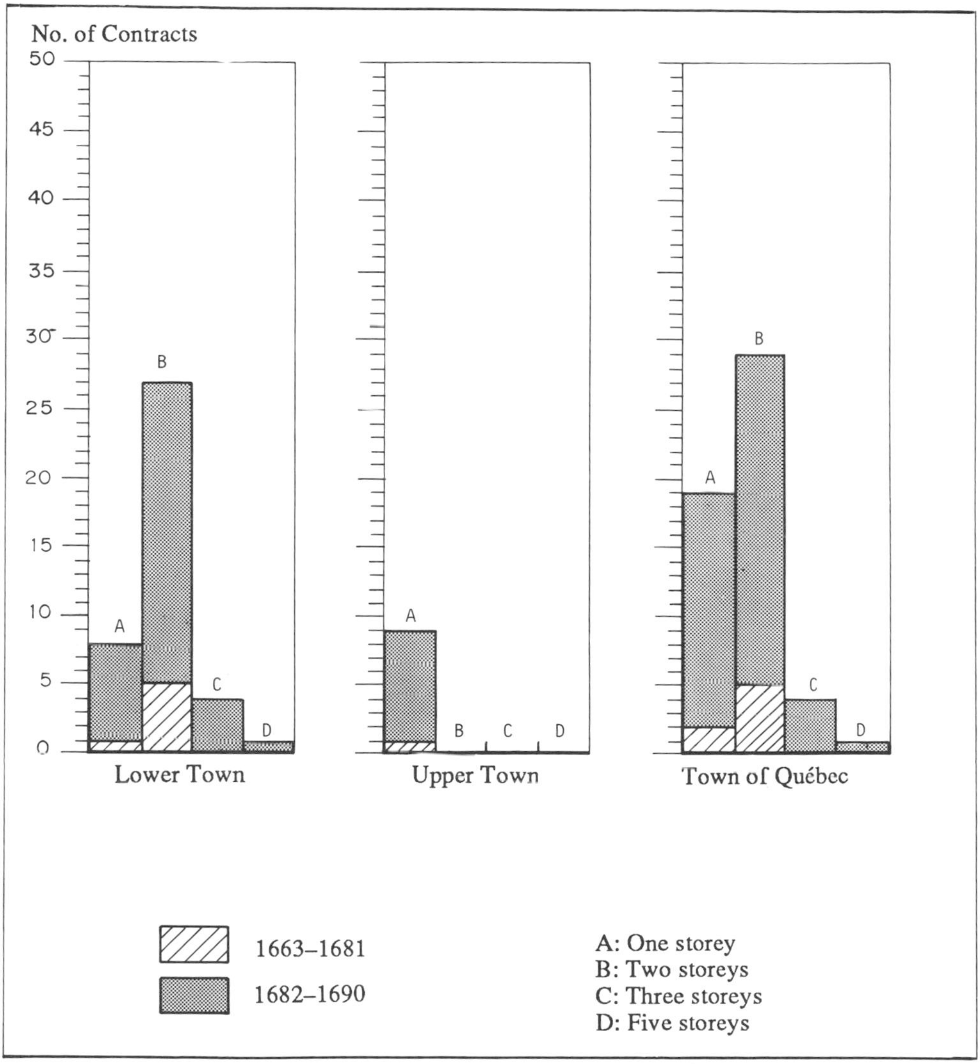

ing an average ground-floor of 645 square *pieds* and a shingle or board roof. This rectangular house, longer than it was wide, had a steeply pitched roof. Variations appeared in Upper Town in the form of a small single-storey half-timbered home with an area of 359 square *pieds*, and in Lower Town the typical house was built of stone and, with two storeys and 720 square *pieds*, was more spacious.

25 8bre 1683
Nº d'ordre 347
Echelle de 100 pieds
a. La grande porte ruinee q'il faut restablir.
b. Muraille neuue restablie.
c. Muraille que l'on a commencé a restablir et que l'hiver empeche de finir.
d. L'angle du NE. d'une terrace fort haute, et qu'il faut restablir a neuf — 1683
CARTE
DU FORT ST LOUIS
DE QUEBEC
Par Iean Baptiste Louis Franquelin
1683

29 "Carte du fort S^t^. Louis de Quebec ... 1683," Jean-Baptiste-Louis Franquelin

Drawn from a peculiar perspective typical of plans dating from the early 17th century, it nevertheless gives an idea of the repairs to Fort Saint-Louis and shows some houses in Lower Town and on côte de la Montagne.

Archives Nationales, France; copy on file, National Archives of Canada, C-16056

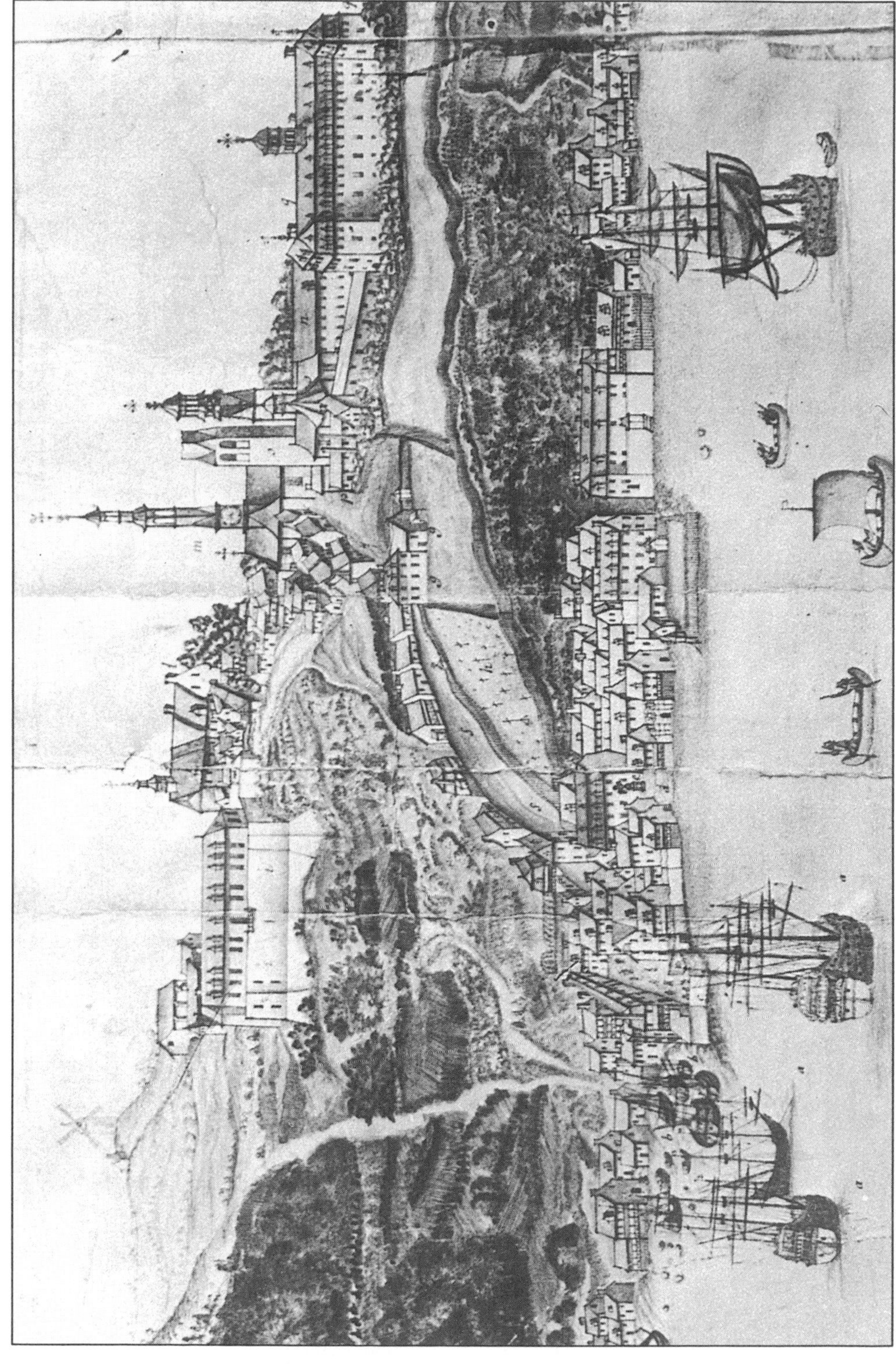

30 "Québec Comme il se voit du côté de l'Est," 1688, Jean-Baptiste-Louis Franquelin

This detail from an inset in Franquelin's view clearly illustrates the two distinct characters of Québec. Lower Town is crowded and boasts more imposing houses, while public and religious buildings dominate Upper Town.

Service historique de la Marine, Vincennes, France, Vol. 40406, No. 6

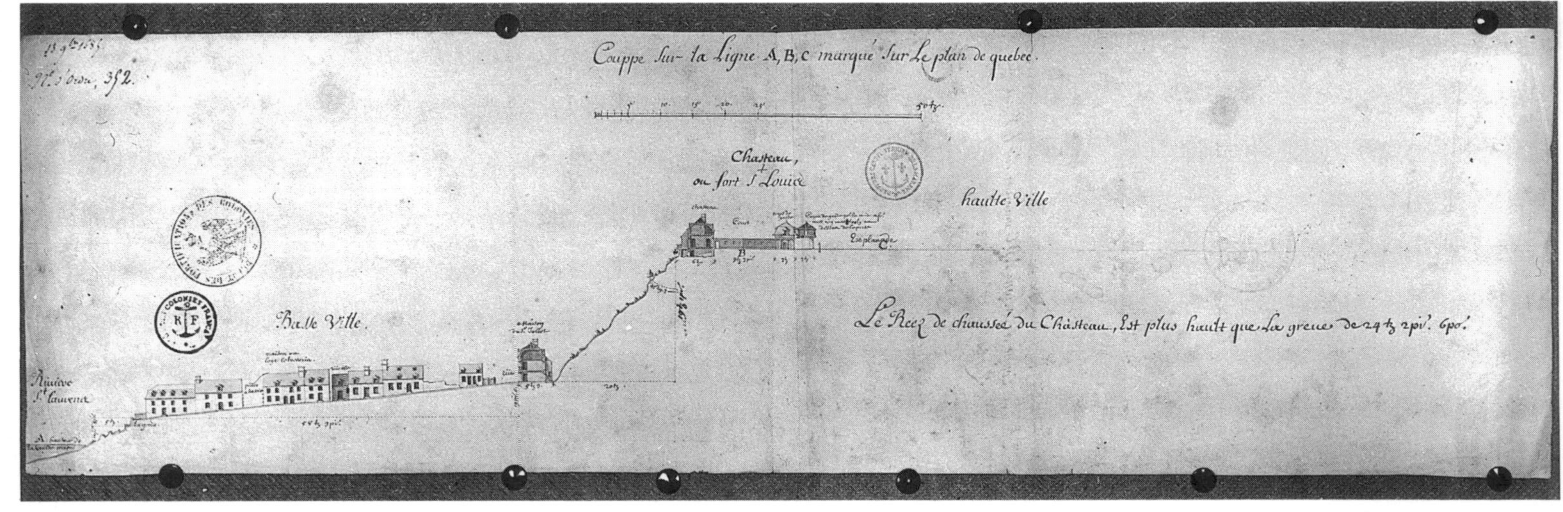

31 "Couppe Sur la Ligne A,B,C marqué Sur Le plan de quebec," 1685, Robert de Villeneuve

This part of the 1685 plan shows an elevation of Fort Saint-Louis and illustrates a few houses in Lower Town on rue Sous-le-Fort.

Archives Nationales, France; copy on file, National Archives of Canada, C-15908

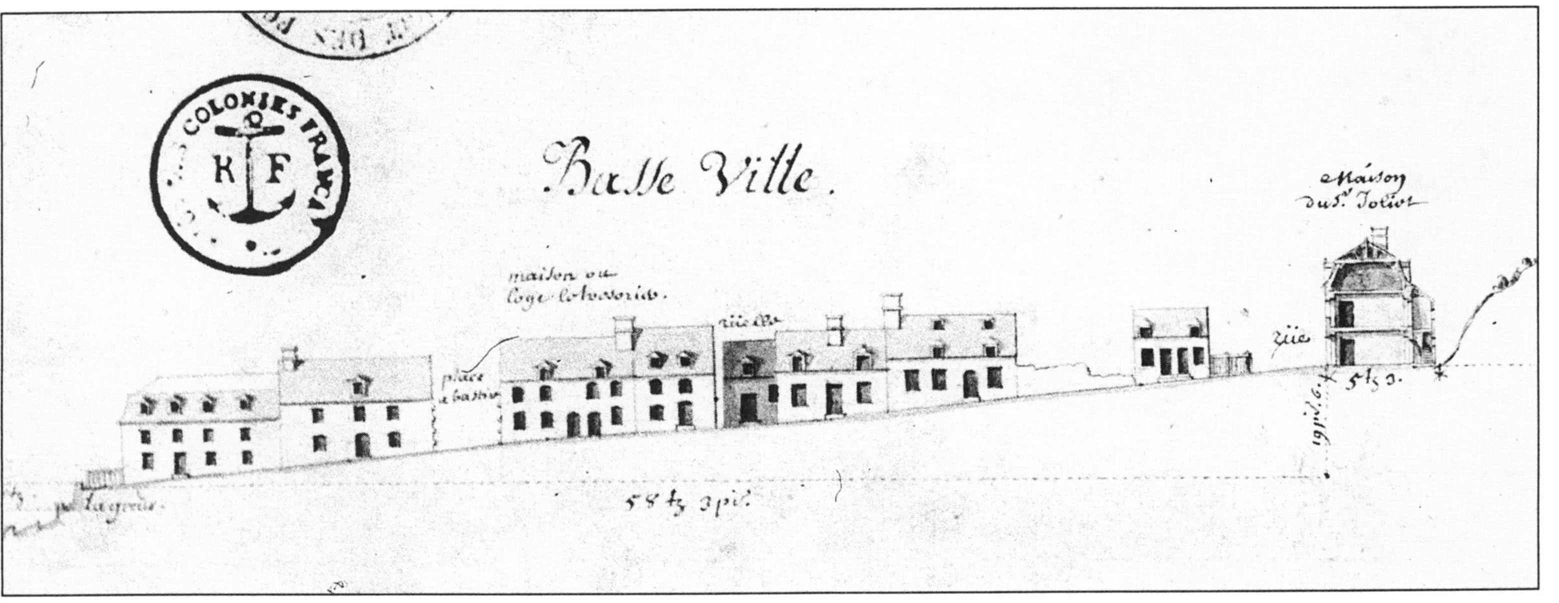

32 Houses on rue Sous-le-Fort, 1685, Robert de Villeneuve

The roof shapes, dormer windows, chimneys, and fenestration are typical of the urban house. On the left between two houses is a vacant lot on which a new dwelling is to be built. On the right the framing and part of the interior layout of Louis Jolliet's house can also be seen.

Archives Nationales, France; copy on file, National Archives of Canada, C-15908

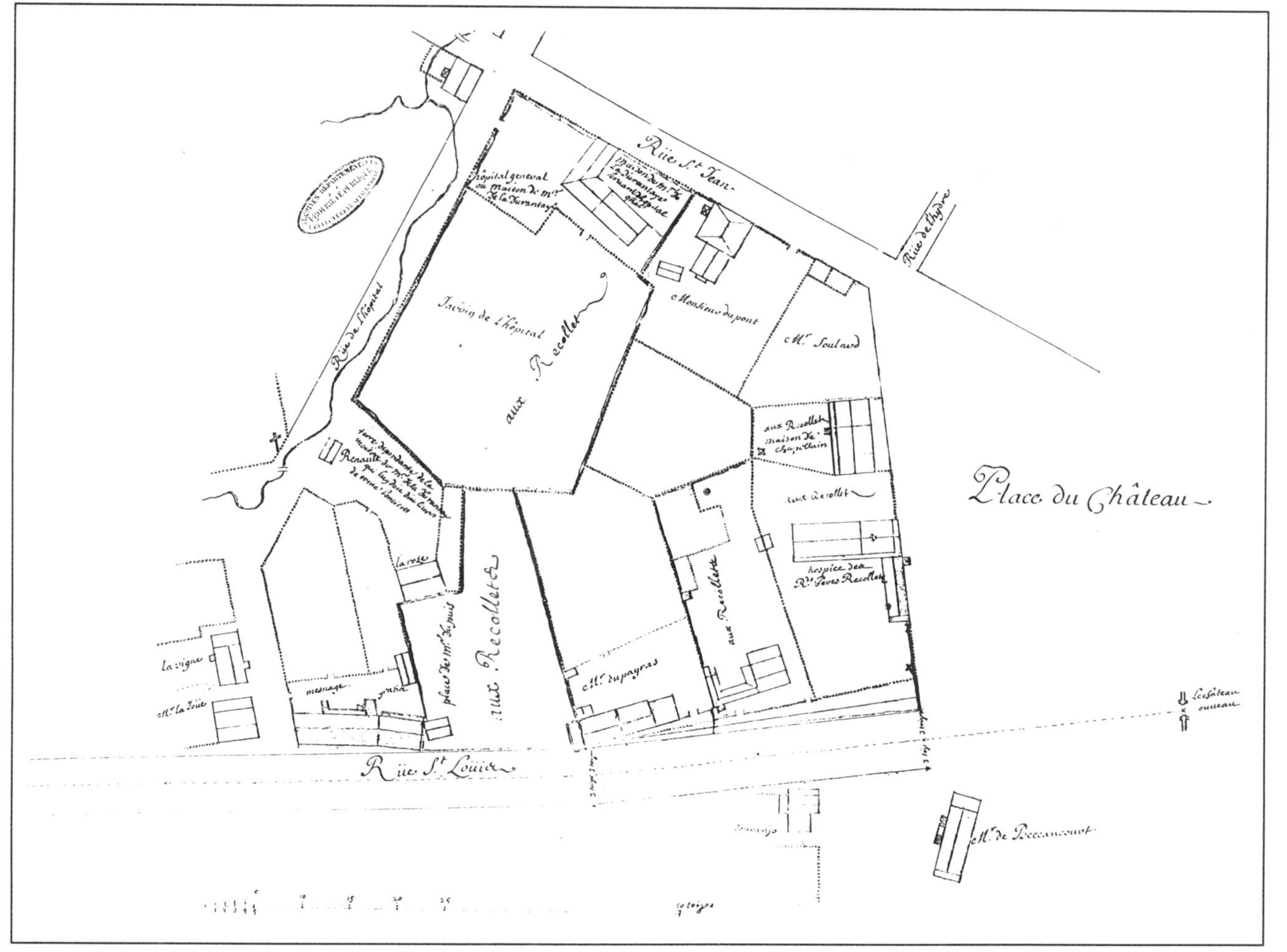
Place du Château
Rüe St Jean
Rüe St Louis
Rüe de l'hôpital
Jardin de l'hôpital
aux Recollets
Monsieur du pont
Mr Soulard
Mr dupayras
place de Mr Dupuis
la vigne
Mr la Joüe
hospice des Rds Peres Recollets

33 Plan of the Récollets' site in Upper Town, 1692, Robert de Villeneuve

Although this plan is not actually signed, the distinctive handwriting undoubtedly shows it to be by de Villeneuve. It illustrates the boundaries of the Récollet land and discusses the allocation of a strip of land leading to rue Saint-Louis. There is an error in the plan: rue Saint-Anne is labelled Saint-Jean. Some of the other names also differ from those commonly used: "Rüe de Lhôpital" for des Jardins, "Rüe de l'hydre" for du Trésor, "Place du Château" for the Place d'Armes, and "hôpital général" for Sieur de la Durantaye's home. Note the width of rue Saint-Louis (36 *pieds*, the largest in Québec), the names of the concession holders, and the presence of a little stream running down rue des Jardins.

Archives Yvelines, Seine-et-Oise, Grandes Ecuries, Versailles; photo by Jean Bélisle

Some maps and sketches of 17th-century Québec illustrate the houses there. The partial map drawn by Franquelin in 1683 provides a good idea of an average dwelling in Lower Town (Fig. 29). A 1688 sketch, also by Franquelin, illustrates differences between Upper and Lower Town and shows some very large residences, including those of Aubert de Lachenaye on rue du Sault-au-Matelot and François Hazeur on rue Saint-Pierre. The small size of houses on côte de la Montagne and rue De Meulles is also of interest (Fig. 30). Villeneuve's 1685 map shows the same feature at the northeast end of rue du Sault-au-Matelot (Fig. 28), and in a cross-section of rue Sous-le-Fort the engineer illustrated well-known houses such as those of Couillard de Lespinay, Maheust, Niel, and Jolliet. Most of these were average-sized, two-storey homes (Figs. 31 and 32). And a map of the neighbourhood around the Récollets' land gives some idea of the area occupied by Upper Town houses (Fig. 33).

These were not the only differences between Upper and Lower Town. At each stage of the analysis, Lower Town activity dominated, mainly because more construction was undertaken there. In turn, patterns established on certain streets such as Notre-Dame, Saint-Pierre, Sault-au-Matelot, and De Meulles influenced development in Lower Town. Also, the house considered typical of Québec was not static but evolved. As a result of the fire in 1682, more and more houses were built of stone; they were larger and had more storeys. Taste in Upper Town was more conservative than in Lower Town.

Did housing construction in Québec represent a novel adaptation to demands of the North American continent that differed from patterns established in the English colonies? Boston's development is quite comparable to that of Québec. The first houses, built from imported materials because of the scarcity of local resources, were single-storey thatched dwellings. By the mid-17th century, considerable progress had been made: "by mid-century larger abodes were being raised; built around a single chimney, they had high-pitched, shingled roofs, and were lighted by small windows with leaded casements and diamond panes."[71] Like Québec, Boston suffered a fire, in 1679. Prior to that date, the most common type of house was built of wood; afterward, there was a tendency toward using brick and stone.

Early conditions in Newport differed little from those in Boston. The availability of wood meant that wooden houses were very common. Since wealthy Newport residents preferred to live in large country houses, the city was slow to develop. As in Québec, the floor space of Newport houses expanded: "by 1670 the old one-room, end-chimney pioneer home had been supplanted by the central chimney type with either two or four rooms on a floor."

Although Philadelphia was founded late in the 17th century, it experienced a remarkable boom in housing construction. Around 1685, brick and wood construction were equally common, but five years later, wood had been abandoned in favour of brick and stone. According to one contemporary observer, the inhabitants "Build all with Stone and Brick now, except the very meanest Sort of People, which Build Framed Houses with Timber ... two Stories high." Charleston boasted only a few houses in 1680, but by 1682 it had approximately one hundred dwellings. Few of its residents used brick; most preferred to build in wood.

Until 1650, houses in New Amsterdam (New York) were similar to those in Boston: built of wood and thatched with straw. Later, prior to the first English occupation in 1664, there was a trend to Dutch brick "alla moderna." The last conquest of the city by the English brought few changes: "English rule in the seventeenth century wrought little visible change in the Dutch town. More houses were erected, some of wood, but the majority as in the past 'built of brick and stone, and covered with red and black tile'. Placed gable-end to the street, and surrounded by gardens and fruit trees, these homes were indeed 'after the manner of Holland.'"

American historian Carl Bridenbaugh's work on the general evolution of these five cities gives us an appreciation of several aspects of Québec's development.[72] He noted that the population transplanted to the new continent lived in primitive temporary dwellings (such as bark shelters in New Amsterdam and huts in Boston and Newport) that were quickly replaced by more lasting buildings of wood, brick, or stone. Bridenbaugh suggested explanations that seem timeless: "the character of the buildings erected in each village was largely determined by the Old World traditions of the inhabitants and by the nature of the materials at hand. The features of the terrain whereon it was located further conditioned the appearance of each community." As in Québec, local material and construction techniques inherited from the mother country influenced housing development much more than climate did.

The originality of housing construction in Québec lay in the use of certain materials like wood and stone in preference to others like brick, tile, and thatch, and in building techniques such as half-timbered houses with stone fill. The town was an example of French construction in North America and was distinct from English colonial towns, all of which, except for New York, resembled towns in England.

Conclusion

The evolution of Québec's urban landscape between 1660 and 1690 shows the dynamic quality of its development: although concessions were granted under the strict seigneurial system, not only the use and layout of town lots but also housing construction underwent changes. Initially the town's territory was part of the land allocated to the trading companies; after 1674 it was Crown land. Obligations and limitations formed part of land grants, whether freehold or seigneurial. By 1663 most lots had been granted and relatively few concessions were granted after that date. The lion's share of land was granted to religious communities and a few prominent property owners.

Descriptions of townhouses illuminate the development of housing construction characteristic of Québec. Although the capital of New France inherited some techniques from France, it became an innovative town in the colony. Well before Montréal and Trois-Rivières it opted for superior residential construction in the form of durable building materials and larger houses. These choices were not dictated by climate, but reflected Québec residents' prosperity and a rational use of local materials. One must be cautious in interpreting features of Québec houses — except for their steeply pitched roofs — as examples of adaptation to climate.

The basic factor in Québec's physical development was its topographically imposed division into Upper and Lower Town. The countryside lay just beyond Upper Town, which boasted the important public and religious buildings. It also had more available space than did Lower Town, where overcrowding was already leading to construction of taller buildings. Most merchants lived in Lower Town, where lot configuration was partly dictated by the river. Not only residents, but also house features — size, number of storeys, and materials used — differed from Upper to Lower Town.

Québec was a product of French colonization in North America. It was an example of urban development born of a desire to create a town on a new continent, a transplanted population, and technical and planning concepts inherited from France. So it is that Québec's physical appearance was typical of a small local or provincial capital in 17th-century France.

Chapter IV
THE PEOPLE AND THE TOWN: POPULATION AND LABOUR FORCE

Human beings are the motor of the urbanization process. Without them there can be no city, only an empty and inert carcass destined to disappear. People create the city; they breathe life into it and give it a future. The city, in turn, influences its creators, for communal life in a given urban space helps shape a particular society.

The urbanization process in Québec therefore cannot be understood without analysing the human element. This is necessary, first of all, so that we may become better acquainted with the town itself: its population, its growth, what it represented in relation to other towns in the colony and to New France as a whole, and its evolution as compared to that of certain towns in the English colonies.

Because its people contribute to a town's image, to the concept of *ville*, the population must also be studied in terms of its distribution by sex, marital status, and age, the size of households, and the number of children and servants. This will prove or disprove certain hypotheses: that during colonization the population is young and essentially composed of bachelors, that males are greatly over-represented, and that the various trades and professions exhibit different demographic patterns.

The labour force is the most dynamic segment of an urban population and the instrument of a town's development. To acquire a better knowledge and understanding of Québec, we must determine what percentage of the population was mobilized into the labour force and whether trades were diversifed. Furthermore, since Québec was in fact being built during the second half of the 17th century, thorough analysis of the sector of the labour force involved in housing construction will be necessary, examining the existence of entrepreneurs, the role craftsmen played, and the establishment of workers' associations. This examination of a segment of the labour force will also explain the attraction that the capital of New France exercised over the region immediately surrounding it (*see* Appendix C).

Population Growth

Prior to 1660 the town of Québec had experienced two distinct periods of settlement: 1608 to 1632 and 1632 to 1659. The first period was that of the trading post. The development of New France was entrusted to individuals or monopoly corporations that, in return for certain privileges, defrayed the country's expenses and saw to its settlement.[1] However, the system had only limited success, primarily because it set the interests of commerce against those of colonization. The companies were interested in the fur trade, an activity that required few people, and did not wish to establish a prosperous colony. Indeed, the figures speak for themselves: 28 people spent winter in Québec in 1608, 60 in 1620, and 76 in 1628.[2]

In 1632, three years after the Kirkes took Québec, a new period began, marked by the first sustained attempts at settlement. After the country was returned to France, the Compagnie des Cents-Associés took the colony's future in hand. Despite a population drop in 1641, no doubt attributable to the Iroquois wars,[3] the number of people in the colony grew from 274 in 1639 to 2000 in 1653, an average annual growth rate of 10.8 per cent (Tables 18 and 19).[4]

The town of Québec had 76 inhabitants in 1628, 240 in 1641, and 600 in 1653,[5] an overall increase of 524 inhabitants, or an average annual growth rate of 6.2 per cent (Table 20).[6] For a 25-year period this represents little growth; nevertheless, Québec accounted for no less than 30 per cent of the colony's population in 1653.

Population growth, both within the town and in the colony as a whole, was due primarily to the Cents-Associés. Its slowness is attributable to the difficulties encountered by the company which, bankrupted by the war, gave up its monopoly and its settlement obligations to the Compagnie des Habitants. However, individuals continued to be the principal instigators of immigration. Robert Giffard, seigneur de Beauport, took an interest in the matter in 1634–35, as did the Compagnie de Beaupré. Religious orders were also responsible for some arrivals (the Jesuits in 1632, the Ursulines and Hospitalières in 1639) and acted as recruiters, especially of indentured labourers, in order to meet their manpower needs.[7]

Table 18
Population of the Town of Québec and of the Colony
1608–1688

Year	Québec		Colony	
	Pop.	Increase	Pop.	Increase
1608	28	—	28	—
1620	60	32	60	32
1628	76	16	76	16
1639	—	—	274	198
1640	—	—	359	85
1641	240	164	240	-119
1650	—	—	675	435
1653	600*	360	2000	1325
1666	547	-53	3215	1215
1667	451**	-96	3918	703
1673	—	—	6705	2787
1675	—	—	7832	1127
1681	1302	851	9677	1845
1685†	1205	-97	10725	1048
1688†	1407	202	10303	-422

* Figures for the town prior to 1666 include the population of the surrounding area.
** The 96-person drop is due to a change in the area attributed to the town for census purposes.
† French population only.

The Compagnie des Cents-Associés was not abolished until 1663, but as early as 1659 the king took an interest in the settlement of the colony and, according to Bishop Laval, sent 300 settlers a year until 1661. This movement, which began in 1659, continued until the war with Holland in 1672. The contingents were mostly made up of indentured labourers, soldiers, and marriageable young women. In 1665, for example, two regular regiments plus civil and military officers, 100 women, and 130 workers disembarked in the colony. Two years later, 92 women and 127 men arrived, followed by 150 young women and 100 indentured labourers in 1671. Troops disembarking at Québec numbered 300 in 1685, 130 in 1686, and 800 in 1687, an increase caused by the war against the Iroquois.[8] Maximum emigration from France to Canada is thus estimated at 3507 persons for the period 1660–69, 540 for the period 1670–79, and 1450 for the period 1680–89. The net number of immigrants for the period 1661–80 was 2542.[9]

Table 19
Growth and Average Annual Growth Rates for the Population of New France 1639–1653 and 1666–1688

1639–1653	absolute increase	1726
	relative increase	629.9%
	intercensus growth rate	151.8%
	average annual growth rate	10.8%
1666–1688	absolute increase	7088
	relative increase	220.5%
	intercensus growth rate	104.9%
	average annual growth rate	4.8%

Absolute increase is simply the difference between the final population and the initial population.

Relative increase is obtained by dividing absolute increase by initial population and multiplying the result by 100.

Table 20
Growth and Average Annual Growth Rates for the Population of the Town of Québec 1628–1653 and 1666–1688

1628–1653	absolute increase	524
	relative increase	689.5%
	intercensus growth rate	155.0%
	average annual growth rate	6.2%
1666–1688	absolute increase	860
	relative increase	157.2%
	intercensus growth rate	88.0%
	average annual growth rate	4.0%

These statistics appear to show that the influx of immigrants lasted until approximately 1670, following which it did not pick up again until the end of the war with Holland in 1679. Louis XIV, embroiled in the conflict, neglected the colony's settlement and even stopped one aspect of it: the last boatload of wives-to-be was sent in 1673.[10]

The population of New France grew at an average annual rate of 4.8 per cent between 1666 and 1688, an overall increase of 7088 inhabitants (Table 19). Despite the low rates of immigration in 1673 and 1675, the colony's population increased by 2787 in the first of those two years and 1127 in the second (Table 18). This growth reflects the high birth rate observed by demographers.[11]

As Québec was the port of entry, the many recruitment campaigns helped to create a transient population there whose ranks were temporarily swollen by soldiers and sailors. However, many newcomers did settle in the Québec area, which, according to Marcel Trudel, accounted for 65.1 per cent of the total population of New France in 1663, while the Montréal region accounted for only 19.7 per cent and the Trois-Rivières region for 15.2 per cent.[12] Québec itself was home to 17 per cent of the colony's population in 1666, 13.5 per cent in 1681, and 13.7 per cent in 1688 (Table 18). These figures clearly illustrate Québec's importance as an urban centre, particularly in light of the fact that the five most populous towns in the English colonies accounted for only 9 per cent of the total population of those colonies in 1690.[13]

Despite a drop in population between 1681 and 1685 resulting from the fire that devastated Lower Town in 1682,[14] Quebec's population increased by 860 between 1666 and 1688, an average annual growth rate of 4.01 per cent, slightly lower that that recorded by the colony as a whole for the same period (Tables 19 and 20).[15] Québec's growth rate can be compared to the rates recorded by four of the English colonies' most heavily populated towns: Philadelphia, Charleston, Boston, and New York (Table 21).[16]

Regarded as the greatest success of English colonization in North America, Philadelphia was still young, having been founded in 1682 by the Quakers, who were settling Pennsylvania. Its average annual growth rate was much higher than Québec's, but was measured over a period of only five years (1685–90).

Charleston was established in 1672 by courtier politicians in Carolina, a colony granted special privileges by the Crown. In 1690 it numbered only 1100 inhabitants, less than the population of Québec. Nevertheless, over a ten-year period it experienced a growth rate almost identical to that of the capital of New France.

Boston was founded in 1630 and had a large influx of immigrants during its early years as the Puritans sought refuge from religious persecution. Between 1660 and 1690 the town recorded a growth rate lower than that of Québec: 2.7 per cent. However, Boston was the largest town in the English colonies and its population was much higher than Québec's: 3000 inhabitants in 1660 and 7000 in 1690.

New York was founded by the Dutch in 1626 and the largest arrival of settlers took place under their rule. The town was conquered by the English in 1664 and re-occupied by the Dutch between 1672 and 1674,

Table 21
Population and Average Annual Rates of Growth of Four Town in the English Colonies

Town	Year	Pop.	Growth Relative	Growth Absolute
Philadelphia	1685	2500	—	—
	1690	4000	1500	60.0%
Intercensus growth rate 46.2%				
Average annual growth rate 9.2%				
Charleston	1680	700	—	—
	1690	1100	400	57.1%
Intercensus growth rate 44.4%				
Average annual growth rate 4.4%				
Boston	1660	3000	—	—
	1690	7000	4000	133.3%
Intercensus growth rate 80.0%				
Average annual growth rate 2.7%				
New York	1660	2400	—	—
	1690	3900	1500	62.5%
Intercensus growth rate 47.6%				
Average annual growth rate 1.6%				

which explains its slow growth. Between 1660 and 1690 the population increased by only 1500, an average annual growth rate of 1.6 per cent.

Overall, Québec, despite its small population, compared favourably to these towns. It was the most populous town in the colony and its growth rate equalled or surpassed that of three of the English colonial towns. Indeed, Québec was of proportionally greater importance to New France than any of these towns were to their colonies, for it could claim a larger percentage of the colonial population.

Demographic Make-Up

The nominal censuses of 1666 and 1681 provide accurate pictures of the population of the town of Québec in the second half of the 17th century. They contain data concerning the distribution of inhabitants by sex, marital status, and age. Some of the data in the 1688 report provide

Table 22
Demographic Make-Up of Québec and New France by Sex
1666, 1681, and 1688 Censuses

	Men		Women	
Year	Que. (%)	N.-F. (%)	Qué. (%)	N.- F. (%)
1666	356 (65.1)	2034 (63.3)	191 (34.9)	1181 (36.7)
1681	705 (54.1)	5375 (55.5)	562 (43.2)	4302 (44.5)
1688	771 (54.8)	5320 (51.6)	636 (45.2)	4749 (46.1)

35 unknown persons (2.7%) were included in the town's population in 1681, and 234 unknown persons (2.3%) were part of the colony's population in 1688.

grounds for comparing the population of Québec with that of the colony. Information concerning the Québec clergy was also recorded in the nominal censuses and provides a basis for studying that group.

As Table 22 shows, the ratio of men to women was disproportionate, the former constantly surpassing the latter both in Québec and in the colony. However, between 1666 and 1688 the gap narrowed, the percentage of men dropping by more than 10 per cent, but by 1688 the sexes were still not evenly balanced, as men represented over 50 per cent of both the town's and the colony's population.[17] In general, Québec followed the trends exhibited by the colony, but a slightly lower percentage of its population was female.

What factors account for the over-representation of males and their proportional decline between 1666 and 1688? Owing to immigration, there were always more men than women in Québec. The town did not really become populated until after 1632, and manpower was its primary need. In the early days most of those recruited were men, and in 1653 there were only 418 women among the 2000 inhabitants of New France.[18] Ten years later, women represented a little more than a third of the population. In 1663 the first boatload of *filles du roi* arrived, and by 1673 some 774 marriageable young women had come to the country. The vast majority of these young women (70 per cent) settled in the Québec region, while only 18 per cent headed for Montréal and 12 per cent for Trois-Rivières.[19]

Immigration dropped after 1672. The disproportionate influx of men subsided[20] and population growth was able to take its natural course. Between 1661 and 1690 there were 1989 more births than deaths in the parish of Notre-Dame de Québec, and this contributed to more evenly balancing the sexes.[21] However, men still outnumbered women in 1688. Having been given a head start, men maintained their lead, notably because the death rate in the colony was lower during the second half of the 17th century than at the beginning of the 18th. While the infant mortality rate remained higher among males, it was counterbalanced somewhat by the high mortality rate among women aged 30 to 45 due to deaths in childbirth.[22]

The coureurs de bois contributed to narrowing the statistical gap between males and females. Although the coureurs de bois were a marginal phenomenon in the Québec region, the fact that they were not recorded in the census reduced the male side of the equation. Around 1681 the number of coureurs de bois in the colony as a whole was estimated to be between 500 and 800.[23]

An imbalance between the sexes in a given population has an impact on marriage patterns. If males are over-represented, it is to be expected that there will be proportionally more married women than married men. Furthermore, because the demand for them is so high, wives will be much younger than their husbands.

According to the figures for Québec, there were more married men than married women in 1666 and 1681, but the opposite was true in 1688 (Table 23). Data for the colony suggest that married men outnumbered married women in all years (Table 24). These discrepancies are partly attributable to recording omissions since, widows and widowers notwithstanding, there should be an equal distribution of married persons between the two sexes.[24] They can also be explained by the fact that some men had wives in France or were recorded as living alone.[25]

To obtain a more accurate picture, marital status must be analysed in terms of the population's composition by sex. Married men were a significantly lower percentage of the total male population than married women in the total female population (Table 23). There were fewer women than men, but they married in proportionately greater numbers; this reflects a shortage in real terms and an over-representation of males. The marriage rate rose with the growth in the female population and its progress toward parity with the male population. By 1681 the number of married men was significantly higher than it had been in 1666.

The marriage rate was lower in Québec than in the colony. Only a quarter of the town's inhabitants were married in 1666 and close to a third in 1688, while in the colony the percentage of the population represented by married people remained at close to a third throughout the period 1666 to 1688 (Tables 23 and 24). Both New France and Québec recorded a drop in the number of married women in 1681, no doubt attributable to the disproportionately high female mortality and the fact that marriageable young women were no longer being sent to New

Table 23
Married and Widowed Population of Québec
1666, 1681, and 1688 Censuses

	Men		Women			
Year	No.	% Male Pop.	No.	% Fem. Pop.	Total No.	% Pop.
1666	71	19.9	67	35.1	138	25.2
1681	180	25.5	175	31.1	355	27.3
1688	213	27.6	235	36.9	448	31.8

Figures for 1666 include 6 widowers, 12 widows, and 7 persons of unknown marital status. The figures for 1681 include 19 widowers, 16 widows, and 35 persons of unknown sex. 61 men (8.7% of the male population) of unknown marital status were excluded from the calculation of the number of men in 1681. In 1688 no distinction was made between the widowed and married population,

Table 24
Married and Widowed Population of the Colony
1666, 1681, and 1688 Censuses

	Men		Women			
Year	No.	% Male Pop.	No.	% Fem. Pop.	Total No.	% Pop.
1666	541	26.6	520	44.0	1061	33.0
1681	1540	28.7	1519	35.3	3059	31.6
1688	1747	32.8	1741	36.7	3488	33.9

Figures for 1666 include 13 widowers and 29 widows. The figures for 1681 include 65 widowers and 58 widows. In 1688 no distinction was made between the widowed and married population. The percentages also take into account 234 persons of unknown sex.

France. Recruitment by the religious orders must also be taken into account: it is estimated that 6 per cent of young women who had reached the age of 15 before 1680 and 4.6 per cent of those who reached 15 between 1680 and 1699 entered religious orders.[26]

Such a marked imbalance between married men and married women as a percentage of their respective populations is no cause for astonishment; it is an essential feature of the matrimonial market at a certain stage. In the beginning, women were in short supply, thus it is not surprising to find that a large proportion of the women recorded in 1666 were married. Furthermore, the *filles du roi* quickly found themselves husbands. In 1671, for example, only 15 of the 165 young women sent out the previous year were still single.[27]

The state encouraged marriage. In 1663 any opposition to the marriage of a *fille du roi* was forbidden except at the publication of the banns. In 1669, fathers were threatened with fines if they did not marry off their sons at 20 and their daughters at 16. The following year the king went so far as to offer 20 *livres* to any person who married at the ages called for in the 1669 decree. The Conseil Souverain ordered parents to declare every six months their reasons for opposing marriages of their sons or daughters and threatened them with arbitrary fines if they did not comply. Furthermore, the council ordered all free volunteers and non-indentured bachelors to marry within 15 days of the arrival of the ships in 1671; those who balked would be barred from hunting, fishing, and the fur trade. In 1671 Intendant Talon applied the council's decree, prohibiting unmarried volunteers from hunting, fishing, or trading in furs.[28]

The low percentage of married persons presupposes a high percentage of unmarried persons (Table 25). The number of bachelors gradually decreased in Québec, both in relation to the total male population (78.1 per cent in 1666, 72.4 per cent in 1688) and to the total number of unmarried persons (69.2 per cent in 1666, 58.2 per cent in 1688). Among women the same was true in relation to the total female population (64.9 per cent in 1666, 63.1 per cent in 1688) except in 1681, when there was a relative growth in the number of unmarried women corresponding to the decrease in the number of married women. An increasing percentage of unmarried persons were female: 30.8 per cent in 1666 and 41.8 per cent in 1688. A growing proportion of women had no choice but to remain single.

The colony exhibited similar trends, but they differed somewhat from the town's. Unmarried persons formed a smaller percentage of the total population, and within the unmarried population, women were less heavily represented than in the town except in 1688. There were not as many unmarried women in the total female population of the colony as in the total female population of the town in 1666 and 1681. Unmarried men, for their part, accounted for a smaller percentage of the male population in the colony, except in 1681, and their numbers decreased steadily.

The predominance of unmarried persons was the second characteristic of the matrimonial market and it illustrates the disparities immigration caused. The over-representation of males partly explains, at least for the period up to 1681, the imbalance between males and females in the unmarried population. Another factor was that in principle, volunteers

Table 25
Children and Unmarried Persons
in the Town of Québec and in the Colony
1666, 1681, and 1688 Censuses

	Men & Male Children			Women & Female Children				
Year	No.	% Male Pop.	% Unmar. Pop.	No.	% Fem. Pop.	% Unmar. Pop.	Total No.	% Pop.
				Québec				
1666	278	78.1	69.2	124	64.9	30.8	402	73.5
1681	464	65.8	54.5	387	68.9	45.5	851	65.4
1688	558	72.4	58.2	401	63.1	41.8	959	68.2
				Colony				
1666	1493	73.4	69.3	661	55.9	30.7	2154	66.9
1681	3835	71.3	57.9	2783	64.7	42.1	6618	68.4
1688	3573	67.2	52.4	3008	63.3	44.1	6815	66.1

The 1666 figures for Québec include 7 men of unknown marital status, and the 1681 figures include 35 persons of unknown sex and 61 men of unknown marital status. The 1688 figures for the colony include 234 unmarried persons of unknown sex.

were not allowed to marry until the expiry of their contracts, which normally lasted three years.[29] It also appears that Canadian women tended to marry immigrants; however, it is not known whether this preference occurred in Québec.[30]

Natural increase and recruitment by religious orders contributed to the rise in the number of unmarried women, as did the change in the male-female ratio. The proportion of males dropped, particularly owing to the absence of the coureurs de bois and to the second Iroquois war, which began under La Barre. This war intensified from 1687 onwards.[31]

Marcel Trudel has said that young countries have young populations. This aptly describes the situation both in Québec and in the colony. In 1666 and 1681 approximately 79.5 per cent of the town's inhabitants were under 41 years of age (Table 26).[32] The population was heavily concentrated in two age groups: 0 to 10 years and 21 to 40 years. The same was true of the colony, except that the percentage of the population under 41 dropped from 86.2 per cent in 1666 to 82.4 per cent in 1681. The population was concentrated in the same age groups as in Québec. However, the percentage of children aged 0 to 10 years was greater in the colony than in the capital, and the reverse was true of young people aged 11 to 20 years, which may indicate that there were more small children in the country than in the town.

Table 26
Age Distribution
in the Town of Québec and the Colony
1666 and 1681 Censuses

	Age									
Year	0–10	%	11–20	%	21–40	%	41–60	%	61+	%
					Québec					
1666	115	21.0	107	19.6	213	38.9	75	13.7	14	2.6
1681	391	30.0	266	20.4	382	29.3	166	12.7	39	2.9
					Colony					
1666	1043	32.4	427	13.3	1303	40.5	306	9.5	57	1.8
1681	3907	40.4	1661	17.2	2404	24.8	1430	14.8	218	2.3

For the town there were 23 persons of unknown age in 1666 (4.2%) and 58 in 1681 (4.5%). For the colony there were 79 persons of unknown age in 1666 (2.5%) and 57 in 1681 (0.6 %).

These data reflect the repercussions of immigration, of people in their prime establishing themselves in the colony. They underline, for both Québec and other parts of the colony, the importance of birth and fertility rates. They also show normal age increments, as all but two age groups accounted for higher percentages of the population in 1681.[33]

Data relating age to marital status reflect the shortage of females and the over-representation of males. Both in Québec and in the colony the married population under the age of 20 consisted entirely of women in two censuses (Tables 27 and 28). In the 1666 census there was a concentration of married women in the 21-to-30 age group whereas in 1681, married women were distributed more evenly between that group and the 31-to-40 age group. The change illustrates the reduction in the surplus of males; in 1681, women married later than in 1666. There were more men in older age groups, 31 to 40 and 41 to 50 years. Men married later than women.[34]

Other differences between men and women are also found in the unmarried population. In Québec in 1666, males were concentrated in two age groups: 0 to 10 years and 21 to 30 years. In 1681 they were more evenly distributed over the various age groups and the under-11 group had tripled (Table 29). Girls were younger than boys: 66 per cent of females were under 15 in 1666; by 1681 the proportion had risen to 75 per cent. The same concentrations were found in the colony as in the town. However, the contrasts between the various age groups were

Table 27
Age Groups among Married Persons in Québec
1666 and 1681 Censuses

	1666					1681				
Age	Male	%	Fem.	%	Total	Male	%	Fem.	%	Total
0–10	—	—	—	—	—	—	—	—	—	—
11–15	—	—	1	1.8	1	—	—	—	—	—
16–20	—	—	6	10.9	6	—	—	19	11.9	19
21–30	14	21.5	27	49.1	41	19	11.8	48	30.2	67
31–40	28	43.1	12	21.8	40	75	46.6	48	30.2	123
41–50	16	24.6	6	10.9	22	44	27.3	36	22.6	80
51–60	6	9.2	3	5.5	9	14	8.7	6	3.8	20
61–70	1	1.5	—	—	1	8	4.9	1	0.6	9
71–80	-	—	—	—	—	1	0.6	1	0.6	2
81–90	-	—	—	—	—	—	—	—	—	—
Total	65		55		120	161		159		320

There were 7 men of unknown status in 1666.

Table 28
Age Groups among Married Persons in the Colony
1666 and 1681 Censuses

	1666					1681				
Age	Male	%	Fem.	%	Total	Male	%	Fem.	%	Total
0–10	—	—	—	—	—	—	—	—	—	—
11–15	—	—	8	1.6	8	—	—	1	0.1	1
16–20	—	—	45	9.2	45	—	—	117	8.0	117
21–30	120	22.7	239	48.7	359	81	5.5	438	30.0	519
31–40	225	42.6	113	23.0	338	591	40.1	459	31.5	1050
41–50	117	22.2	54	10.9	171	489	33.2	319	21.9	808
51–60	45	8.5	19	3.9	64	216	14.7	93	6.4	309
61–70	14	2.7	12	2.4	26	74	5.0	23	1.6	97
71–80	5	0.9	1	0.2	6	16	1.1	5	0.3	21
81–90	2	0.4	—	—	2	6	0.4	4	0.3	10
Total	528		491		1019	1473*		1459*		2932

* 2 unknown persons excluded.
† The table does not take widows or widowers into account.

Table 29
Age Groups of Children and Unmarried Persons in Québec
1666 and 1681 Censuses

	1666					1681				
Age	Male	%	Fem.	%	Total	Male	%	Fem.	%	Total
0–10	62	24.0	53	42.7	115	188	40.6	203	52.5	391
11–15	19	7.4	29	23.4	48	67	14.5	87	22.5	154
16–20	44	17.1	8	6.5	52	51	11.0	37	9.6	88
21–30	85	32.9	10	8.1	95	68	14.7	20	5.2	88
31–40	23	8.9	9	7.3	32	51	11.0	16	4.1	67
41–50	10	3.9	6	4.8	16	16	3.5	8	2.1	24
51–60	9	3.5	7	5.6	16	12	2.5	6	1.6	18
61–70	5	1.9	2	1.6	7	4	0.9	6	1.6	10
71–80	1	0.4	—	—	1	4	0.9	4	1.0	8
81–90	—	—	—	—	—	2	0.4	—	—	2
Total	258*		124		382	463**		387		850

* 7 men of unknown status and 20 of unknown age are excluded.
** One person of unknown age not included.

Table 30
Age Groups of Children and Unmarried Persons in the Colony
1666 and 1681 Censuses

	1666					1681				
Age	Male	%	Fem.	%	Total	Male	%	Fem.	%	Total
0–10	546	38.2	497	77.2	1043	1986	52.5	1921	69.0	3907
11–15	110	7.7	91	14.1	201	457	12.1	456	16.4	913
16–20	153	10.7	20	3.1	173	369	9.8	261	9.4	630
21–30	455	31.8	22	3.4	477	445	11.8	74	2.7	519
31–40	111	7.8	3	0.5	114	267	7.1	25	0.9	292
41–50	30	2.1	3	0.5	33	155	4.1	19	0.7	174
51–60	16	1.1	6	0.9	22	67	1.8	7	0.3	74
61–70	8	0.6	2	0.3	10	22	0.6	13	0.5	35
71–80	1	0.1	—	—	1	9	0.2	5	0.2	14
81–90	1	0.1	—	—	1	5	0.1	2	0.1	7
Total	1431*		644**		2075	3782†		2783		6565

* 62 unknown persons excluded.
** 17 unknown persons excluded.
† 53 unknown persons excluded.

Table 31
Québec Clergy
1666 and 1681 Censuses

Religious Community	1666 No.	1666 Avg. Age	1681 No.	1681 Avg. Age
Seminary	8 priests	29.0	25 priests	32.6
Jesuits	10 priests	49.6	8 priests	56.5
	7 lay brothers	51.9	7 lay brothers	48.6
Ursulines	9 nuns	50.6	21 nuns	38.1
	9 lay sisters	31.9	7 lay sisters	40.9
Hôtel-Dieu (Hospitalières)	13 nuns	38.9	19 nuns	38.2
	4 lay sisters	32.5	7 lay sisters	42.1
Totals	25 males		40 males	
	35 females		54 females	

sharper than in the town and reflected the disparities between the two sexes (Table 30).[35]

The Québec clergy was made up of four religious communities: the seminary, the Jesuits, the Ursulines, and the Hôtel-Dieu. They accounted for 10.9 per cent of the town's population in 1666 and 7.2 per cent in 1681. During the intervening period they grew at an average annual rate of 2.9 per cent, as their numbers rose from 60 to 94 (Table 31).

There were more women than men in the clergy. The 1666 census indicated that members of religious orders, particularly the Jesuits and Ursulines, were relatively old. The seminary recorded the lowest average age, as it had been founded recently, while the three other orders had been established during the first half of the 17th century. Most of the clergy had come from France; only one priest and five nuns were recruited in the colony.[36]

By 1681 three of the orders had grown considerably; however, the Jesuits had decreased in number and their average age remained high. Among the Ursulines and Hospitalières, *mères* were getting younger but *soeurs* were getting older. Overall, the clergy was drawing more heavily on the colony for new members: 11 priests and 23 nuns (19 of them from Québec) were natives of New France.

Population Distribution
Households

Determining a population's composition is not enough; people's choice of lifestyle and living partners must also be viewed. Between 1666 and 1681 the structure of households in Québec changed and the various socio-professional categories exhibited different behaviour.

In 1666 there were 102 households[37] in the town of Québec, more than 34 per cent consisting of a single person (Table 32). The four-person household constituted the second most common type of living arrangement. By 1681, individuals living alone represented only 20.3 per cent of the 231 households in the town, the most frequent being a two- or three-person household. These changes were due to a decrease in the number of unmarried persons and a drop in immigration.

A more telling picture of households in Québec can be obtained by setting aside persons living alone and considering only groups of people enumerated together, generally families in the true sense and including servants, relatives, apprentices, or boarders.[38] These data (67 households in 1666 and 184 households in 1681) can be classified according to 15 socio-professional categories (Table 33).[39]

Classification by profession partly confirms Edward Shorter's hypothesis that in cities "sharp differences in the size and composition of households turn up according to income and social status. The higher the income or the more elevated the social class, the larger and more complex the household."[40] The average number of persons per household was 5.5 in 1666 and 5.4 in 1681. In 1666, senior officials and government clerks had households much larger than average; after them came members of the building trades, innkeepers and merchants, and labourers.

Each group seems to have had its own distinct pattern of family behaviour, for which there were various explanations. Senior officials had large families because they were all married with many children (*see* Appendix D).[41] The same was true of government clerks. Furthermore, servants' presence contributed significantly to household size (2 per household). Among members of the building trades the number of children was high, while among innkeepers and merchants, servants were more significant (2.2 per household).

The number of their children (3.3 per household) set labourers apart from the average. Shorter had seen the opposite occur, noting that "poverty and wage labor meant that few children would be in residence with the parents." Perhaps the roots of this behaviour are to be found in a

Table 32
Québec Households by Size, 1666 and 1681 Censuses

No. of Persons	1666 Frequency	1666 %	1681 Frequency	1681 %
1	35	34.3	47	20.3
2	8	7.8	29	12.6
3	9	8.8	41	17.7
4	17	16.7	13	5.6
5	9	8.8	21	9.1
6	5	4.9	18	7.8
7	3	2.9	17	7.4
8	4	3.9	16	6.9
9	2	1.9	12	5.2
10	4	3.9	10	4.3
11	2	1.9	2	0.9
12	3	2.9	1	0.4
13	—	—	—	—
14	—	—	2	0.9
15	—	—	1	0.4
16	1	0.9	—	—
Total	102	100.0	231	100.0

The garrison, the governor's household, and the intendant's household are excluded from the figures for 1681. This table does not take the clergy into account.

hope that more labour would be available within the family and that the children's income would supplement that of the household head.

Essentially the same categories were above average in 1681 as in 1666. Senior officials' households had slightly diminished in size, but still remained in the lead. Notaries and surgeons had overtaken government clerks, who had slid to third place, with innkeepers and merchants close behind. Among tradespeople, builders had lost ground to ironworkers and tailors.

The statistics in Table 33 also reveal more general trends. They reflect households' aging in 1681 as compared to 1666, particularly in terms of the number of children per family, which increased from 2.2 to 2.9. They also show that the number of servants dropped per household (from 1.4 in 1666 to 0.5 in 1681) and that they were unevenly distributed among households, professionals and merchants accounting for the largest share.

Table 33
Number of Persons, Children, and Servants per Household by Socio-Professional Category 1666 and 1681 Censuses

Category	1666			1681		
	Persons	Children	Servants	Persons	Children	Servants
Professionals						
Senior officials	8.5	4.8	1.8	7.6	3.9	1.4
Notaries, surgeons and others	5.0	0.0	3.0	6.6	2.8	1.2
Tradespeople and shopkeepers						
Innkeepers and merchants	6.0	1.6	2.2	6.1	2.9	1.4
Food trade	4.0	0.5	1.5	4.8	2.7	0.3
Craftsmen						
Art and luxury items	—	—	—	3.0*	1.0*	0.0
Clothing	2.0*	0.0	0.0	5.8	3.4	0.2
Wood and furniture	4.0	2.0	0.0	4.9	2.5	0.7
Leather	3.0	0.5	0.5	3.7	1.7	0.0
Building construction	6.7	3.7	1.0	4.4	2.4	0.1
Iron	5.5	2.4	1.0	5.9	3.2	0.3
Other	—	—	—	7.0**	4.5	0.0
Salaried workers						
Labourers	5.7	3.3	0.3	4.5	2.3	0.3
Government clerks	8.3	4.3	2.0	6.2	4.0	0.2
Military	—	—	—	4.0	1.5	0.3
Unknown	5.2	2.0	1.5	4.9	2.8	0.3
Averages	5.5	2.2	1.4	5.4	2.9	0.5

* One household only.
** Two households: one ship's carpenter and one caulker.

Clergy households were complex. The seminary and the Jesuits housed 67 individuals in 1666, of whom 13 were servants and 20 were boarders. The Ursulines and the Hospitalières had a total of 74 persons including 15 servants and some 24 boarders (*see* Appendix D). By 1681 the male orders were housing 91 people, the female orders, 107; and servant numbers had increased considerably in both (*see* Appendix E).

The Labour Force according to the 1666 and 1681 Censuses

In 1665 Intendant Talon drew up a list of workers able to ply their trades in Canada and comprising 19 trades from bakers to tile makers.[42] Trades in the colony were diversified even at that early date.

In 1666 thirty-five trades were being practised in the town of Québec and 119 people were thus occupied, representing 21.8 per cent of the recorded population (Table 34).[43] More than half were registered as heads of households and among them they exercised 24 trades. Within the group, merchants, joiners, and law officers were most numerous.

Servants and indentured workers formed a large part of the labour force. In the 1666 census, 50 indentured workers, 41 indentured household servants, 23 household servants, and 7 maids were enumerated. The indentured workers, who had to serve 36 months, accounted for the greatest variety of occupations, 19 practising 13 trades between them (Table 35). Indentured household workers, bound by contract, accounted for just two nailsmiths. Eleven different trades were found among the household servants and maids, from shoemakers to unskilled labourers.

Indentured workers and household servants of all categories numbered 121 in all, representing 22.1 per cent of the reported population. This percentage is extremely high, particularly when compared with the percentage of people practising trades. However, 30.6 per cent of the persons in this category were skilled in 20 trades, most frequently masonry (Table 35).

A total of 20 non-resident volunteers[44] made up the other component of the labour force in 1666. They were represented in ten different trades, "worker" being most common. A very small proportion of the urban population practised any kind of trade and those most frequently reported were merchant, worker, joiner, edge-tool maker, and tailor.

The 1681 census allows more detailed analysis of the labour force than does the 1666 census. Over the 15 years the number of trades had increased only to 43 and occupied only 186 persons. The relative size of the labour force had significantly decreased as workers represented only 14.3 per cent of the population (Table 36). Servants were also playing less important parts in the trades; only 14 were reported, in ten different occupations. Almost all were apprentices, mostly in iron work (Table 38).

As Table 36 shows, four trades dominated in 1681: merchant, law officer, joiner, and tailor. Some of these occupations were found in the 14

Table 34
Distribution of Trades in Québec in 1666
By Household Heads, Servants, and Others

Trade	Household Heads	Servants	Indentured Servants	Indentured Workers	Volunteers	Total
Armourer-ironsmith	3	—	—	—	—	3
Arquebusier	2	—	—	—	—	2
Bailiff	3	—	—	—	—	3
Baker	—	—	—	—	1	1
Boatman	1	—	—	—	—	1
Brewer	1	—	—	—	—	1
Candlemaker	—	—	—	1	—	1
Carpenter	2	—	—	1	—	3
Clerk	1	—	—	—	—	1
Confectioner	1	—	—	1	—	2
Cooper	3	1	—	1	—	5
Edge-tool maker	4	1	—	1	2	8
Foundry worker	1	—	—	—	—	1
Furrier	—	—	—	1	—	1
Gardener	1	1	—	—	—	2
Illegible	—	—	—	1	—	1
Joiner	5	2	—	1	—	8
Labourer	—	4	—	—	8	12
Law officer	5	—	—	—	—	5
Mason	2	1	—	4	—	7
Merchant	15	—	—	—	3	18
Music teacher	—	1	—	—	—	1
Nailsmith	1	—	2	—	—	3
Notary	2	—	—	—	—	2
Pastrycook	1	—	—	—	—	1
Ropemaker	—	—	—	—	1	1
Sailor	—	—	—	1	1	2
School teacher	—	1	—	—	—	1
Ship's pilot	1	—	—	—	—	1
Shoemaker	2	1	—	2	1	6
Stone carter	—	—	—	1	1	2
Surgeon*	1	—	—	1	—	2
Sword cutler	1	—	—	—	—	1
Tailor	3	2	—	2	1	8
Tinsmith	—	—	—	—	1	1
Weaver	—	1	—	—	—	1

Totals:
household heads: 62 individuals, 24 trades
servants: 16 individuals, 11 trades
indentured servants: 2 individuals, 1 trade
indentured workers: 19 ndividuals, 13 trades
volunteers: 20 individuals, 10 trades. (Volunteers are non-residents.)

Total: 119 individuals, 35 trades

* 1 Jesuit doctor not included.

Table 35
Trades Practised by Québec Servants in 1666

50 Indentured Workers	41 Indentured Servants	30 Servants and Maids
1 candlemaker	2 nailsmiths	1 cooper
1 carpenter		1 edge-tool maker
1 confectioner		1 gardener
1 cooper		2 joiners
1 edge-tool maker		4 labourers
1 furrier		1 mason
1 illegible		1 music teacher
1 joiner		1 school teacher
4 masons		1 shoemaker
1 sailor		2 tailors
2 shoemakers		1 weaver
1 surgeon		
1 stone carter		
2 tailors		

trades listed as common to Upper and Lower Town (Table 37). However, there were disparities between these two parts of Québec.

In Upper Town ten socio-professional categories encompassed 20 trades and covered 43 persons or 23.1 per cent of the reported labour force. The building trades were dominant in Upper Town: carpenter, roofer, and mason. They were followed by the wood-working and furniture trades: joiner and turner (Table 39).

In Lower Town 33 trades occupied 103 persons, or 55.4 per cent of the labour force. Tradespeople and shopkeepers accounted for the largest proportion of the population by far, followed by ironworkers and labourers (most of whom were sailors), then garment workers, and members of the wood-working and furniture crafts (Table 40).

As successive governors and intendants lamented, workers were too few in Québec. The problem, already existing in 1666 despite the large number of indentured labourers and servants, worsened during the last quarter of the 17th century. The minimal diversification of trades during the period between the two censuses was certainly due to industry's lack of success in the colony.[45] It is also clear that Québec was a town of traders, although Upper and Lower Town projected distinct images that seemed to indicate spatial segregation.

The town's labour force evolved between 1666 and 1681. The decrease in the number of indentured labourers and servants is particularly striking, surely suggesting that the town had attained a certain degree of

Table 36
Trades in Québec in 1681

Trade	Upper Town	Lower Town	Unspecified Location	Servants and Others	Total
Arquebusier	—	3	—	2 (1 apprentice)	5
Bailiff	1	1	5	—	7
Baker	—	2	—	1	3
Butcher	1	2	—	—	3
Carpenter	5	2	1	—	8
Cartographer	—	1	—	—	1
Caterer	1	1	—	—	2
Caulker	—	1	—	—	1
Clerk	1	—	—	—	1
Clogmaker	—	1	—	—	1
Constable	—	—	1	—	1
Confectioner	—	2	—	—	2
Cooper	—	3	—	1 apprentice	4
Cook	—	1	—	1	2
Cutler	—	1	—	—	1
Edge-tool maker	1	6	—	1 apprentice	8
Executioner	—	—	—	1	1
Explorer	—	2	—	—	2
Gunner	—	1	—	—	1
Innkeeper	—	1	—	—	1
Joiner	8	3	1	—	12
Law officer and others	4	2	10	—	16
Locksmith	—	3	—	2 (1 apprentice)	5
Mason	4	1	—	—	5
Merchant	3	30	—	—	33
Nailsmith	—	3	—	3 apprentices	6
Notary	—	—	2	1 clerk	3
Recorder	—	—	2	—	2
Roofer	2	—	—	—	2
Sailor	—	7	—	—	7
Servant*	—	2	—	—	2
Ship's carpenter	—	2	—	—	2
Shoemaker	1	3	—	—	4
Soldier	4	3	—	—	7
Stonecutter	—	1	—	—	1
Surgeon	1	2	—	1 apprentice	4
Surveyor	1	—	—	—	1
Tavernkeeper	—	1	—	—	1
Tailor	3	8	—	1	12
Tapestry maker	1	—	—	—	1
Turner	1	1	—	—	2
Vinegar merchant	1	—	—	—	1
Wheelwright	2	—	—	—	2

Totals: Upper Town: 46 individuals, 20 trades; Lower Town: 103 individuals, 33 trades; unspecified location: 22 individuals, 7 trades; servants and others: 15 individuals, 11 trades.
Total: 186 individuals, 43 trades.

* These servants are household heads.
Members of religious orders, including 4 lay brothers, and 21 garrison soldiers were excluded from this table.

Table 37
Trades Common to Upper and Lower Town in 1681

Trade	Upper Town	Lower Town
Bailiff	1	1
Butcher	1	2
Carpenter	5	2
Caterer	1	1
Edge-tool maker	1	6
Joiner	8	3
Law officer and others	4	2
Mason	4	1
Merchant	3	30
Shoemaker	1	3
Soldier	4	3
Surgeon	1	2
Tailor	3	8
Turner	1	1
Total 14 trades	38	65

Table 38
Socio-Professional Classification of Servants and Others, 1681

Category	Trade	Total Persons
Professionals	1 apprentice surgeon	
	1 clerk	2
Tradespeople and shopkeepers		
Food trade	1 baker	
	1 cook	2
Craftsmen		
Clothing	1 tailor	1
Wood and furniture	1 apprentice cooper	1
Iron	1 arquebusier	
	1 apprentice arquebusier	
	3 apprentice nailsmiths	
	1 locksmith	
	1 apprentice locksmith	
	1 apprentice edge-tool maker	8
Total: 5	10	14

Table 39
Trades in Upper Town in 1681 and Socio-Professional Classification

Category	Trade	Total Persons
Professionals	1 surveyor*	
	1 surgeon	
	4 law officers and others	6
Tradespeople and shopkeepers	1 butcher	
	3 merchants	
	1 caterer	
	1 vinegar merchant*	6
Craftsmen		
Art and luxury items	1 tapestry maker*	1
Clothing	3 tailors	3
Wood and furniture	8 joiners	
	1 turner	9
Leather	1 shoemaker	1
Building trades	5 carpenters	
	2 roofers*	
	4 masons	11
Iron	2 wheelwrights*	
	1 edge-tool maker	3
		28
Salaried workers	1 clerk*	
	1 bailiff	2
Military	4 soldiers and others	4
Total: 10	20	46

* Trades exclusive to Upper Town (6).

Table 40
Trades in Lower Town in 1681
and Socio-Professional Classification

Category	Trade	Total Persons
Professionals	1 cartographer*	
	2 surgeons	
	2 law officers and others	5
Tradespeople and shopkeepers	2 butchers	
	2 bakers*	
	1 tavernkeeper	
	1 cook*	
	1 innkeeper*	
	30 merchants	
	2 confectioners*	
	1 caterer	40
Craftsmen		
Clothing	1 clogmaker*	9
	8 tailors	
Wood and furniture	3 joiners	
	3 coopers*	
	1 turner	7
Leather	3 shoemakers	3
Building	2 carpenters	
	1 mason	
	1 stonecutter*	4
Iron	3 arquebusiers*	
	3 nailsmiths*	
	1 cutler*	
	3 locksmiths*	
	6 edge-tool makers	16
Others	1 caulker*	
	2 ship's carpenters	
	2 explorers*	5
		44
Salaried workers	2 servants*	
	1 bailiff	
	7 sailors*	10
Military	1 gunner*	
	3 soldiers and others	4
Total: 10	33	103

* Trades exclusive to Lower Town (18).

maturity and was no longer forced to rely on workers bound by contract to swell its inhabitants' ranks, but could also attract free men.

The Labour Force and Housing Construction

The building trades are of particular interest not only because of their importance within the labour force,[46] but also because Québec was literally under construction between 1663 and 1690. Focussing on these trades and studying the behaviour of a specific group working within a major industry will provide us with a very different view of the labour force than do the censuses.[47] It will also contribute to our understanding of the urban house's evolution.

What follows is an overview of the most important basic craftsmen: masons, carpenters and joiners, and roofers. Who were the builders? Did they work alone or in partnership? To what extent were workers from outside Québec called upon? Of the entries in construction contracts, 40.9 per cent were for masons, 47.7 per cent for carpenters and joiners, and 10.4 per cent for roofers. Only three entries (1.0 per cent) provide no information as to the craftsmen's trade.[48]

Masons

Nine masons accounted for 68.9 per cent of the entries for this group. Five were particularly active, as 50.0 per cent of the entries concerned them. The two most prominent were André Couteron and Louis Lavergne, with 13.1 per cent and 11.5 per cent of the entries respectively (Table 41). They were the two masons most in demand between 1663 and 1690. Short biographies of the five most prominent masons will explain who these craftsmen were and why masons like Baillif and Le Rouge were not more active.

Two masons, Baillif and Le Rouge, are already well known and brief studies of them have been published, notably in the *Dictionnaire biographique du Canada*. **Claude Baillif *dit* Regnault** (ca. 1635–98), hired by Bishop Laval to teach at the seminary's school of industrial arts for three years, arrived in Québec in 1675.[49] His name first appears in a construction contract in 1679 and he was then identified as an architect and plaster worker. To these titles he added that of contracting mason in

Table 41
Frequency (Five or More Entries) of Craftsmen's Names in Construction Contracts for the Three Basic Trades 1663–1690

Masons	No. of Entries	%*
Baillif, Claude	9	7.4
Couteron, André	16	13.1
Dumas, Gabriel	7	5.7
Duplais, Sylvain	10	8.2
Jourdain, Guillaume	5	4.1
Lavergne, Louis	14	11.5
Le Rouge, Jean	12	9.8
Renault, Antoine	5	4.1
Roy, Étienne	6	4.9
Total	84	68.9

Carpenters and Joiners	No. of Entries	%*
Bédard, Jacques	6	4.2
Caillé, Jean	6	4.2
Chesnier, Jean	7	4.9
Choret, Robert	5	3.5
Dupille, Rémi	5	3.5
Leclerc, Robert	7	4.9
Marchand, Jean	6	4.2
Ménage, Pierre	7	4.9
Paillard, Léonard	16	11.3
Réaume, René	12	8.5
Total	77	54.2

Roofers	No. of Entries	%*
Gacien, Pierre	24	77.4

* Percentages are calculated on the basis of total entries for each trade including names mentioned less than five times: 122 for masons, 142 for carpenters and joiners, and 31 for roofers.

1691. Baillif continued to work in construction in Québec until 1697 and resided in rue du Sault-au-Matelot from 1682 to 1696.[50]

Baillif's name appeared only nine times in the housing contracts studied, representing just 7.4 per cent of the total entries for masons. The man who has been called the best-known and most prolific building contractor in New France in the 17th century does not figure prominently in housing contracts made between 1663 and 1690 because he had little interest in private construction and was primarily involved in building for public authorities and religious institutions. He was commissioned to build the platform of the Batterie Royale in 1683 and a wing of the Québec prison in 1687;[51] however, his major field of activity was religious architecture. He worked on the Québec cathedral in 1686 and was awarded the contract for the construction of Notre-Dame-des-Victoires in 1687 and the one for the bishop's palace in 1690.

Claude Baillif worked chiefly but not exclusively in Québec, sometimes doing jobs out of town, as in 1679 when Charles Aubert de Lachenaye hired him to build Maison Blanche and in 1688 when Bishop Saint-Vallier asked him to undertake construction of the church at Sainte-Anne-de-Beaupré. Two years later he was called on to build the manse for the church at Saint-Joseph-de-la-Pointe-Lévis.

The kinds of contracts listed do not do justice to Baillif's role, which was an important one in various activities (hiring, employing apprentices, handling supply contracts, etc.) connected with house building. A better estimate of his real importance to that sector can be reached by looking at his activities as an entrepreneur.

According to Antoine Furetière's dictionary, an entrepreneur in the 17th century was "one who undertakes or contracts for a building or some other construction; said especially of Architects who undertake to erect a building at a fixed price."[52] A contractor was responsible for a construction project; he oversaw it. A priori, he was unlike masons in that he apparently did no physical work on site. Rather, he let supply contracts, hired workers (masons, stonecutters, etc.), and supervised the work. He was the boss.

Can Baillif be considered an entrepreneur? As a contracting party he most often worked alone; we know of only two partnerships of his, neither of which lasted long. In 1682–83 he took on three jobs in partnership with Jean Le Rouge and Jean Poliquain, then in 1683 he signed five contracts in association with Jean Le Rouge alone.

What set Baillif apart from other masons was how many men he hired. In the course of ten years, from 1679 to 1689, he hired no fewer than 28 men, most when he was engaged in various contracts: 4 in 1682, 8 in 1683, and another 8 in 1684.[53] Masons, labourers, joiners, and stonecutters were among those he took on. Of the masons, two were to be particularly active between 1663 and 1690: Antoine Renault, who was hired in 1681 and 1686, and André Couteron, who signed on in the summer of 1683. Workmen whose main period of activity was in the early years of the 18th century are also among those hired, especially Joseph Maillou, who signed on in 1683, 1686, and 1689, and his brother Jean-Baptiste Maillou *dit* Desmoulins, whom Baillif employed in 1685 and again in 1689.[54] Very often Baillif did his hiring out of town. In 1682 he brought in a mason from Petite-Rivière, in 1682 and 1684 he hired another from Pointe-aux-Trembles, and thrice during 1683–84 he used workers from Île d'Orléans.[55]

Training workers through apprenticeship was another contractor-like trait in Baillif. Between 1684 and 1690 this architect trained five workmen in masonry and stonecutting. Again, Jean-Baptiste Maillou's name comes up, Baillif taking him on as an apprentice in 1685. There were also Pierre de la Faye, whose apprenticeship was from 1684 to 1687; Jean Parent, from Beauport, who was apprenticed from 1687 to 1692; and François Desnoyers, who began his two-year apprenticeship in 1690.[56] Baillif thus contributed to creating a pool of skilled labour in Québec, and in at least one case the future craftsman did not come from the capital. His apprentices were taken on almost at the rate of one a year.

Baillif acted like an entrepreneur when contracting for materials and when performing subcontracts for someone else. There were two types of supply contract, one where Baillif supplied the goods and another where he ordered them. Except for 1682, when he agreed to supply Master Gunner Jean Levrard with labour and materials for a house to be built on côte de la Montagne, the first type of contract was rare. The other type took the form of agreements for transport or for manufacture of materials required by Baillif. In 1683, for instance, Baillif twice contracted Pierre Maufay of Côte Saint-Michel to transport materials such as sand, lime, and stone needed for his jobs in Lower Town or on the cathedral. In 1684 he ordered stone from the Cap-aux-Diamants quarry from two habitants, one living at Charlesbourg and the other at Beauport.

There seem to have been more cases where Baillif did subcontracting. In 1682 he agreed to have Pierre Gacien roof Jean Levrard's house, in 1683 he hired two joiners to work on Louis Jolliet's house on rue Sous-le-Fort, and in 1684 he signed two contracts for the same house, one with a carter and another with two carpenters. Of all the masons studied, Baillif is the only one that engaged in that kind of activity, fitting Furetière's definition of an entrepreneur exactly.

Baillif's other function was as an architect.[57] With Le Rouge, he is one of the few to have left estimates. In 1683 he did an estimate for the Niel house on rue Sous-le-Fort; then, with Le Rouge, he did another for the same house and for the Maheust house. He was on his own when he prepared four estimates for Pierre Moisan's residence on rue De Meulles: for the masonry, carpentry, joinery, and locksmithing.[58] Baillif also drew up a few plans, such as those for the Maison Blanche chimneys in 1679 and for rebuilding Eustache Lambert Dumont's house on rue Notre-Dame in 1687.

Baillif's real importance is not reflected by his name's frequency in contract records. As well as being one of those who truly deserved the name of entrepreneur, he was one of the principal architects of the reconstruction of Lower Town after the 1682 fire.

Jean Le Rouge (1639–1712) came to the colony around 1667 and was sworn in as surveyor for the seigneurial jurisdiction of Québec by Intendant Talon in November 1672.[59] The first time he was mentioned in construction contracts, in 1672, he was called a master mason and surveyor; in 1676, a stonecutter as well, and two years later, an entrepreneur. Le Rouge had a long career that apparently ended only in 1702. A resident of Québec from 1669 on, he also moved frequently: rue Sainte-Anne from 1683 to 1687, rue Notre-Dame in 1688, and rue du Sault-au-Matelot in 1701.

Le Rouge was in third place among masons (Table 41), so he did build quite a few houses. Among his major projects were building part of Charles Aubert de Lachenaye's house on rue du Sault-au-Matelot in 1679, repairing the Hôtel-Dieu in 1681, building the Jesuits' house on rue Saint-Pierre in 1683, and building the Château Saint-Louis powder magazine in 1685. Le Rouge confined his masonry work to Québec, and outside the town performed only one contract, to build a house on Île d'Orléans in 1674 in partnership with Jean Poliquain.

Unlike Baillif, Le Rouge often worked with partners. Between 1672 and 1683 he did so 13 times; as early as 1672 he had contracted with Jean Poliquain and Jacques Charrier. In 1675 he signed another contract with Jean Jobin. He also worked with Poliquain, as a sole partner, in 1674, then again in 1682–83. He collaborated with Poliquain and Baillif in 1682–83, and in the latter year, with Baillif alone.

Between 1676 and 1684 Le Rouge hired 18 workmen, including three in partnership with Baillif in 1683. His frenetic hiring activity during that same year, with ten contracts, left his partner in the shade; all ten hands were masons except for three labourers. Of these, Antoine Renault signed his contract in 1683 and Louis Lavergne in 1678, and André Couteron was hired in 1678 and 1683. Jean Le Rouge did his hiring out of town, as his workers came from Beaupré, Petite-Rivière, or Île d'Orléans, whence six were recruited in 1683 alone.

Since he hired so many men, Le Rouge can, like Baillif, be considered an entrepreneur. Where he differed from his colleague, however, was in apprenticeship and subcontracting.

Supply contracts for building materials are another indication of Le Rouge's activity as an entrepreneur. On two occasions, in 1676 and 1683, he offered to cut and supply stone, but he was more ordinarily the buyer in such transactions. He let five materials-transport contracts between 1676 and 1685, including one with Baillif, and a stonecutting contract in 1685. Le Rouge in that case used out-of-town labour: a Charlesbourg carter and quarryman, a Saint-Jean carter, etc.

Le Rouge saw himself as an architect, but the title fits him less well than it did Baillif. On his own he drew up only one estimate, for Jean-Baptiste Couillard de Lespinay's house on rue Sous-le-Fort. He did make another estimate, in partnership with Baillif and Poliquain, for Louis Niort de Lanoraie's house.

Like Baillif, Le Rouge appears to have been instrumental in the reconstruction of Lower Town after the 1682 fire. His case was different from those of three other less-well-known masons, André Couteron, Louis Lavergne, and Sylvain Duplais, who hired and trained practically nobody. Sylvain Duplais was the only one of the three who had an apprentice (in 1689).

André Couteron (ca. 1649–1702) is the mason whose name appears most often in building contracts. Nothing is known of his origins or his arrival in the colony. The first time he was mentioned was in the contracts for 1677 as a master mason living at Côte Saint-Michel near Cap-Rouge. He took up residence in Québec about 1678 and lived at various addresses there: côte de la Montagne in 1679–80; Cul-de-Sac, 1680 and 1682; Upper Town, 1681; De Meulles and Cul-de-Sac between 1685 and 1688. He was active until about 1701 and worked almost exclusively on house construction in Québec. Outside the town he did one job at Côte de Lauzon in 1677 and another in 1680 on Île d'Orléans. Apart from repairs to the Sulpicians' *magasin* in 1681 and various jobs for the Récollets the following year, he was not mentioned in any contract relating to religious or public buildings prior to 1690.

Although he plied a specialized trade, Couteron was more the workman-labourer type of mason. He seldom worked alone; from 1677 to 1688 he did some 17 jobs with a partner. Until 1687 he worked closely with Louis Lavergne, on ten jobs. In 1680 he was associated with Gabriel Dumast for three contracts, then with François Ducarreau in 1682 and Mathieu Lagrange in 1688.[60] During these jobs Couteron's behaviour was not that of a contractor or entrepreneur: four times he hired himself out. Le Rouge employed him in 1678 and 1683; in 1682 he signed on with François Ducarreau, who transferred his contract to Baillif the following year; and in the same year, together with Ducarreau, he took service with the Récollets.

Though Couteron did hire hands, he did so very much less than Baillif and most often within a partnership. With Ducarreau in 1682 he hired a mason from Île d'Orléans, and he employed another mason in 1686 with Lavergne; in 1688, with Mathieu Lagrange, he took on a labourer. On the two occasions when Couteron acted on his own he engaged a mason, from Lorette in 1678 and from Lauzon in 1687.

Neither were building materials supply-contracts a major interest for Couteron. Out of five such contracts he let only one on his own, when a habitant from the seigneurie of Lauzon was to supply him with shingles in 1680. The other four were with partners: a habitant from Saint-Joseph agreed in 1680 to supply him and Gabriel Dumast with stone, and in 1681 he and Lavergne engaged a carter from the Saint-Charles River. That same year, still with Lavergne, he had dealings with a lime merchant from Côte de Lauzon, and seven years later a carter from Saint-Jean agreed to transport materials for him and Lagrange.

André Couteron was the busiest mason over the period 1663–90, but although he holds first place for number of entries, he was not the most important figure in Québec house construction. In his partnerships, his hiring, and his supply contracting Couteron could not rival such true entrepreneurs as Baillif and Le Rouge.

Little information is available on the career of **Louis Lavergne** (16??–87) even though he was the second most important mason. He was first mentioned in 1672, in 1684 he was called a master mason and stonecutter, and in 1687 he appeared in the records for the last time. Like Couteron, Lavergne moved several times. In 1675 he was living at La Canardière, from 1677 to 1679 and in 1681–82 he lived in Côte Saint-Michel, in 1680 he was briefly in Upper Town, and five years later he was said to live on rue De Meulles.

Between 1672 and 1687 Lavergne does not seem to have worked outside Québec; even in town he undertook only a few big jobs. In 1679 Aubert de Lachesnaye called on him to build a house at Sault-au-Matelot. During the following two years Lavergne worked with Couteron on the Sulpicians' *magasin* on rue Notre-Dame. In 1684 he collaborated with Sylvain Duplais on the construction of François Pachot's house on rue Saint-Pierre. In 1685, again with Couteron, he took on the masonry for Jean Lebert's house.

Lavergne was probably the mason who entered into the most partnerships. During his active period he worked on 23 jobs with other masons: with André Couteron he did five contracts in 1677–78, three in 1680–81, and three more between 1685 and 1687. In 1682 he had a new partner, Guillaume Jourdain, for three contracts and for two other contracts in 1684. In the latter year he also teamed up with Duplais for five contracts.

Lavergne did even fewer hiring and supply contracts than Couteron. In 1678 he hired himself out to Le Rouge, but also, with Couteron, hired a mason. In 1684 he did the same with Sylvain Duplais. In 1681, again with Couteron, he bought lime from Lauzon; in 1683 he made a deal with Léonard Paillard of Beauport for fireplace jambs; however, this was really more of an exchange, since Lavergne promised to replace the jambs the following year.

With ten entries **Sylvain Duplais** (ca. 1658–1703) was a slightly more important figure than Baillif (Table 41). He first appeared in the records in 1679 and kept on until about 1696. Until 1682 Duplais lived at Petite-Rivière; he moved to Québec the following year and during 1688–89 lived on rue De Meulles.

Duplais's achievements include, with his uncle Louis Duplais, construction of a house for Pierre Normand Labrière in 1680; in 1686, with Guillaume Jourdain, he worked for François Pachot on rue Saint-Pierre; and in 1686–87, with the same partner, he worked at the Ursuline convent. Duplais also worked out of town. In 1682, for instance, he did jobs at Côte Saint-François-Xavier and Côte Saint-Michel; in 1687 he and Jourdain built a lime kiln at Lauzon. Even from these few hints it seems a fair guess that he seldom worked alone. From 1679 to 1687 he worked with a partner on 16 jobs. In addition to Lavergne, he worked with his uncle on 3 of them, in 1679 and 1680, then with Guillaume Jourdain on 8 more in 1686–87.

Of the three masons considered secondary, Duplais was the one who showed the most interest in hiring. Baillif employed him full-time for a while in 1682, then between 1684 and 1689 Duplais signed nine labour contracts, including seven with Jourdain for a partner in 1686–87. The workmen they took on, insofar as we are told where they came from, were exclusively from Québec.

It is possible to compare Duplais, Couteron, and Lavergne in the area of materials supply-contracts. Duplais entered into only two such contracts, both with Guillaume Jourdain. These two arranged for Joseph Giffard, seigneur of Beauport, to supply them with stone and lime for François Pachot's house, and they let a transport contract to a carter from Saint-François.

Carpenters

Five carpenters account for 34.5 per cent of the entries for all such tradesmen: Léonard Paillard, René Réaume, Pierre Ménage, Robert Leclerc, and Jean Chesnier.[61]

Léonard Paillard ***dit*** **Le Poitevin** (1647–1729), arrived in Canada in about 1670 as an indentured servant. By 1672 he was apprenticed to Jean Lemire, *charpentier du roi* and syndic of Québec. His initial contract called for a three-year training period; however, in 1674 Lemire lent his apprentice to Pierre Mercereau for a year. The temporary arrangement became permanent the following year, when Mercereau undertook to teach Paillard his trade for three years. Their agreement also stipulated that all work and all profits would be shared between them, so it was not so much an apprenticeship as a partnership.

In 1678, when his name showed up for the first time in the contracts, Paillard was called a master millwright; he lived at the time in Petit-Village (Petite-Auvergne), Beauport, and stayed there until 1684, when he moved to Québec. His first residence was on rue Saint-Anne, but he soon moved to rue du Sault-au-Matelot, where he remained from 1684 to 1687. He then moved to Montréal permanently.[62]

Statistically Paillard takes first place among carpenters (Table 41). Within Québec he undertook only a few major projects, working on Louis Jolliet's house in 1684 with Robert Leclerc, then by himself in 1685, and in 1687 doing repairs to the Mont-Carmel mill. However, outside the town limits he undertook many different projects. Peter N. Moogk, author of Paillard's biography in the *Dictionnaire biographique du Canada*, claimed that his career as a millwright was slow to develop and that his talent was not recognized until he arrived in the Montréal area (in 1687);[63] however, such was not the case. From 1678 to 1686 Paillard built six mills in several different seigneuries. First came a windmill built for Aubert de Lachenaye at Pointe-aux-Lièvres, then the following year another windmill was built at Saint-François, where he was to build yet another for the Jesuits in 1682. In 1680 and 1681 he built two gristmills, the first in the seigneurie of La Durantaye and the second at Pointe-aux-Écureuils (Bélair). Finally, in 1686, Pierre Boucher of Boucherville contracted with him for a windmill.

Paillard rarely had a partner; he signed only two such contracts, with Robert Leclerc in 1684 and 1685. But he did not work alone. From 1679 until the end of his stay in Québec he took on three apprentices. In 1679 he agreed to teach his trade for three years to Edme Guyart of Petit-Village de Beauport. Then in 1687 he enrolled another Beauport inhabitant, Joseph Creste, as an apprentice house-builder and millwright. At the same time, Jean Froment also began his apprenticeship with Paillard, but for two years only.

Paillard seldom entered into contracts for the supply of building materials, and then only as supplier. In 1682, for instance, he supplied Pierre Nolan with timber for the construction of Nolan's house in Lower Town, in 1683 he supplied fireplace jambs to Louis Lavergne, and in 1684 he supplied Nicolas Marion de La Fontaine, a merchant, with cedar beams.

René Réaume (1643–1722), called a master carpenter, appeared in the contracts for 1666. From 1667 until 1679 at least he lived on the Saint-Charles River; he is recorded to have been in Québec in 1681, living on rue des Jardins, but it was only a short stay as in 1683 he was in Côte Saint-Bernard, then in 1685 and 1688 in Charlesbourg. In 1689 Réaume had a residence in La Canardière and another on rue des Jardins.

Réaume was active until 1696 and was second among carpenters, with 12 entries (8.5 per cent). He did not seem to have undertaken any big projects. In 1677 in partnership with René Renault he entered into a contract with Charles Bazire, *receveur des droits du Domaine*, to build a house. In 1683 he and Jean Giron took on the repair of the retaining wall at côte de la Montagne; since the wall had been destroyed in the fire of 1682 the road had become impassable, the earth no longer being held back. These were Réaume's only two partnerships.

Outside Québec Réaume took on only two jobs: a barn in Charlesbourg in 1667 and in 1674 shoring for a mill ramp at Bazire on the Saint-Charles River. On that occasion Réaume had three habitants deliver timber, and in 1675 two workers from Saint-Joseph were to supply him with beams and planking. Réaume entered into only one other supply contract: in 1681 he delivered beams and ribbing to the king's bailiff, Jean Levasseur. Réaume took on only one apprentice, Pierre Gaultier, in 1674, for a term of two and a half years.

Pierre Ménage (ca. 1648–1715) came to New France during Intendant Jean Talon's first term. In 1669 he bought a dwelling on the Saint-Charles River and remained there until 1674, at which time he took up residence in Québec.[64] From then until 1682 he is known to have lived in Upper Town, probably on rue Saint-Louis, as he was certainly there in 1686.

First recorded in construction contracts in 1672, the name Ménage was still to be found there in 1701, in which year he signed his last contract and retired from the construction business. He was the second *charpentier du roi* in Québec, having received the title in 1675, and seems to have confined his work to the capital. In 1675 Ménage built the Jacquet house, which is "[the] sole surviving complete example of a

17th century house in the city."[65] In addition he entered into several big contracts with Jean Caillé: one in 1683 for the Jesuit house on rue Saint-Pierre; another, in 1685, for Jacques Lebert's house (the contract included plans and estimates that may have been done by both carpenters); and a third for François Pachot's residence, built in 1686. Religious orders also patronized Ménage: in 1681 he and Jean Marchand worked on the Hôtel-Dieu; in 1686, still with Caillé, he took on two contracts for the Ursuline convent; and two years later the two partners were working together again, this time on the Québec cathedral and the Lower Town church.

Ménage engaged in many partnerships: 12 between 1672 and 1688, his favourite partner being Jean Caillé, with whom he undertook six contracts from 1683 to 1686. The only hired help Ménage had was one apprentice, who was taken on for three years in 1673.

Ménage entered into only three supply contracts, all before 1680. In 1672, with Marchand, he supplied the timber for Nicolas Follain's building, probably at La Potasse, for Follain had a monopoly on potash and pearl-ash production in New France. Two years later Ménage called on a habitant from Grande Allée to carry the sand he needed for a house he was building in Upper Town. Then in 1679 certain habitants from L'Auvergne, in the seigneurie of Notre-Dame-des-Anges, agreed to supply him with the stakes he needed for the work at La Potasse.

Robert Leclerc (1650–1731) was mentioned for the first time in 1667 when he was Jean Soullard's domestic servant. In 1669 he seems to have been in Beauport, and in 1681 he was said to be from Québec. He lived there at least until 1716; from 1682 to 1685 he had resided on rue Saint-Louis. His professional activity peaked in the 1690s and may have continued until 1705.

Leclerc, who accounted for as many entries as Pierre Ménage, does not seem to have been as active. He undertook few jobs outside Québec: a stable at Côte Saint-Michel in 1681 and a barn at La Canardière in 1685 for Thimothée Roussel, a Québec surgeon. For work within the town he limited himself to two partnerships: he worked with Paillard in 1684–85 on three contracts, and from 1687 to 1689 he shared four contracts with Jean Marchand.

The work done during the first partnership included a subcontract Baillif let in 1684 for the Jolliet house; the following year Leclerc and Paillard worked on Pierre Nolan's house on rue Saint-Pierre. Leclerc and Marchand rebuilt La Potasse in 1687, then worked on Eustache Lambert-Dumont's residence on rue Notre-Dame. In 1688 they were employed on rue Saint-Pierre for Nicolas Dupont de Neuville.

The last carpenter on the list, **Jean Chesnier** (ca. 1622–99), received the title master carpenter in 1674 and had as many entries as Robert Leclerc. Chesnier had a long career, extending from 1656 to 1689, during which he lived in four different communities: from 1657 to 1667 he resided in Québec, then in Dombourg from 1671 to 1677; in 1688 he is listed as residing once more in Québec, and the following year he moved to Pointe-aux-Trembles.

Chesnier worked on, among other buildings, the Montréal warehouse on rue Notre-Dame for Barbe de Boulogne in 1666, then on it again for the Sulpicians in 1671. With Antoine Rouillard he entered into two contracts in 1666. He worked with Claude Carpentier in 1671, and with his son Jean Chesnier in 1688 he contracted to build a house on rue Sous-le-Fort for Jean-Baptiste Couillard de Lespinay. Chesnier seems, like Leclerc, to have done almost nothing in supply contracts. In 1671 Jean Poidras, a master joiner from Upper Town, agreed to prepare, bleach, tongue and groove, and lay a number of beams and planks to repair and roof the Montréal warehouse. In exchange Chesnier agreed to build a house for Poidras in Upper Town.[66]

Roofers

Unlike the other two trades studied above, roofing involved few people. **Louis Creste**, a slater from Beauport, was listed as having performed only one contract, on the house of Claude Charron de la Barre on rue Notre-Dame in 1679. **Pierre Dron** (1668–86), also called a slater, signed an agreement in 1679. His term at the Québec seminary, which was to have been for three years, was cut short on condition that he roof a house belonging to the seminary at Anse-à-Puiseaux, a contract to that effect being drawn up that year between Dron and the seminary bursar. He reappeared in the record of building contracts only in 1683, when he and his partner Robert Pépin had to break off their roofing work on the belfry of the Récollet hospice in Upper Town.

The career of **Robert Pépin** (1643–86) was more interesting. He lived in Beauport from 1668 to 1675 and from 1678 to 1680; after 1681 he took up residence in Upper Town. Pépin seems to have worked mainly for religious communities and specialized in slate roofs. In 1668 he contracted with the Jesuits for "slates 3½ *pouces* thick and for laying the necessary planking for the roof of their new church" near the Jesuit college. In 1670 he slated part of the Hôtel-Dieu roof, and in 1671 roofed the Montréal warehouse and also the Ursulines' belfry and part of their convent in the same material. Under private contracts he roofed a house for François Hazeur in 1684 and another for Jacques Lebert in 1685.

He is said to have done some work outside Québec. In 1672 he was hired to roof Jean-François Bourdon de Dombourg's mill in Pointe-aux-Trembles. Six years later the Notre-Dame de Beauport *fabrique* hired him to work on their parish church. And in 1680 he slated the Récollets' residence in the seigneurie of Notre-Dame-des-Anges.

The names of these three roofers do not appear in Table 41 because individually they do not account for five entries in the list of contracts. One name only appeared there, that of Pierre Gacien, who accounted for 77.4 per cent of all roofers' entries. This enormous preponderance shows that roofing was a monopoly.

Strangely enough, there seems to be no complete study of **Pierre Gacien *dit* Tourangeau** (ca. 1653–1728) even though he was the most important roofer in Québec[67] at the turn of the 18th century. Gacien's name turned up in the contracts for the first time in 1678. In 1679 he was referred to as a master slater; in 1680 he was called a master roofer in slates or shingles, and in the same year he gained the added title of thatcher. He lived in Upper Town after 1680. Two years later he was on rue Saint-Louis, where he stayed from 1686 to 1688. He lived also on rue Buade, in 1684 and — what seems impossible unless he had two houses — in 1687–88. In 1688 he was also said to reside on rue Saint-Anne.

In spite of his importance, little is known of Gacien's career. Apart from the Ursulines' belfry, which he roofed with slate in 1688, and the roof of a mill in Neuville, he did not venture outside Québec and confined his trade to private houses. In 1678, for instance, he worked on Claude Bermen de la Martinière's house on rue Saint-Louis and on Nicolas Cliche's in 1680. He also roofed André Couteron's house in 1681, the tailor André de Chaune's in 1683, and in 1687 that of Gabriel Gosselin, a merchant on rue Sous-le-Fort.

Gacien did not sign any supply contracts, and hiring and training staff were secondary activities with him. In 1681 Louis Duplais signed an open-ended contract with Gacien to make shingles; he promised, in addition, to "employ his time in the woods of the Seigneurie of Saint-Bernard, near Saint-Joseph."[68] Apparently Duplais became a logger, so we can assume that Gacien obtained his timber from his own lands. The only other man Gacien hired was Étienne Michelon, in 1682.[69] He took on only one apprentice: Alexandre Biron of Québec, aged 14, began a four-year apprenticeship with Gacien in 1686.

* * *

Moving beyond raw statistics are the descriptions of the lives and activities of these 14 craftsmen, defining who they were and revealing, as far as might be, why each did as much or as little house building as he did. In any case, how could mere statistics allow us to truely assess a Baillif or a Le Rouge? By examining the labour force in general through these 14 men we can get a new insight into the lives of Québec construction workers between 1663 and 1690.

Any conclusions from this examination are only valid for the trades under study and only for a small number of people; however, they do represent wider tendencies. At the level of entries, the representation of the three trades was uneven. Carpenters outpaced masons to some extent and accounted for a higher overall total. There are two possible reasons for this difference: first, carpenters were more in demand owing to the prevalent styles of house construction that favoured wood over masonry, especially for private houses, whether made entirely of wood or half-timbered; and second, the Lower Town fire of 1682. Wooden frames and roofs would have required more extensive repair after the fire than relatively fireproof masonry walls. Though roofers were very rarely mentioned in the contracts, that may be because such work did not require many labourers; a few workmen sufficed.

It was important to know if these workers lived in Québec. According to the biographies, 9 of the 14 craftsmen lived outside the town at the beginning of their careers. This proportion is the more significant if one reflects that for 34.9 per cent of the contracts analysed, the labour force came from out of town. Within the town itself, workmen originated in four different areas. In Upper Town they mainly lived in the areas of Saint-Louis and des Jardins, and Saint-Anne and Buade streets. In Lower Town there were two foci: rue De Meulles and rue du Sault-au-Matelot. Was there perhaps a certain spatial segregation, at least in Lower Town? Workmen would, according to that theory, be concentrated in distinct working-class districts apart from the areas, especially around the Place Royale, where merchants lived. In addition, even though some workmen (Couteron, Le Rouge) displayed remarkable mobility, it appears that a tradesman's place of residence had an influence on the contracts he obtained. Baillif, for instance, who lived on rue du Sault-au-Matelot, worked extensively for residents of that street and the immediate vicinity.

Each profession had its own work patterns, but masons seem to have been very polarized, as two distinct types of individuals appeared. The first type of mason was apparently incapable of working alone and always had a partner on site. Such masons specialized in private houses and did not work on public buildings or ones belonging to the religious.

He seldom hired men or entered into supply contracts, and if he did so it was with a partner. Like Duplais, he often worked out of town. Couteron and Lavergne exemplify this category; they have the most contract entries and were probably the easiest for people to hire as their time was not taken up with institutional work.

The second kind of mason was very different. He kept every job site to himself and accepted many jobs on public and religious buildings. He hired often and was even known to take on hands who were much in demand. He entered into numerous supply contracts and also let subcontracts. As well, he helped train new labourers through apprenticeships. He also drew up specifications and estimates.

Carpenters' work patterns were less evident (Table 41). Among carpenters there were no real entrepreneurs despite the presence of a Paillard and a Réaume. Parnerships were frequent with them, too, so that they are more like masons of the first category in that regard. Of all entries for masons, 27 are for partnerships (22.1 per cent of the entries for this group), while 30 partnerships of carpenters were listed (21.1 per cent of the total). Some activities were almost unknown among carpenters: hiring was rare and there were few supply contracts. True, apprentices were more evenly distributed among them, but the number of their apprentices hardly compares with the number masons took on.

Two categories of carpenter can be defined based on the kind of contracts they entered: one category consists of those who, like Paillard and Réaume, confined their activities to in-town house building, and the other category consists of those, like Ménage, who worked on public and religious buildings.

A similar classification can be applied to roofers. The first category would include such men as Gacien; the model for the second is Pépin.

Insofar as house building was a thriving industry in Québec, it can serve as a barometer for the status of the town's labour force and as a measure of the raw-material supply situation. When men were to be hired, in all cases except Duplais's, they had to be brought from out of town, and the same held true when apprentices were taken on. Supplies, too, were obtained outside the town: Île d'Orléans, Beauport, Charlesbourg, Côte Saint-Michel, and Saint-Bernard. The fire of 1682 had a great effect, as it caused a great upsurge in construction in Québec and drew men and materials into the capital from outlying areas. That men had to be brought in from out of town shows the scarcity of workers and craftsmen in Québec in spite of its well-qualified labour force. In addition, with a few exceptions such as the Cap-aux-Diamants quarry, the town was not self-sufficient in building materials.

Conclusion

Québec's population had a colonial makeup, a somewhat artificial character because of the immigrants (brides, indentured servants, soldiers) and various measures intended to encourage growth (dowries, bonuses, marriage ordinances, and so on). The greatest wave of immigration kept on until 1672, and it is surprising to see how the town's rate of growth compares to those of the principal towns in the English colonies.

Québec's situation in the colony was exceptional in that it had the highest urban population in New France; in that regard its development was more vigorous than that of the most populous towns of the English colonies, undoubtedly because it was the colony's capital, the main port of entry, and an administrative and religious centre.

Québec's population had certain points in common with the rest of New France. Immigration had led to a preponderance of males. Although that eased in later years, in the 17th century there were always more men than women, both in Québec and in the rest of the colony. The imbalance affected the "marriage mart." In proportion to their numbers, women married earlier and more often than men since they were in such demand. However, the population was mainly composed of young and single persons.

Differences did exist between population trends in the town and in the colony. For example, its marriage rate and natural increase were lower than in the colony as a whole, which showed a lesser disproportion of males — and so proportionately more females — than the town. The colony at large had younger children and fewer single persons than the town. Population trends were quite different in town and country:

> *The town takes in more people than the country, but it loses more, too. Positive factors in population growth (births, immigration, internal migration) are more significant there than in the country; losses, though, through death or departure, are more frequent. It appears that the mixing of population was more intense in the towns in New France than in the country, as is typical of many other countries.*[70]

Most of the clergy of New France were found in Québec, although all four religious communities in town became less important in its population mix between 1666 and 1681. There were on the whole more women than men in the religious population, for the female communities were very dynamic, much like the seminary, while the Jesuits' membership was declining. In comparison to 1666, Canadian-born members were becoming more numerous by 1681.

Unlike most of the lay population, the religious tended to form complex households having numerous domestic servants and lodgers. Analysis of lay households between 1666 and 1681 shows a drop in the number of people living alone, and the most common household size decreased from 4 to 2 or 3 persons. Great disparities among households appeared along socio-professional lines, but in both 1666 and 1681 the average number of persons to a household was 5.5.

In general, examination of population distribution reinforces the view that a household is larger if the wealth and social position of the head of the family are greater. Between 1666 and 1681 two salient points emerged: the number of children increased and the number of domestic servants dropped sharply. In contrast to the 1666 situation, servants were in 1681 more frequently found in the houses of merchants and those in the liberal professions.

The labour-force study shows how little Québec trades diversified from 1666 to 1681 and reveals the decrease of workers in all categories between these years. It also points up the importance of indentured workers and domestic servants, especially in the 1666 census, when workers in these categories plied a great variety of trades. Not only had their numbers greatly decreased by 1681, but they then seldom practised any trade other than as apprentices.

When the last nominal census was taken, certain labour-market differences could be detected between Upper Town and Lower Town. In Upper Town, building tradesmen were best represented, whereas Lower Town had mainly merchants and ironworkers. In addition, the number and diversity of trades was stronger in Lower Town, whose population was also larger than Upper Town's.

Examining the labour force available to the house-building trade shows that there were skilled workers in Québec and large differences between the various trades' activity levels. We have looked at certain categories of workman within these trades, studied a few exceptional careers, and seen that there were entrepreneurs in the housing sector. Also, Québec was a magnet for the regional economy, and indeed it drove the economies of the adjoining seigneuries by providing an outlet for their materials and workers. Through its craftsmen who took on apprentices, the town even contributed to the training of specialized workers.

CONCLUSION

Québec is an example of how urbanization proceeds in a colonial context. It was similar in concept to cities and towns in France despite the fact that it lacked a defensive wall. However, from a legal standpoint Québec did not evolve as French cities did. It was established at a time when the kings of France were seeking control over the kingdom's cities; as a result, it experienced only a brief period of independent aldermanic government.

A new town on a new continent, Québec was born of the desire of the Compagnie des Cents-Associés to found an urban centre in New France. It was first a company town, but fell under royal jurisdiction during the second half of the 17th century.

Government was omnipresent. The colonial government was generally responsible for the town's administration, but this did not preclude the establishment of what were actually municipal controlling structures. France played a key role, either through the king and the minister of the Marine or through the trading companies despite an attempt at centralization. The law officials also had a role to play in the town's government, and there was a hierarchical division of power and responsibility and the establishment of offices and institutions with very specific duties, such as those of the *grand voyer*. However, true power lay in the hands of the intendant, the Conseil Souverain, and the Prévôté, in that order.

Urban development in Québec followed the rules of the seigneurial system, as the capital of New France was a *censive*, later made part of the royal domain. City administrators implemented notions of town planning prevalent in France during the 17th century and put forward various urban-development projects in attempts to solve the problem of crowding in Lower Town. Almost all of the land grants in the town were made before 1660. Changes in the urban landscape provide a clear picture of the town's latent energy, particularly evident in the building contracts, with their trend towards better housing. Half-timbered construction gave way to stone construction, with increases in house size and storeys.

Demographic and labour-force analyses are essential factors in all urban studies. Cities reflect their inhabitants and in that sense Québec was a colonial creation. Immigration was controlled and depended on France. Québec's population was mainly made up of a disproportionate number of young single men. Study of the town's households and labour force reveals the gradual aging of the town, as witnessed by, among other points, a reduction in the number of servants and the lack of diversification of trades. Workers involved in residential construction followed several trades and showed behavioural differences according to trade.

This study of urbanization to better understand the town's dynamics turned out to be complex. Québec was by turns an administrative capital, a merchant city, and a religious and military centre. It was a hub of interrelated activities. One notices numerous differences between Upper and Lower Town in regard to land use and subdivision, evolution of residential housing, distribution of the labour force and various trades, and demography. Lower Town was more densely populated and therefore featured a larger number of concessions, construction contracts, and houses than Upper Town. Growth in these areas went hand in hand with the increase in population and in the number of households. Québec was in fact composed of two towns that were in many respects dissimilar.

Some urban problems were related to demography and population distribution. The concentration of merchants in Lower Town led to crowding. The existence of a transient population brought about the prostitution and begging that afflicted the town. Prostitution was also due to the disproportionately high male population. Bylaws dealt mainly with trades between 1663 and 1690; those governing servants were confined to a specific period and disappeared completely after 1676, undoubtedly due to the drop in the number of servants between the censuses of 1666 and 1681. The number of bylaws governing trade must be viewed in relation to the preponderance of merchants among tradesmen and the need to regulate supply within the town.

A few general conclusions can be drawn from the various subjects dealt with in this book. Colonial and "municipal" authorities practised a form of state intervention and tried to standardize residents' attitudes or behaviour. This intervention can be seen not only in bylaws, but also in the granting of concessions, the road alignments that the *grand voyer* decreed, the implementation of town planning, and the ordinances governing marriage; however, it encountered some resistance from residents who, in a few instances, flouted the bylaws.

Québec's development followed a different path from that of other towns in the colony. It constituted a supply and services centre for all of New France and consequently drained part of the colony's energies. The town had its own society, with various classes and a ruling elite made up of senior government officials, merchants, and prosperous craftsmen, and including the most important families, who owned the biggest houses.

Québec was, without doubt, unique in New France. At various times and in various respects it was the colony's crossroads: administrative, religious, demographic, etc. Later, compared to other towns in the colony, it became a vanguard of town planning in New France, reflecting the image of French cities and towns of the day. Québec completely illustrates urban complexity where nothing is static, where all changes.

Jacques-René de Brisay de Denonville
Archives du Séminaire de Québec, album 5G

Alexandre de Prouville de Tracy
National Archives of Canada, C-12177

J.-B. Colbert, marquis de Seignelay
National Archives of Canada, C-09627

Daniel de Rémy de Courcelle
National Archives of Canada, C-10684

Jean-Baptiste Colbert
Musée du Louvre, Paris

Jean Talon
Monastère des Augustines de l'Hôtel-Dieu, Québec

Appendix A
PRINCIPAL ADMINISTRATORS OF THE COLONY AND TOWN OF QUÉBEC, 1660–1690

1. **Secrétaires d'État à la Marine**
   - Jean-Baptiste Colbert, 1669–83
   - Jean-Baptiste Colbert, marquis de Seignelay, 1683–90, son of the above
   - Louis Phélypeaux, comte de Pontchartrain, 1690–99

2. **Governors**
   - Pierre de Voyer d'Argenson, 1657–61
   - Pierre Dubois Davaugour, 1661–63
   - Augustin de Saffray de Mézy, 1663–65
   - Daniel de Rémy de Courcelle, 1665–72
   - Louis de Buade de Frontenac et de Palluau, 1672–82, 1689–98
   - Joseph-Antoine Le Febvre de La Barre, 1682–85
   - Jacques-René de Brisay de Denonville, 1685–89

   Between 1665 and 1667 the government of New France was entrusted to Lieutenant-General Alexandre de Prouville de Tracy.

3. **Intendants**
   - Louis Robert de Fortel, appointed 21 March 1663 but never came to Canada
   - Jean Talon, in office from 1665 to 1668 and from 1670 to 1672
   - Claude de Boutroue d'Aubigny, 1668–70
   - Jacques Duchesneau de La Doussinière et d'Ambault, 1675–82
   - Jacques Demeulle, 1682–86
   - Jean Bochart de Champigny, 1686–1702

   Between 1672 and 1675 there was no intendant to replace Talon; Frontenac governed the colony alone.

4. **Prévôté of Québec**

   A. Lieutenants-general
      - Louis-Théandre Chartier de Lotbinière, 1 May 1666 to 25 October 1677
      - René-Louis Chartier de Lotbinière, 1 May 1677 to 1 June 1703

B. *Procureurs du roi*
- Jean-Baptiste Peuvret Demesnu, 5 May 1666 until 1675. (Up to 1674 Demesnu was also *procureur fiscal*.)
- Louis Boulduc, 15 April 1676 until he was suspended on 28 April 1681
- Pierre Duquet de la Chesnaye, substitute in 1675–76 and 1681–86
- Paul Dupuy de Lisloye, 17 October 1686 until his appointment as *lieutenant particulier* in 1695

C. *Greffiers*
- Gilles Rageot, 5 May 1666 to 3 January 1692
- François Genaple de Bellefonds, 1685 to 24 May 1686

5. *Grands voyers*
- René Robinau de Bécancour, 1657; 29 March 1667 to 24 May 1689
- Pierre Robinau de Bécancour, son of preceding, 24 May 1689 to 1729
- François Genaple de Bellefonds, clerk to the *grand voyer* June 1685 to 6 October 1709

Appendix B
METHODOLOGY USED IN ANALYSING CONSTRUCTION CONTRACTS

During the period from 1660 to 1690, a total of 516 contracts were drawn up for the town of Québec. I kept 229, rejecting 287 that did not reflect private housing construction in Québec.[1] The contracts chosen for the analysis are of three kinds, corresponding to the three main stages of construction: masonry, carpentry, and roofing. Work that might indicate erection of or repairs or additions to houses or other buildings (shops, sheds, warehouses) as distinct entities are included among these kinds of contracts.

Although the term "masonry" does refer to any construction made of stone held together by mortar or to part of a work,[2] the masonry category only includes those contracts specifying the use of masonry, in whole or in part, in building either a house or other structure. To use certain expressions from the "Inventaire des marchés de construction des Archives nationales à Québec, XVIIe et XVIIIe siècles," I looked at only those contracts where the artisans undertook to "do the masonry work of a house" or "to build a house of stone or using *colombage pierroté*." Work done on common walls was omitted as being difficult to analyse adequately, especially within the framework of the defined goal. A common wall is common to two buildings and it was therefore impossible to incorporate that sort of thing into the general data. Some figures (number of contracts, dimensions, and so forth) would have been duplicated, skewing the total statistics. Contracts whose sole object was chimney construction were also passed over.

Under the heading of frame, a general term used when talking about part of the roof or walls of a house, are grouped contracts for building houses made of wood and half-timbering.[3] This category includes contracts for the roof, an essential part of a house frame. All woodworking and carpentry contracts were kept for the analysis except those having to do with both outside (shutters, galleries, porches) and inside finishing. Roofing posed no problem as to definition, and I considered only the roof itself and the materials used in it.

How valid is the sample represented by these contracts, and how far do they reflect housing construction activity in Québec? They do not represent the total number of houses built in Québec from 1660 to 1690, more especially because of the under-registration of the contracts reviewed in the "Inventaire." For example, not all contracts written under private seal were listed. For the 229 contracts analysed, the statistics shown in Chapter III concern the building of houses in 87.8 per cent of all cases; only 13 contracts (5.7 per cent) have to do with the erection of different structures (shops, etc.) and 15 contracts (6.6 per cent) deal with house repairs or additions.

Appendix C
DEMOGRAPHY AND THE LABOUR FORCE: RESEARCH AND METHODOLOGY

Between 1660 and 1690 the census was taken five times in Canada (1666, 1667, 1681, 1685, and 1688), the first three being nominal lists. To study the population of the town and of the colony, only three censuses were used: those of 1666, 1681, and 1688. The 1667 census was not considered because it did not cover the same territory of the town as the 1666 census.[1] The other two that were used allowed analysis of the growth of the town and New France at given times.

Microfilmed originals of the 1666 and 1681 Québec censuses were studied as well as data published by the Université de Montréal research team on historical demography.[2] Several works were also consulted to outline short biographies of each individual listed, to rectify dates of birth, and to eliminate errors and duplicate entries.[3] Even at that, the final statistics do not match those of some demographers.[4]

Population figures for Québec in 1688 and for the colony at the time of the three censuses come from *Recensements du Canada 1665 à 1871*.[5] The statistics for 1666 concern households, population, sex, marital status, age groups, age versus marital status, professions, and trades. The king's troops were not counted in that census, and the absence of some 30 ecclesiastical and religious people, four of whom resided in Québec, was noted. Moreover, the category "professions and trades" excluded clergy, nobility, civil servants, and farmers. The 1681 census had the same categories as the one for 1666; however, to the latter were added the number of *arpents* under cultivation and the number of animals. It did not include Amerindians nor coureurs de bois. The 1688 census did not give the number of households and mentioned just two age groups: over and under 15 years of age for men, over and under 12 years of age for women. It also gave information on the number of houses, land clearings, crops, and cattle, and it did distinguish between the French and indigenous populations.

The *Recensements du Canada 1665 à 1871* is an imperfect source. In 1666, for example, the population of the colony was overestimated by 1.0 per cent when 33 people were counted twice, and it was underestimated by 11.1 per cent because 397 individuals were not put on the census rolls. That is why the figures given for the colony in the different tables in Chapter IV must only be used as indications. They do not at all reflect any absolute mathematical precision, simply an idea of the colony's demographic evolution, thus making it possible to make certain comparisons with Québec.[6]

Appendix D
RAW DATA BY SOCIO-PROFESSIONAL CATEGORY 1666 CENSUS

1. Clergy

A. Men

- 2 households
- 25 *religieux* and 1 clerk
- 13 servants (8 with trades)
- 20 boarders and 8 lay brothers

- Total: 67 persons

B. Women

- 2 households
- 35 *religieuses*
- 15 servants (3 with trades)
- 24 boarders and others

- Total: 74 persons

2. Liberal Professions

A. Senior civil servants

- 4 households
- 4 married couples
- 19 children (4.75 per household)
- 7 servants (3 with trades; 1.75 per household)

- Total: 34 persons (8.5 per household)
- 1 widower living alone

B. Notaries, surgeons, surveyors, teachers

- 2 households
- 2 married couples
- 6 servants (1 with a trade; 3.0 per household)

- Total: 10 persons (5.0 per household)
- 1 bachelor living alone

3. Businesspeople and Shopkeepers

A. Tavernkeepers and merchants

- 16 households
- 13 married couples, 2 widowers, 1 not known

- 25 children (1.6 per household)
- 35 servants (9 with trades; 2.2 per household)
- 5 relatives

- Total: 93 persons (6.0 per household)
- 1 married man and 2 bachelors living alone

B. Food trades
- 2 households
- 2 married couples
- 1 child (0.5 per household)
- 3 servants (2 with trades; 1.5 per household)

- Total: 8 persons (4.0 per household)
- 2 bachelors living alone

4. Craftsmen

A. Art and luxury trades: none

B. Clothing trades
- 1 household
- 1 married couple

- Total: 2 persons (2.0)
- 1 married man and 2 bachelors living alone

C. Woodworking and furniture trades
- 6 households
- 6 married couples
- 12 children (2.0 per household)

- Total: 24 persons (4.0 per household)
- 2 married men living alone

D. Leatherworking trades
- 2 households
- 2 married couples
- 1 child (0.5 per household)
- 1 servant (0.5 per household)

- Total: 6 persons (3.0 per household)

- 1 bachelor living alone

E. Construction trades
- 3 households
- 3 married couples
- 11 children (3.7 per household)
- 3 servants (1 with a trade; 1.0 per household)

- Total: 20 persons (6.7 per household)
- 1 widower and 1 bachelor living alone

F. Ironworking trades
- 8 households
- 8 married couples
- 19 children (2.4 per household)
- 1 boarder
- 8 servants (4 with trades; 1.0 per household)

- Total: 44 persons (5.5 per household)
- 1 widower and 6 bachelors living alone

G. Miscellaneous
- 1 bachelor living alone

5. **Salaried Workers**

A. Labourers
- 3 households
- 3 married couples
- 10 children (3.3 per household)
- 1 servant (0.33 per household)

- Total: 17 persons (5.7 per household)
- 9 bachelors living alone

B. Clerks and officeholders
- 3 households
- 3 married couples
- 13 children (4.3 per household)
- 6 servants (2.0 per household)

- Total: 25 persons (8.3 per household)
- 1 bachelor living alone

6. **Military:** none

7. **Not known**
- 17 households
- 9 married couples, 7 widowers, 1 not known
- 34 children (2.0 per household)
- 25 servants (2 with trades; 1.5 per household)
- 3 relatives

- Total: 88 persons (5.2 per household)
- 1 widower and 1 married man living alone

Totals (religious excepted)
- 67 households (56 married couples, 9 widowers, 2 not known)
- 145 children
- 95 servants (22 with trades, or 23% of the total)
- 9 relatives and others

- Total: 371 persons
- 35 persons living alone (26 bachelors, 5 married men, and 4 widowers)

Averages per household
- 2.2 children
- 1.4 servants
- 0.1 relative or other
- 5.5 persons

Clergy
- 4 households
- 60 *religieux* and *religieuses*
- 1 clerk
- 28 servants (11 with trades, or 39%)
- 52 boarders and others

- Total: 141 persons

Grand Total
- 71 households
- 145 children
- 61 relatives and others
- 123 servants (33 with trades, or 27% of the total)

- Total: 512 persons
- 35 persons living alone

Notes
"Servants" includes household help as such, indentured servants and those not indentured.
Persons living alone are not considered households.

Appendix E
RAW DATA BY SOCIO-PROFESSIONAL CATEGORY 1681 CENSUS

1. **Clergy**

   A. Men
   - 2 households
   - 40 *religieux*
   - 28 servants (3 with trades)
   - 23 boarders and lay brothers

   - Total: 91 persons

   B. Women
   - 2 households
   - 54 *religieuses*
   - 28 servants and 1 maid serving someone other than the *religieuses*
   - 24 boarders, Indian women and others

   - Total: 107 persons

2. **Liberal Professions**

   A. Senior civil servants
   - 14 households
   - 11 married couples, 2 widows, 1 bachelor
   - 51 children (3.9 average over 13 households)
   - 19 servants (1.4 average over 14 households)
   - 5 relatives and others
   - 6 not known

   - Total: 106 persons (7.6 per household)

   B. Notaries, surgeons, surveyors, teachers
   - 5 households
   - 4 married couples, 1 widower
   - 14 children (2.8 per household)
   - 6 servants (1.2 per household, including 1 apprentice and 1 clerk)
   - 2 not known

   - Total: 33 persons (6.6 per household)

3. **Businesspeople and Shopkeepers**

   A. Tavernkeepers and merchants
      - 22 households
      - 17 married couples, 3 widows, 1 widower, 1 bachelor
      - 60 children (2.9 average over 21 households)
      - 31 servants (1.4 per household)
      - 4 relatives and others
      - 1 not known

      - Total: 135 persons (6.1 per household)
      - 3 bachelors and 6 unknown persons living alone

   B. Food trades
      - 6 households
      - 5 married couples, 1 widower
      - 16 children (2.7 per household)
      - 2 servants (0.33 per household)

      - Total: 29 persons (4.8 per household)
      - 1 widower and 2 unknown persons living alone

4. **Craftsmen**

   A. Art and luxury trades
      - 1 household
      - 1 married couple
      - 1 child

      - Total: 3 persons

   B. Clothing trades
      - 9 households
      - 9 married couples
      - 31 children (3.4 per household)
      - 2 servants (0.2 per household)
      - 1 relative or other

      - Total: 52 persons (5.8 per household)
      - 3 bachelors living alone

   C. Woodworking and furniture trades
      - 15 households
      - 13 married couples, 1 widower, 1 not known
      - 38 children (2.5 per household)
      - 1 servant (0.07 per household)
      - 6 relatives and others

      - Total: 73 persons (4.9 per household)
      - 1 unknown person living alone

D. Leatherworking trades
- 3 households
- 3 married couples
- 5 children (1.7 per household)

- Total: 11 persons (3.7 per household)
- 1 unknown person living alone

E. Construction trades
- 14 households
- 14 married couples
- 33 children (2.4 per household)
- 1 servant (0.07 per household)

- Total: 62 persons (4.4 per household)
- 2 bachelors and 1 widower living alone

F. Ironworking trades
- 18 households
- 16 married couples, 1 widower, 1 not known
- 58 children (3.2 per household)
- 6 servants (0.33 per household, 6 apprentices)
- 7 relatives and others
- 1 not known

- Total: 106 persons (5.5 per household)
- 1 bachelor living alone

G. Miscellaneous
- 2 households
- 2 married couples
- 9 children (4.5 per household)
- 1 relative or other

- Total: 14 persons (7.0 per household)
- 1 bachelor living alone

5. Salaried Workers

A. Labourers
- 4 households
- 4 married couples
- 9 children (2.3 per household)
- 1 servant (0.25 per household)

- Total: 18 persons (4.5 per household)
- 6 unknown persons and 1 bachelor living alone

B. Clerks and officeholders
   - 10 households
   - 10 married couples
   - 40 children (4.0 per household)
   - 2 servants (0.2 per household)

   - Total: 62 persons (6.2 per household)
   - 1 unknown person and 1 bachelor living alone

6. Military
- 6 households
- 6 married couples
- 9 children (1.5 per household)
- 2 servants (0.33 per household)
- 1 not known

- Total: 24 persons (4.0 per household)

7. Not Known
- 55 households
- 41 married couples, 8 widows, 4 widowers, 1 bachelor, and 1 not known
- 155 children (2.8 per household)
- 14 servants (0.25 per household)
- 3 relatives and others
- 3 not known

- Total: 271 persons (4.9 per household)
- 7 bachelors, 1 widower and 8 unknown persons living alone

Totals (religious excepted)
- 184 households (156 married couples, 22 widowed, 4 bachelors, 2 not known)
- 529 children
- 87 servants
- 27 relatives and others
- 14 not known

- Total: 999 persons
- 47 persons living alone (19 bachelors, 3 widowers, 25 not known)

Averages per household
- 2.9 children
- 0.5 servant
- 0.2 relative or other
- 0.1 not known
- 5.4 persons

Clergy
- 4 households
- 94 *religieux* and *religieuses*
- 56 servants (3 with trades) plus 1 maid
- 47 boarders and others

- Total: 198 persons

Grand total
- 188 households
- 529 children
- 74 relatives and others
- 143 servants and 1 maid serving a lay person
- 14 not known

- Total: 1197 persons
- 47 persons living alone

Notes

"Servants" includes apprentices.

Persons living alone are not considered households.

The garrison, the governor's house, and the intendant's house are not included in these data.

List of Abbreviations

ANC	Archives nationales, France. Fonds des colonies.
ANQQ	Archives nationales du Québec à Québec
ANSOM	Archives nationales, France. Section Outre-Mer.
APT	*APT Bulletin: The Association for Preservation Technology/Association pour la préservation et ses techniques*
ASQ	Archives du Séminaire de Québec
BRH	*Bulletin des recherches historiques*
CHR	*Canadian Historical Review*
DBC	*Dictionnaire biographique du Canada*
DFC	Dépôt des fortifications des colonies
NA	National Archives of Canada
NF	Nouvelle-France
PUF	Presses universitaires de France
PUL	Presses de l'Université Laval
PUM	Presses de l'Université de Montréal
RAPQ	*Rapport de l'archiviste de la province de Québec*
RHAF	*Revue d'histoire de l'Amérique française*

ENDNOTES

Introduction

1 Quebec (Province), Législature, *Jugements et délibérations du Conseil Souverain de la Nouvelle-France* (Québec: A. Côté and Joseph Dussault, 1885–91) (hereafter cited as *Jugements et délibérations*), Vol. 2, pp. 56, 58–59, 542–43.
2 Ibid., p. 860.
3 Gaston Bardet, *L'urbanisme* (Paris: PUF, 1977), pp. 5–7, 18–19.

Chapter I
The Concept of *Ville*

1 Yvon Desloges, "L'étude du passé urbain et ses nombreuses approches; un bilan historique," *Bulletin de recherches*, No. 197, Parks Canada, Ottawa, June 1983.
2 Jacqueline Beaujeu-Garnier and Georges Chabot, *Traité de géographie urbaine* (Paris: Librairie Armand Colin, 1963), p. 30.
3 Ibid.; Arnold Whittick, ed., *Encyclopedia of Urban Planning* (New York: McGraw-Hill, 1974). For an assessment of the terms "urban" and "rural" on the basis of population and density criteria, *see* Pierre George, *Précis de géographie urbaine* (Paris: PUF, 1974), pp. 11–16, and Arthur E. Smailes, *The Geography of Towns* (Chicago: Aldine Publishing, 1968), p. 34ff.
4 Jacqueline Beaujeu-Garnier and Georges Chabot, op. cit., p. 104.
5 Georges Duby and Jacques Le Goff, eds., *Histoire de la France urbaine* (Paris: Seuil, 1980), Vol. 2, La ville médiévale. Des Carolingiens à la Renaissance, p. 23.
6 Regarding the creation of the office of intendant, *see* Maurice Bordes, "Les intendants de province aux XVIIe et XVIIIe siècles," *L'information historique*, Vol. 30, No. 3 (May–June 1968), pp. 107–20.
7 In this section on the legal evolution of the concept of *ville* in France, I drew heavily on Charles Petit-Dutaillis, *Les communes françaises. Caractères et évolution des origines au XVIIIe siècle* (Paris: Albin Michel, 1970), passim.
8 Pierre Chaunu and Richard Gascon, "La France du mouvement: Les commerces et les villes," in Fernand Braudel and Ernest Labrousse, *Histoire économique et sociale de la France* (Paris: PUF, 1977), Tome 1: De 1450 à 1660, Vol. 1: L'état et la ville, p. 408.
9 Antoine Furetière, *Dictionnaire universel, Contenant généralement tous les Mots François tant vieux que modernes, & les Termes des Sciences et des Arts* (The Hague: Arnoud and Reinier Leers, 1701), Vol. 3, s.v. "ville."
10 Jean-Claude Perrot, *Genèse d'une ville moderne, Caen au XVIIIe siècle* (Paris and The Hague: Mouton & Co. and École des Hautes Études en sciences sociales, 1975), Vol. 1, pp. 29–37.
11 Pierre Goubert, *L'Ancien régime* (Paris: Librairie Armand Colin, 1973), Vol. 1: La société, p. 166.
12 Fernand Braudel, *Civilisation matérielle et capitalisme (XVe–XVIIIe siècle)*(Paris: Armand Colin, 1967), Vol. 1, p. 378.
13 Ibid., p. 370; Pierre Goubert, op. cit., p. 171.
14 Pierre Goubert, op. cit., pp. 165–79. Regarding the *société d'ordre* and social class, *see also* Roland Mousnier, *Les hiérarchies sociales de 1450 à nos jours* (Paris: PUF, 1969), pp. 30–35, 60–82.
15 Marcel Trudel, *Histoire de la Nouvelle-France* (Montréal: Fides, 1966), Vol. 2, Le comptoir, 1604–1627 (hereafter cited as Le Comptoir), p. 253. Regarding Québec's founding, *see also* Marcel Trudel, *Les débuts du régime seigneurial au Ca-*

nada (Montréal: Fides, 1974) (hereafter cited as *Les débuts du régime seigneurial*).

16 Antoine Furetière, op. cit., Vol. 2, s.v. "habitation."

17 Lucien Campeau, *Les Cents-Associés et le peuplement de la Nouvelle-France (1633–1663)* (Montréal: Éditions Bellarmin, 1974) (hereafter cited as *Les Cents-Associés*), p. 20. Unlike this historian, I was unable to establish with precision the date the site of the town was selected.

18 Jesuits, *Relation des Jésuites* (Montréal: Éditions du Jour, 1972), Vol. 1, p. 41.

19 ANC, F^3, Vol. 3, fol. 135–135v, 15 Jan. 1637, "Concession faite par la Compagnie de la Nouvelle france à Maître Jean de Beauvais Commissaire de la Marine pour l'établissement et dotation d'une Maison de Religieuses à Quebek." The designated site for the town of Québec was frequently mentioned in documents prior to 1660.

20 Marcel Trudel, *Les débuts du régime seigneurial*, pp. 82–87. Similar land reclamation took place in Montréal from 1648 onwards and in Trois-Rivières from 1649 onwards.

21 Regarding Montmagny's plan, *see* Marc Lafrance, "Évolution physique et politiques urbaines: Québec sous le régime français," *Revue d'histoire urbaine/Urban History Review*, année 1975, No. 3 (Feb. 1976), pp. 3–22. Definitions of town plans can be found in Jean Gottmann, "Plans de villes des deux côtés de l'Atlantique," *Mélanges géographiques canadiens offerts à Raoul Blanchard* (Québec: PUL, 1959), pp. 237–42.

22 The following refer to some uses of the possessive: ANC, B, Vol. 4, fol. 64–64v, 4 June 1672, "Lettre du Roy à Mr Talon Sur le Sujet des Volontaires du Canada"; ibid., Vol. 7, fol. 180–180v, 12 May 1678, "Ordonnance pour lentretenement d'Un garde magasin, d'Un armurier, et dun canonier dans la Ville de Quebek"; ibid., Vol. 8, fols. 44–45, 29 May 1680, "Arrest pour la confirmation des concessions accordées par Mrs de Frontenac et Duchesneau depuis le XIj^e^ octobre 1676. jusques au 6e septembre 1679."

23 ANC, F^3, Vol. 4, fol. 109v, 23 March 1673, "Reglement de Police, fait par M. Le Comte de frontenac gouverneur Et Lieutenant général pour Le Roy en Canada."

24 Ibid., fol. 110ff., and "Permission donnée par M. de Frontenac aux échevins de Québec de faire bâtir des étaux et boutiques le long des murs du magasin du roi (15 avril 1673)," in Quebec (Province), Archives, *Ordonnances, commissions, etc., etc., des gouverneurs et des intendants de la Nouvelle-France, 1639–1706*, (Beauceville: L'Éclaireur, 1924) (hereafter cited as *Ordonnances, commissions*), Vol. 1, pp. 141–43.

25 Regarding the inhabitants' privileges, *see*, for example, "règlement sur le commerce de la Nouvelle-France dressé par M. de Meulles et accepté par le Conseil Souverain (21 février 1683)" in Quebec (Province), Archives, *Ordonnances, commissions*, Vol. 2, pp. 12–16.

26 On this *see* Jeanne Garnier's request to the Conseil Souverain on 20 March 1684, in Quebec (Province), Législature, *Jugements et délibérations*, Vol. 2, pp. 937–39. Another concept typical of the 17th century maintained that craftsmen constituted "the most solid foundation of cities and towns"; *see* ANC, $C^{11}A$, Vol. 7, fols. 121–122v, "Placet des habitants de Montréal à Denonville," 30 Oct. 1685.

27 André Charbonneau, Yvon Desloges, and Marc Lafrance, *Québec; ville fortifiée du XVIIe au XIXe siècle* (Québec: Éditions du Pélican and Parks Canada, 1982), pp. 22–31.

28 Marcel Trudel, *Le terrier du Saint-Laurent en 1663* (Ottawa: Éditions de l'Université d'Ottawa, 1973) (hereafter cited as *Le terrier du Saint-Laurent*), p. 157; "Mandement au sujet du retranchement et de l'institution de quelques fêtes," in H. Têtu and C.-O. Gagnon, eds., *Mandements, lettres pastorales et circulaires des évêques de Québec* (Québec: A. Côté, 1887), Vol. 1, p. 71.

29 Traditional historiography blames the failure of the aldermanic system in New France on the inhabitants' lack of participation in the colony's administration and on the absolutist practices of Louis XIV and Colbert. In the case of cities and towns, royal policy in urban matters and the practice of administrative trusteeship, which had continued since the reign of Louis XII, obviously explain the aldermanic system's failure and the lack of popular participation in government decision-making.

30 Roland Mousnier, "Paris, capitale politique au Moyen Age et dans les temps modernes (environ 1200 à 1789)," in Roland Mousnier, *La plume, la faucille et le marteau. Institutions et société en France du Moyen Age à la Révolution* (Paris: PUF, 1970), p. 95.

Chapter II
The Administration of the Town of Québec

1 *See*, among others, Gustave Lanctôt, *L'administration de la Nouvelle-France* (Montréal: Éditions du Jour, 1971) (hereafter cited as *L'administration de la Nouvelle-France)*, and André Vachon, *L'administration de la Nouvelle-France, 1627-1760* (Québec: PUL, 1970) (hereafter cited as *L'administration de la Nouvelle-France*).

2 For an examination of the scope of royal power, *see* Pierre Goubert, op. cit., Vol. 2: Les pouvoirs, pp. 21–40. On the rise of absolutism, *see* Hubert Méthivier, *Le siècle de Louis XIV* (Paris: PUF, 1975), pp. 50ff., and Jean Brissaud, *A History of French Public Law* (London: John Murray, 1915), pp. 388–90.

3 R. La Rocque de Roquebrune, "La direction de la Nouvelle-France par le Ministère de la Marine," *RHAF*, Vol. 5, No. 4 (March 1953), p. 474.

4 Quebec (Province), Assemblée législative, *Édits, ordonnances royaux, déclarations et arrêts du Conseil d'État concernant le Canada* (Québec: E.-R. Fréchette, 1854–56) (hereafter cited as *Édits, ordonnances*), Vol. 1, p. 33; ANC, B, Vol. 4, fols. 67–69; ANC, C^{11}A, Vol. 5, fols. 101–105v, 9 May 1679. This decree mentions the order given to Duchesneau in 1675 to revoke half of any lands that had been granted but had not been cleared for cultivation for over ten years.

5 ANC, B, Vol. 1, fol. 127, 10 May 1669; ibid., Vol. 7, fols. 41v and 45–45v, 20 May 1676.

6 ANC, F^3, Vol. 5, fols. 244–45, 10 June 1679. The definition given for *papiers terriers* is based on Richard Colebrook Harris, *The Seigneurial System in Early Canada: A Geographical Study* (Madison: Univ. of Wisconsin, 1968), p. 229.

7 ANQQ, NF25, pièce No. 150½, 7 Oct. 1682.

8 ANC, B, Vol. 6, fol. 30, Colbert to Frontenac, 17 May 1674; ibid., Vol. 7, fol. 77–77v, Colbert to Duchesneau, 28 April 1677; ibid., Vol. 1, fol. 80v, mémoire from the king to Talon, 27 March 1665; ibid., Vol. 6, mémoire from the king to Duchesneau, 7 June 1675; ANC, C^{11}A, Vol. 3, fol. 218-218v, "Arrêt pour les Réglements de police et l'Etablisseme.[t] des Juges du Canada," 4 June 1672.

9 ANC, B, Vol. 13, fol. 163, mémoire from the king to Denonville, 30 March 1687.

10 *See* analysis of the charter granted to the Compagnie des Cents-Associés in J. Delalande, *Le Conseil Souverain de la Nouvelle-France* (Québec: Ls-A. Proulx, 1927), pp. 21–26.

11 ANC, C^{11}A, Vol. 1, fol. 241v; Gustave Lanctôt, *Histoire du Canada* (Montréal: Librairie Beauchemin, 1964), Vol. 1, Des origines au régime royal, pp. 279–82.

12 André Vachon, *L'administration de la Nouvelle-France*, pp. 19–23; NA, MG5, B1, Vol. 4, fols. 522–23, "Arrêt portant règlement de la conduite qui doit être tenue pour la traite des pelleteries de la Nouvelle-France," 13 May 1659.

13 Quebec (Province), Assemblée législative, *Édits, ordonnances*, Vol. 1, pp. 30–32, "Délibération de la Compagnie de la Nouvelle-France pour l'abandon du Canada à Sa Majesté très chrétienne," "Abandon et démission du Canada au roi par la Compagnie de la Nouvelle-France," 24 Feb. 1663, and "Acceptation du roi de la démission de la Compagnie de la Nouvelle-France," March 1663.

14 Ibid., Vol. 1, pp. 40–48, "Etablissement de la Compagnie des Indes Occidentales"; ibid., Vol. 3, pp. 36–37, "Commission d'Agent-Général de la Compagnie des Indes Occidentales, pour M. Le Barroys, du 8e Avril 1665."

15 Quebec (Province), Archives, *Ordonnances, commissions*, Vol. 1, pp. 32–45, "Ordonnance de Mm. de Tracy, de Courcelles et Talon sur les demandes de M. Lebarroys, agent général de la Compagnie des Indes Occidentales (9 septembre 1666)."

16 The king authorized Tracy, Talon, and Courcelle to make these appointments and they did so. Later, in 1674, the company exercised its right and presented the councillors to the king; *see* Villeray's appointment on 3 Oct. 1674 in Quebec (Province), Législature, *Jugements et délibérations*, Vol. 1, pp. 859–62, and those of Lotbinière and D'Auteuil in ANQQ, NF12, Vol. 1, fol. 51–51v.

17 André Vachon, "La restauration de la Tour de Babel, ou 'La vie à Québec au milieu du XVIIe siècle,'" *RHAF*, Vol. 24, No. 2 (Sept. 1970) (hereafter cited as "La restauration de la Tour de Babel"), pp. 183–84; Émile Salone, *La colonisation de la Nouvelle-France, étude sur les origines de la nation canadienne-française* (Trois-Rivières: Boréal Express, 1970), p. 178.

18 Quebec (Province), Assemblée legislative, *Édits, ordonnances*, Vol. 3, pp. 86–88; Quebec (Province), Législature, *Jugements et délibérations*, Vol. 1, pp. 497–99, 594; ANQQ, NF12, tome 1, lettre A, 5 May 1666; Quebec (Province), Archives, *Inventaire des procès-verbaux des grands voyers conservés aux Archives de la Province de Québec ... par Pierre-Georges Roy* (Beauceville: L'Éclaireur, 1923–32) (hereafter cited as *Inventaire des procès-verbaux*), Vol. 5, pp. 141–43.

19 Quebec (Province), Assemblée législative, *Édits, ordonnances*, Vol. 1, pp. 74–78.

20 ANC, B, Vol. 11, fols. 83v–95, "Instruction que le Roy veut estre remise entre les mains du Sr Marquis de Denonville choisy par Sa Ma^{té} pour gouverneur et Son Lieutenent general en la nouvelle france," 10 March 1685; ibid., Vol. 7, fol. 45, "Lettres patentes portant pouvoir aux Srs Comte de Frontenac et du chesneau de conceder les terres du Canada," 20 May 1676.

21 Ibid., Vol. 7, fol. 30, "Lettre du roi à Frontenac," 15 April 1676.

22 ANC, C^{11}A, Vol. 6, fol. 242, Seignelay to La Barre, 10 April 1684. Regarding the formulation of bylaws, *see* ibid., Vol. 7, fols. 190–92, "Extrait des responses aux lettres receues de Canada," 18 Feb. 1687; with regard to the general role of the governor, *see* ANC, B, Vol. 15, fols. 85–98v, "Instruction pour le Sr Comte de Frontenac gouyerneur et Lieutenant g^{nâl} pour le Roy dans les Pays de la Domination de Sa Ma^{té} en l'Amerique septentrionalle," 7 June 1689.

23 ANC, B, Vol. 1, fols. 71–73v, "Pouvoir d'Intendant de la Justice police & finances en Canada pour le Sr Talon," 23 March 1665.

24 Ibid., fol. 127–127v, "Pouvoir d'Intendant de la Justice police et finances en Canada pour Mr Talon," 10 May 1669; Quebec (Province), Assemblée législative, *Édits, ordonnances*, Vol. 1, pp. 72–73, "Arrêt du Conseil d' État qui ordonne à M. Talon de faire des Réglements de Police," 4 June 1672.

25 The first signs of Talon's town-planning policy appeared in the creation of villages around Québec. The desired form of these *bourgs* reflected principles of appropriateness to the landscape and layouts advocated by theorists of his time. These villages were, in effect, created. Charlesbourg, for example, is square with radiating axes.

26 ANC, F^{3}, Vol. 4, fol. 116–116v, bylaws by Frontenac, 23 March 1673.

27 ANSOM, DFC, Amérique septentrionale, N^{o} d'ordre 374, procès-verbal of De Lajoue for changes in the water system for the Hôtel-Dieu, 8 Nov. 1708.

28 ANC, C^{11}A, Vol. 3, fol. 235–235v, mémoire from Frontenac to Colbert, 2 Nov. 1672.

29 ANC, F^{3}, Vol. 4, fols. 109–118v, 23 March 1673.

30 ANSOM, DFC, Amérique septentrionale, n° d'ordre 344, 1683.

31 ANC, B, Vol. 11, fol. 28v, Seignelay to Demeulle, 10 April 1684; ANC, C^{11}A, Vol. 6, fol. 412v, Demeulle to Seignelay, 12 Nov. 1684.

32 ANC, C^{11}A, Vol. 7, fol. 143, Demeulle to Seignelay, 28 Sept. 1685; ibid., Vol. 6, fol. 411, Demeulle to Seignelay, 12 Nov. 1684.

33 ANC, B, Vol. 11, fols. 95–100, the king to Demeulle, 10 March 1685.

34 ANC, C^{11}A, Vol. 7, fol. 145–145v, Demeulle to Seignelay, 28 Sept. 1685.

35 Ibid, Vol. 8, fol. 19v, Denonville to Seignelay, 8 May 1686; ibid., Vol. 10, fols. 11v–12, Denonville and Champigny to Seignelay, 6 Nov. 1688.

36 ANQQ, NF12, Vol. 2, fol. 25, concession of the location of the Lower Town battery to Denys de Vitré, 10 Sept. 1683; ibid., Vol. 2, fols. 49v–50v, concession of the location of the Lower Town battery to the Jesuits, 16 Sept. 1683.

37 ASQ, Polygraphie 19, No. 39, 22 Oct. 1683.

38 Noël Baillargeon, *Le Séminaire de Québec de 1685 à 1760* (Québec: PUL, 1977), Vol. 1, p. 21f.

39 ANQQ, greffe of Pierre Duquet, 11 Nov. 1683; ANQQ, NF1, chemise No. 10, 3rd document, 30 April 1684; ANQQ, NF10, cahier A, pièce No. 32, 2 June 1689.

40 ANC, E, carton No. 15, confirmation of a Lower Town concession to Claude Baillif, 31 May 1686.

41 ANC, C^{11}A, Vol. 7, fols. 240–42v, mémoire from the bourgeois of Lower Town to Seignelay, after 15 June 1685.

42 Quebec (Province), Archives, *Ordonnances, commissions,* Vol. 2, pp. 110–12, 8 June 1685; ANC, C^{11}A, Vol. 7, fols. 240–44v, after 15 June 1685.

43 ANC, C^{11}A, Vol. 7, fol. 105v, Denonville to Seignelay, 13 Nov. 1685.

44 ANC, B, Vol. 12, fol. 37v, mémoire from the king to Denonville, 31 May 1686, ANC, C^{11}A, Vol. 8, fol. 250v, Champigny to the minister, 16 Nov. 1686.

45 ANQQ, NF1, chemise No. 9, pièce No. 2, 3 Jan. 1673. The former concession and the expansion of 1673 are located on the present rue de l'Escalier, corner of côte de la Montagne.

46 NA, MG5, B1, Vol. 5-2, pp. 98–99, Frontenac to Colbert, 13 Nov. 1673; ANC, F^{3}, Vol. 4, fols. 114–115, 23 March 1673; ANQQ, NF12, Vol. 2, fol. 33, 20 June 1674.

47 Duchesneau's procès-verbal is reproduced in the text of the alignment of 12 May 1689; ANQQ, NF10, cahier A, pièce No. 27. The plan almost certainly resembles the one shown in Figure 26.

48 ANQQ, greffe of Genaple, 23 Feb. 1683.

49 Quebec (Province), Archives, *Ordonnances, commissions*, Vol. 2, pp. 174–78, 15 June 1688.

50 *See*, for example, the grant of a site on rue De Meulles to Gabriel Lemieux on 26 August 1658; ANQQ, NF25, pièce No. 38. The expression "a mesme retz de chaussée" simply requires that the alignment of the street or other buildings be respected.

51 ANQQ, NF4, cahier 3, fol. 27–27v, 5 April 1689.

52 Ibid., cahier 3, fol. 32, 25 April 1689; ANQQ, NF10, cahier A, pièce No. 28, 13 May 1689.

53 Quebec (Province), Législature, *Jugements et délibérations*, Vol. 2, p. 638, 16 Aug. 1681; Quebec (Province), Archives, *Ordonnances, commissions*, Vol. 2, pp. 45–46, 28 Aug. 1683.

54 ANC, B, Vol. 11, fol. 14, Seignelay to La Barre, 10 April 1684; ANC, C^{11}A, Vol. 7, fol. 192, "articles a adjouster a l'instruction du Gouverneur," 18 Feb. 1685.

55 This was true of Denonville and Frontenac. On the former, *see* ANC, B, Vol. 11, fol. 95, 10 March 1685; on the latter, ibid., Vol. 15, fol. 98v, 7 June 1689.

56 These were only some of the duties of an *intendant de marine. See* "Code des armées navales, ou recueil des édits, déclarations, ordonnances et règlemens, sur le fait de la marine du roi, Depuis le commencement du regne de Louis XIV, jusques & y compris l'Ordonnance de 1689, conférés avec les Ordonnances postérieures sous le même regne & sous celui de Louis XV, jusques en 1757," reproduced in Vol. 3 of Richebourg and Boismeslé, *Histoire generale de la marine, contenant Son origine chez tous les Peuples du monde, Ses progrès, Son état actuel, & les Expéditions Maritimes, anciennes et modernes* (Paris: Antoine Boudet, 1758) (hereafter cited as "Code des armées navales"), pp. 70–72.

57 ANC, F^3, Vol. 6, fols. 43–44, 21 Sept. 1683; ibid., fols. 48–49, 16 Oct. 1683.

58 ANC, C^{11}A, Vol. 2, fol. 160, 3 Nov. 1665; ANC, F^3, Vol. 4, fol. 117–117v, 23 March 1673; ANC, C^{11}A, Vol. 11, fol. 196, 15 March 1691, and Vol. 20, fol. 70–70v, Callière and Beauharnois to the minister, 3 Nov. 1702. On a harbour master's duties, *see* De Merville, *Ordonnance de la Marine, Du mois d'Aoust 1681. Commentée & Conférée Sur les anciennes Ordonnances, le Droit Romain, & les nouveaux Reglemens* (Paris: Guillaume Cavelier, 1714), Vol. 4, pp. 381–84, and the "Code des armées navales," pp. 72–74, 287–88.

59 J. Delalande, op. cit., p. 60.

60 On the functions of the various tribunals, *see* Pierre Goubert, op. cit., Vol. 2, Les pouvoirs, pp. 98ff.

61 For details about the successive changes in the council's duties, *see* Gustave Lanctôt, *L'administration de la Nouvelle-France*, pp. 109–122; Quebec (Province), Législature, *Jugements et délibérations*, Vol. 2, p. 13; Quebec (Province), Assemblée législative, *Édits, ordonnances*, Vol. 1, pp. 83–84, "Déclaration du Roi qui confirme et règle L'Etablissement du Conseil Souverain de Canada," 5 June 1675.

62 Quebec (Province), Législature, *Jugements et délibérations*, Vol. 1, p. 274, 3 Sept. 1664; p. 348, 13 May 1665; p. 355, 29 May 1665: p. 400, 6 June 1667; pp. 409–410, 20 June 1667; p. 276, 13 Sept. 1664; pp. 622–23, 4 Aug. 1670.

63 Ibid., Vol. 1, pp. 788–89, 29 Jan. 1674. This bylaw, promulgated anew in May 1676, did not remain theoretical. For example, in 1681 Jean Guyon du Buisson and Jean Le Rouge had to have their compasses and instruments calibrated by Martin Boutet de Saint-Martin before aligning lands in Beauport. *See* Quebec (Province), Archives, *Ordonnances, commissions*, Vol. 1, pp. 199–200, and Quebec (Province), Législature, *Jugements et délibérations*, Vol. 2, p. 462, 20 Jan. 1681.

64 ANC, B, Vol. 6, fol. 31, Colbert to Frontenac, 17 May 1674.

65 Quebec (Province), Législature, *Jugements et délibérations*, Vol. 3, p. 329, 21 March 1689; p. 111, 27 Jan. 1687; pp. 330–31, 21 March 1689; p. 385, 30 Jan. 1690.

66 The case of Charles Roger Descoulombiers in 1670 was considered a legal case. A further example occurred in 1689, when the council ruled on the demolition of a wall that encroached upon rue Champlain; Quebec (Province), Législature, *Jugements et délibérations*, Vol. 3, pp. 375–76, 19 Dec. 1689.

67 Ibid., Vol. 1, p. 215, 25 June 1664; pp. 269–70, 27 Aug. 1664; p. 431, 23 July 1667.

68 Quebec (Province), Archives, *Ordonnances, commissions*, Vol. 1, p. 196; Quebec (Province), Législature, *Jugements et délibérations*, Vol. 3, pp. 111, 331.

69 Analysis of bylaws is based essentially on Volumes 1 to 3 of Quebec (Province), Législature, *Jugements et délibérations*, and on Volume 1 of Quebec (Province), Archives, *Ordonnances, commissions*. A few scattered documents were traced in ANC, B, C^{11}A, and F^3.

70 On this subject *see* W.J. Eccles, *Frontenac, The Courtier Governor* (Toronto: McClelland and Stewart, 1972), pp. 39–50, 131–44, 145–48, 149–53.

71 Stall rental was enforced as early as 1677, when certain butchers were fined the amount of their rental. The rental appears to have been an annual practice; in 1683 Demeulle gave butchers permission to set up their booths on the Place Royale for one year.

72 In 1685 Demeulle tried unsuccessfully to introduce tile as a roofing material. Tile and slate were used primarily on the town's many public and religious buildings.

73 In 1686 Québec received leather buckets from France and distributed them throughout the town. In regulations of 1687 the Conseil Souverain considered building wells in Upper and Lower Town not only for individuals' use, but also for the "public good" in case of fire.

74 These requirements were not theoretical. For instance, in 1681 François Viennay Pachot, who became one of the best-known merchants in Québec, requested the right to enjoy the privileges granted to other inhabitants of the colony, citing that he was married to a local girl, had established his store in Lower Town, lived there with his family, and wished to remain in Canada.

75 There remains some ambiguity about the Québec market. As early as 1673 Frontenac laid down its location and determined the days on which it would open, but his directives do not appear to have been put into effect. In April 1676 Demeulle was once again ordered to establish a market in Québec. Countless recommendations about it were received from France until 1689. In 1673 Frontenac planned to set up butchers' stalls in the Lower Town marketplace and they did exist from at least that year onwards.

76 There was no further mention of prostitution in bylaws after 1676. The subject was referred to only in official correspondence, which does not describe a situation prevailing only in Québec. Thus in 1677 Duchesneau denounced drunkenness, luxury, and the debauchery of young women. The minister ordered the Conseil Souverain to punish them in accordance with French ordinances and exhorted the bishop of Québec to combat such vices. In 1686 Denonville complained of a number of "rogues" and women of ill repute, suggesting that they be sent back to France. The king ordered him instead to form companies of soldiers to prevent the debauchery of young men and to assign women of ill repute to hard public labour (drawing water, serving masons, sawing wood), so that their punishment would serve as an example.

77 M. Guyot, *Répertoire universel et raisonné de jurisprudence civile, criminelle, canonique et bénéficiale* (Paris: Panckoucke, 1783), Vol. 64, s.v. "voirie."

78 "Saillies" refers to any object (vestibule, staircase, balcony) that projects beyond the alignment of a building and is likely to encroach on the public thoroughfare. On the inspection of streets and highways, *see* Ivanhoë Caron, "Historique de la voirie dans la province de Québec," *BRH*, Vol. 39, No. 4 (April 1933), pp. 199–200.

79 Antoine Furetière, op. cit., Vol. 3, s.v. "voyer" and "voyrie." M. Guyot, loc. cit. The possible attribution of street inspections to peace officers helps one to comprehend the lieutenant-general's role in this area.

80 Jean-Louis Harouel, "Les fonctions de l'alignement dans l'organisme urbain," *Dix-huitième siècle*, No. 9 (1977), p. 137. This special issue, entitled "Le sain et le malsain," of the periodical is devoted to various urban problems. In France the office of the *grand voyer* was done away with in 1626 and road administration was turned over to the Bureaux des finances; in Paris it was only in 1693 that four general commissioners of roads were appointed. For more information, *see* Marcel Marion, *Dictionnaire des institutions de la France aux XVIIe et XVIIIe siècles* (Paris: A. and J. Picard, 1968), pp. 561–62.

81 I did not consult the text of the 1607 edict nor those of the various regulations. The information is taken from Jean-Louis Harouel, op. cit., pp. 135ff., and from M. Guyot, loc. cit.

82 Quebec (Province), Archives, *Inventaire des procès-verbaux*, Vol. 5, pp. 141–43. That de Bécancour was a shareholder of the company certainly had something to do with this appointment.
83 Quebec (Province), Législature, *Jugements et délibérations*, Vol. 2, p. 462, 20 Jan. 1681; Vol. 2, pp. 462–63, 20 Jan. 1681; Vol. 3, pp. 375–76, 19 Dec. 1689.
84 ANQQ, NF10, cahier A, pièce No. 5, 5 Sept. 1682; pièce No. 41, 9 July 1689.
85 ASQ, Registre A, fols. 39v–40v (pp. 80–82), 17 July 1683; collated copy of 6 May 1710.
86 Antoine Furetière, op. cit., Vol. 1, s.v. "alignement."
87 ANC, F^3, Vol. 4, fol. 119–119v, 15 April 1673; ANQQ, NF25, pièce No. 123, 1 June 1675. This last document has yet to be found.
88 M. Guyot, op. cit., Vol. 2, s.v. "alignement." In Volume 57 Guyot defined street: "as the beauty of towns lies primarily in the alignment of its Streets, the ordinances & particularly the king's statement of 16 June 1693 do now forbid not only the construction of a new house, but also the reconstruction & repair of walls bordering the Street in towns & outlying districts, & even in villages, until the location & building line have been marked out by officers of the administration."
89 Jean-Louis Harouel, op. cit., pp. 135, 138–39.
90 M. Guyot, loc. cit., stated that a builder or mason who did not have the building line marked out before demolishing a party wall at the ground-floor level became responsible for changes, usurpation of bequeathed property rights, and encroachment. The stipulation seems to conform with article 11 of Chapter 2 of the Coutume de Paris, which deals with the use and maintenance of party walls. For more information, *see* François Miville-Deschênes, "Les lois de la construction et de la propriété des édifices dans la Coutume de Paris," term paper, Université Laval, Québec, 1976, p. 20.
91 Pièces 13 to 41 of the certificates issued from 7 June 1685 to 9 July 1689 are part of a register Genaple kept.
92 ANQQ, NF10, cahier A, pièce No. 17, 12 June 1687. On this site, *see* Figures 15 and 16.
93 Ibid., pièce No. 4, 30 Oct. 1681. Mention is made here of a certificate of land survey issued to Louis Marin Boucher on 17 March 1678, signed by de Bécancour and filed in his record office, but the document has yet to be found. On boundary markers, *see* Figures 23 and 24.
94 Ibid., pièce No. 11, 5 June 1685. The bend in rue du Sault-au-Matelot was to be modified in 1687, when a building alignment was granted to André Parent by Genaple; ibid., pièce No. 22, 3 July 1687.
95 In 1700 the Académie d'architecture recommended a minimal width for main public roads in order to allow the passage of two carriages travelling side by side. In 1698 Vauban advocated a width of 36 *pieds* for such roads, particularly those used for military purposes. This information, provided to me by my colleague Marc Lafrance, is taken from B.F. Bélidor, *La science des Ingénieurs dans la conduite des travaux de fortification et d'architecture civile* (Paris: C. Jombert, 1729), Book 4, p. 60.
96 ANC, $C^{11}A$, Vol. 7, fol. 246, 14 Nov. 1685.
97 Jean-Claude Marsan, *Montréal en évolution. Historique du développement de l'architecture et de l'environnement montréalais* (Montréal: Fides, 1974), pp. 93–97.
98 Peter N. Moogk, *Building a House in New France: An Account of the Perplexities of Client and Craftsmen in Early Canada* (Toronto: McClelland and Stewart, 1977), pp. 14, 16.
99 Carl Bridenbaugh, *Cities in the Wilderness: The First Century of Urban Life in America, 1625–1742* (London: Oxford Univ. Press, 1971), pp. 13–19.
100 ANC, $C^{11}A$, Vol. 5, fol. 167, Duchesneau to Colbert, 13 Nov. 1680.

101 *DBC*, Vol. 1, pp. 588–89.

102 J.-B. Gareau, "La Prévôté de Québec: ses officiers — ses registres," in *RAPQ pour 1943–1944* (Québec: Rédempti Paradis, 1944), pp. 51–146; Pierre-Georges Roy, *La ville de Québec sous le régime français* (Québec: Rédempti Paradis, 1930), 2 vols.; John Alexander Dickinson, *Justice et justiciables. La procédure civile à la Prévôté de Québec, 1667–1759* (Québec: PUL, 1982), 289 pages.

103 André Lachance, *La justice criminelle du roi au Canada au XVIIIe siècle. Tribunaux et officers* (Québec: PUL, 1978) (hereafter cited as *La justice criminelle*), pp. 8–9. Lachance maintained that the Conseil Souverain heard no lower court cases between 23 Sept. 1665 and 6 Dec. 1666. Gareau, however, claimed that the Prévôté was in place as early as 2 Nov. 1666.

104 Quebec (Province), Assemblée législative, *Édits, ordonnances*, Vol. 3, pp. 86–88; *DBC*, Vol. 1, pp. 573–74.

105 J.-B. Gareau, op. cit., p. 61. Counsellor Louis Rouer de Villeray presided over the hearings until Chartier de Lotbinière was installed in his post.

106 Quebec (Province), Assemblée législative, *Édits, ordonnances*, Vol. 1, pp. 77–78, Dec. 1674; ANC, C^{11}A, Vol. 4, fols. 167-68, May 1677; J.-B. Gareau, op. cit., p. 56; ANQQ, NF12, Vol. 1, fols. 56v–57, 13 May 1675.

107 Quebec (Province), Assemblée législative, *Édits, ordonnances*, Vol. 3, pp. 87–88.

108 Quebec (Province), Archives, *Ordonnances, commissions*, Vol. 1, pp. 39–40, 9 Sept. 1666. I use the term "government of Québec" as Marcel Trudel defined it in *Atlas de la Nouvelle-France* (Québec: PUL, 1968), pp. 174–75. It includes the seigneuries from Grondines to Mille-Vaches on the north shore and from Deschaillons to Mitis on the south shore.

109 Quebec (Province), Archives, *Ordonnances, commissions*, Vol. 1, pp. 39–40. The installation of Chartier de Lotbinière and the powers of the Prévôte were subject to Talon's approval. For Boutroue's role, *see* J.-B. Gareau, op. cit., p. 54. From 1682 to 1686 Intendant Demeulle also took over control of lower court cases; John Alexander Dickinson, op. cit., p. 102.

110 Quebec (Province), Assemblée législative, *Édits, ordonnances*, Vol. 1, pp. 236–38, June 1679.

111 John Alexander Dickinson, op. cit., pp. 48–50.

112 *See*, for example, an ordinance issued on 10 March 1685 forbidding the lieutenant-general from holding hearings in his house (ANC, B, Vol. 11, fol. 111–111v) and one ordering Prévôté officers not to exceed the rates set by the regulation of 1678 (ibid., Vol. 11, fols. 111v–112).

113 René-Louis Chartier de Lotbinière was given his new post as early as 1 May 1677; he began exercising his responsibilities only after his father resigned. Quebec (Province), Législature, *Jugements et délibérations*, Vol. 2, pp. 168–69, 25 Oct. 1677.

114 Quebec (Province), Archives, *Ordonnances, commissions*, Vol. 1, p. 40, 9 Sept. 1666; NA, MG5, B1, Vol. 5–2, pp. 94–96, Frontenac to Colbert, 13 Nov. 1673; ANC, B, Vol. 6, fol. 30, Colbert to Frontenac, 17 May 1674.

115 ANC, B, Vol. 6, fol. 97v, the king to Frontenac, 22 April 1675; fol. 144, 30 May 1675. The same instructions are found in Champigny's commission; *see* ANC, B, Vol. 12, fols. 3–5, 24 April 1686; Quebec (Province), Législature, *Jugements et délibérations*, Vol. 3, pp. 10–11, 4 Feb. 1686; pp. 109–11, 27 Jan. 1687.

116 Quebec (Province), Législature, *Jugements et délibérations*, Vol. 3, pp. 109–11, 27 Jan. 1687; pp. 205–206, 26 Jan. 1688.

117 ANC, C^{11}A, Vol. 6, fols. 102–103v, 4 Aug. 1682; Quebec (Province), Législature, *Jugements et délibérations*, Vol. 2, pp. 100–101, 11 Jan. 1677; ANC, C^{11}A, Vol. 5, fol. 149, [circa 1717].

118 André Vachon, "La restauration de la Tour de Babel," pp. 188–92: a critique of an article by Jacques Mathieu published in that journal in Dec. 1969. Also by Ma-

thieu, *see* "Les causes devant la Prévôté de Québec en 1667," *Histoire sociale/Social History*, No. 3 (April 1969), pp. 101–111.

119 The Prévôté registration of administrative ordinances from the intendant and the Conseil Souverain confirms that the role of the lieutenant-general was to enforce rather than to initiate bylaws. *See*, in particular, Volume 2 of Quebec (Province), Archives, *Inventaire des insinuations de la Prévôté de Québec ... par Pierre-Georges Roy* (Beauceville: L'Éclaireur, 1936–39).

120 ANQQ, NF4, cahier 1, fols. 46-47, concession of three-quarters of an *arpent* on the Quai Champlain to Philippe Gaultier de Comporté, 7 Nov. 1672. After the revocation of the Compagnie des Indes Occidentales, the lieutenant-general no longer seemed to have played that role.

121 Quebec (Province), Archives, *Papier terrier de la Compagnie des Indes occidentales, 1667–1668 ... par Pierre-Georges Roy* (Beauceville: L'Éclaireur, 1931), passim. Although a *terrier* did exist as early as 1661–62, this is the first to have been preserved. In 1673 Chartier de Lotbinière received 400 *livres* to be used to produce another *terrier*; *see* Quebec (Province), Législature, *Jugements et délibérations*, Vol. 1, p. 751, 3 July 1673. The definition given for *aveux et dénombrements* is based on Richard Colebrook Harris, *The Seigneurial System in Early Canada: A Geographical Study* (Madison: Univ. of Wisconsin, 1968), p. 229.

122 ANC, $C^{11}A$, Vol. 6, fols. 140v–141, 10 April 1684. Admiralty cases relate to a number of things including the outfitting, sale, and allocation of vessels, as well as chartering and loading them, and also prizes and wrecks. For further information, *see* De Merville, op. cit., Book 1, pp. 15–31; ANC, $C^{11}A$, Vol. 11, fol. 202, Frontenac and Champigny to Pontchartrain, 10 May 1691, and Vol. 11, fol. 254v, Champigny to Pontchartrain, 10 May 1691. For three other admiralty cases appealed to the Conseil Souverain, *see* Quebec (Province), Législature, *Jugements et délibérations*, Vol. 3, pp. 77–78, 24 Sept. 1686; pp. 240–41, 27 July 1688; pp. 264–65, 25 Oct. 1688.

123 Quebec (Province), Archives, *Ordonnances, commissions*, Vol. 2, pp. 93–96, 13 April 1685. What is referred to here is the current rue Champlain, which under the French régime was also called rue De Meulles.

124 ANQQ, NF10, cahier A, pièce No. 18, 26 June 1687; ibid., pièce No. 19, 28 June 1687. In the first volume of his dictionary, Furetière pointed out that it was common practice for law officers to assist the *grand voyer* in determining the alignments for houses situated at corners of streets. Antoine Furetière, op. cit., s.v. "alignement." ANQQ, NF10, cahier A, pièce No. 22, 3 July 1687; pièce No. 30, 16 May 1689.

125 ANC, $C^{11}A$, Vol. 6, fol. 195, Demeulle to Seignelay, 4 Nov. 1683, but I have no information as to whether the *procureurs du roi* in Québec were as active as those in Montréal. For additional information on the latter, *see* Gustave Lanctôt, "Le régime municipal en Nouvelle-France," *Culture*, Vol. 9, No. 3 (1948), p. 271.

126 John Alexander Dickinson, op. cit., pp. 71–75; André Lachance, *La justice criminelle*, p. 28.

127 Concerning the *lieutenant général de police*, *see* Jacques Saint-Germain, *La Reynie et la police au Grand Siècle d'après de nombreux documents inédits* (Paris: Hachette, 1962), p. 26ff. Under an edict issued in Oct. 1699 that office, completely separate from that of the lieutenant-general responsible for civil and criminal matters, was established in all towns within the realm.

128 Quebec (Province), Législature, *Jugements et délibérations*, Vol. 1, p. 18, 10 Oct. 1663; p. 57, 14 Nov. 1663; pp. 169–70, 9 April 1664.

129 Ibid., pp. 278–80, 19 Sept. 1664; ANC, F^3, Vol. 78, fols. 5–6, 21 Sept. 1664. For information on the disputes between Bishop Laval and Mézy, *see* the latter's biography in *DBC*, Vol. 1, pp. 600–604.

130 Quebec (Province), Législature, *Jugements et délibérations*, Vol. 1, p. 291, 3 Nov. 1664; p. 305, 17 Dec. 1664; pp. 340–41, 29 April 1665; pp. 372–73, 24 Jan.

1667; p. 377, 14 Feb. 1667; p. 387, 28 March 1667; pp. 433–34, 30 July 1667; ANC, F^3, Vol. 4, fols. 75–76v, 1672.

131 Quebec (Province), Législature, *Jugements et délibérations*, Vol. 1, pp. 251–52, 6 Aug. 1664; pp. 285–86, 22 Oct. 1664; p. 292, 5 Nov. 1664; pp. 293–94, 6 Nov. 1664; pp. 294–96, 8 Nov. 1664; pp. 299–300, 19 Nov. 1664; p. 305, 17 Dec. 1664; p. 307, 24 Dec. 1664; p. 309, 31 Dec. 1664; p. 417, 4 July 1667; pp. 433–34, 30 July 1667. The fact that Bishop Laval had not yet settled his differences with Mézy explains his refusal to provide the *monitoire* Lemire requested.

132 Quebec (Province), Législature, *Jugements et délibérations*, Vol. 1, pp. 92–93, 16 Jan. 1664; pp. 193–94, 10 June 1664; pp. 637–38, 20 Oct. 1670; ANC, F^3, Vol. 4, fol. 75, 1672; Thomas Chapais, *Jean Talon, intendant de la Nouvelle-France*, (Québec: S.-A. Demers, 1904), pp. 263–64; Émile Salone, op. cit., pp. 149–50, 212, 420.

133 Quebec (Province), Législature, *Jugements et délibérations*, Vol. 1, p. 287, 15 Oct. 1664; p. 613, 28 April 1670; pp. 698–99, 24 Oct. 1672; ANC, F^3, Vol. 4, fol. 104–104v, Oct. 1672.

134 Quebec (Province), Législature, *Jugements et délibérations*, Vol. 1, pp. 476–79, 5 March 1668; p. 524, 30 Oct. 1668; pp. 549–50, 19 March 1669; pp. 636–37, 15 Sept. 1670.

135 Émile Salone, op. cit., pp. 207–11; Quebec (Province), Législature, *Jugements et délibérations*, Vol. 1, pp. 524–27, 30 Oct. 1668; Quebec (Province), Assemblée législative, *Édits, ordonnances*, Vol. 1, p. 76, Dec. 1674.

136 Quebec (Province), Assemblée législative, *Édits, ordonnances*, Vol. 1, p. 130, 23 March 1673; ANC, F^3, Vol. 4, fol. 21, excerpt of a letter from Colbert to Frontenac, 13 June 1673; Pierre-Georges Roy, "Le procès de l'abbé de Fénelon devant le Conseil Souverain de la Nouvelle-France en 1674," *RAPQ, 1921–1922* (Québec: Ls.-A. Proulx, 1922), pp. 147–49 and 150, 11 and 12 May 1674. Re Abbé Fénelon's case, *see RAPQ* issue mentioned above, pp. 124–88, as well as the *DBC*, Vol. 1, pp. 613–15.

137 ANC, B, Vol. 6, fol. 30–30v, Colbert to Frontenac, 17 May 1674; ANC, $C^{11}A$, Vol. 4, fol. 62–62v, Frontenac to Colbert, 12 Nov. 1674.

138 Quebec (Province), Assemblée législative, *Édits, ordonnances*, Vol. 1, p. 130, 23 March 1673; Quebec (Province), Législature, *Jugements et délibérations*, Vol. 1, p. 763, 21 Aug. 1673; pp. 956–57, 15 July 1675; Vol. 2, pp. 139–41, 5 July 1677.

139 Quebec (Province), Assemblée législative, *Édits, ordonnances*, Vol. 1, pp. 141–43, 15 April 1673; Quebec (Province), Législature, *Jugements et délibérations*, Vol. 2, pp. 126–27, 26 April 1677; pp. 139–41, 5 July 1677; pp. 147–48, 27 July 1677.

140 Quebec (Province), Législature, *Jugements et délibérations*, Vol. 1, p. 763, 21 Aug. 1673; pp. 763–65, 21 Aug. 1673; p. 767, 4 Sept. 1673; p. 850, 25 Sept. 1674; pp. 938–39, 14 June 1675; pp. 956–57, 15 July 1675.

141 ANQQ, NF1, chemise No. 9, pièce No. 6, 23 March 1677; Allana G. Reid, "Representative Assemblies in New France," *CHR*, Vol. 27, No. 1 (March 1946), pp. 19–20.

Chapter III
The Urban Landscape
An Evolving Town

1 Raoul Blanchard, "Québec esquisse de géographie urbaine," in *L'Est du Canada français: "Province de Québec"* (Montréal: Librairie Beauchemin, 1935), Vol. 2, pp. 159ff. Here "location" means the geographic location of the town, while "site" — "the place most suited to daily life" — refers to peoples' adaptation to the geo-

graphic location. These remarks are taken from Jacqueline Beaujeu-Garnier and Georges Chabot, op. cit., p. 111.

2 Marc Lafrance, "Étude sur l'évolution physique de la ville de Québec 1608–1763," manuscript on file, National Historic Sites Directorate, Canadian Parks Service, Ottawa, 1972 (hereafter cited as "Étude sur l'évolution physique"), pp. 10, 11–17.

3 Marcel Trudel, *Les débuts du régime seigneurial*, pp. 81, 86–87, 208. The measurements given in this section on concessions are measures of area; the text therefore refers to square *toises* and *arpents*. According to Marcel Trudel, the average size of lots in Lower Town was 0.2 square *arpents* or 95.2 square *toises*. However, 95.2 square *toises* equals 0.105 square *arpents*, not 0.2 square *arpents*.

4 Marcel Trudel, *Le terrier du Saint-Laurent*, pp. 160–79; *see also* maps 18, 20, 21, and 22.

5 Marc Lafrance, "Étude sur l'évolution physique," pp. 14–15.

6 Marcel Trudel, *Le terrier du Saint-Laurent*, p. 181, 188; *see also* map 24.

7 Ibid., *Les débuts du régime seigneurial*, p. 209.

8 Ibid., *Le terrier du Saint-Laurent*, pp. 164–65, 168–69, 172–73, 177–78, maps 21–23.

9 Ibid., *Les débuts du régime seigneurial*, pp. 209–210.

10 Ibid., *Le terrier du Saint-Laurent*, pp. 159, 161, 170, 200, maps 19, 23, 25.

11 Ibid., *Les débuts du régime seigneurial*, p. 210.

12 Marc Lafrance, "Étude sur l'évolution physique," p. 30.

13 Ibid., pp. 15, 17–19.

14 Marc Lafrance, "Étude sur l'évolution physique," p. 26.

15 ANC, C^{11}A, Vol. 5, fol. 338v, the king to Duchesneau, 30 April 1681; ANQQ, NF12, "Registre des insinuations du Conseil supérieur," Vol. 1, fol. 90v, 27 Oct. 1681.

16 ANC, C^{11}A, Vol. 5, fol. 388–388v, Frontenac to the king, 2 Nov. 1681; Vol. 6, fol. 244v, the king to La Barre, 10 April 1684; Vol. 8, fol. 166, summary of Denonville's letters of 11, 15, and 16 Nov. 1686. ANC, B, Vol. 13, fol. 165, the king to Denonville and Champigny, 30 March 1687; ANQQ, NF10, cahier A, pièce No. 27, 12 May 1689.

17 Most of the information is taken from the intendants' registers, ANQQ, NF4, cahier No. 3.

18 Letter from Marie de l'Incarnation to her son, 26 August 1644, quoted in Marc Lafrance, "Étude sur l'évolution physique," p. 52.

19 Pierre Boucher, *Histoire Veritable et Naturelle Des Moeurs & Productions du Pays De La Nouvelle France Vulgairement dite Le Canada* (Boucherville: Société Historique de Boucherville, 1964), p. 140.

20 Louis-Armand de Lom d'Arce, baron de Lahontan, *Voyages du Baron de La Hontan dans l'Amerique Septentrionale* Vol. 1, p. 17. (Montréal: *Éditions Élysée*, 1974).

21 Marthe Lacombe and Doris Drolet-Dubé, "Inventaire des marchés de construction des Archives nationales à Québec, XVIIe et XVIIIe siècles," *History and Archaeology/Histoire et Archéologie*, No. 17 (1977) (hereafter cited as "Inventaire des marchés de construction").

22 Since Upper Town and Lower Town could not be broken down, the figures for côte de la Montagne had to be considered separately in Table 9. Under the "Québec" heading are all contracts for which there was inadequate information about their precise location.

23 In Table 10 "Lower Town" includes contracts for which there was no street name plus data for Place Royale (where the Place Royale square is located) and for the Cul-de-Sac, which was not considered separately as a street. In the 17th century this name applied both to a street and to the Lower Town port area.

24 ANC, $C^{11}A$, Vol. 6, fol. 101, 4 Aug. 1682, procès-verbal by Chartier de Lotbinière on the Lower Town fire; Quebec (Province), Archives, *Ordonnances, commissions*, Vol. 1, pp. 322–23, 9 Sept. 1682.
25 The column "Framing and Roofing" simply covers double contracts where the workmen agreed to build the frame and to put the roof on the house. Twenty-one per cent of the framing contracts were such double contracts.
26 Georges Gauthier-Larouche, *Évolution de la maison rurale traditionnelle dans la région de Québec (étude ethnographique)* (Québec: PUL, 1974), p. 67.
27 For various classifications *see* Georges Gauthier-Larouche, op. cit., p. 67; A.J.H. Richardson, "A Comparative Historical Study of Timber Building in Canada," *APT*, Vol. 5, No. 3 (1973) (hereafter cited as "Comparative Historical Study"), p. 77; Yves Laframboise, *L'architecture traditionnelle au Québec. Glossaire illustré de la maison aux 17e et 18e siècles* (Montréal: Éditions de l'Homme, 1975), p. 26.
28 *See* the definitions of these types of assemblage in Yves Laframboise, op. cit., pp. 47ff.
29 Ibid., p. 26. For further information on the various ways of framing walls, *see* Laframboise's work.
30 Peter N. Moogk, op. cit., pp. 30–32.
31 Yves Laframboise, op. cit., p. 26. However, he included *pièce-sur-pièce* under the generic heading of "framing." A.J.H. Richardson saw it as a different construction method; A.J.H. Richardson, "Comparative Historical Study," p. 79.
32 Georges Gauthier-Larouche, op. cit., p. 67; Yves Laframboise, op. cit., p. 26. Half-timbered construction is included with other types of wood construction because of the importance of wood in it.
33 Yves Laframboise, op. cit., p. 97, and Marius Barbeau, "Notre ancienne architecture," *La Revue du Québec industriel*, Vol. 5, No. 2 (1940), p. 4.
34 André Charbonneau, "Les carrières de pierre dans la région de Québec sous le régime français", in *Exercices des métiers de la pierre et de l'argile*, ed. Jean-Claude Dupont (Québec: Célat, 1988), pp. 173–209.
35 Marius Barbeau, op. cit., pp. 4–5.
36 Peter N. Moogk, op. cit., pp. 23–24, 27. He pointed out, however, that the movement began in the 1680s in Québec's case.
37 A.J.H. Richardson, "Comparative Historical Study," p. 80.
38 Ibid., p. 78.
39 Georges Gauthier-Larouche, op. cit., p. 65.
40 Robert-Lionel Séguin, *La maison en Nouvelle-France* (Ottawa: Musée national du Canada, 1968), pp. 11–12.
41 Peter N. Moogk, op. cit., pp. 27–29. For a critique on the distinctive nature of the *pièce-sur-pièce* style in New France, *see* the review of Moogk's work by Yvon Desloges, Alain Rainville, and Serge Saint-Pierre, "Building a House in New France. An Account of the Perplexities of Client and Craftsmen in Early Canada," *The Journal of Canadian Art History/Annales d'histoire de l'art canadien*, Vol. 4, No. 2 (1977/78), pp. 162–63.
42 A.J.H. Richardson, "Comparative Historical Study," pp. 78–79.
43 Peter N. Moogk, op. cit., p. 49.
44 Georges Gauthier-Larouche, op. cit., p. 37.
45 A.J.H. Richardson, "Comparative Historical Study," p. 77.
46 Ibid., "Early Wood Construction in New France," manuscript on file, History and Archaeology, Quebec Regional Office, Parks Service, Environment Canada, Québec, May 1964, p. 2.
47 *See*, for example, Marc Lafrance, "Étude sur l'évolution physique," op. cit., p. 51.
48 Ramsay Traquair, *The Old Architecture of Quebec. A Study of the Buildings Erected in New France from the Earliest Explorers to the Middle of the Nineteenth Century* (Toronto: Macmillan, 1947), p. 16.

49 A.J.H. Richardson, "Early Wood Construction in New France," manuscript on file, History and Archaeology, Quebec Regional Office, Parks Service, Environment Canada, Québec, May 1964, p. 2. The *pièce-sur-pièce* style was found in the Pyrenees and Landes, the region south of Bordeaux.
50 Peter N. Moogk, op. cit., p. 23.
51 Ibid., p. 30.
52 Georges Gauthier-Larouche (op. cit., p. 66) expressed the same opinion regarding the Quebec countryside in the 18th century.
53 Robert-Lionel Séguin, op. cit., p. 30.
54 Peter N. Moogk, op. cit., pp. 34, 60. *See also* the review by Yvon Desloges, Alain Rainville, and Serge Saint-Pierre, op. cit., pp. 160–61.
55 For an overview of the legislation, *see* Chapter II and the first chapter of Peter N. Moogk, op. cit.
56 Georges Gauthier-Larouche, op. cit., pp. 59–97; Peter N. Moogk, op. cit., pp. 22–24, 28–30.
57 Peter N. Moogk, op. cit., pp. 28–29; A.J.H. Richardson, "Comparative Historical Study," p. 83.
58 Georges Gauthier-Larouche, op. cit., p. 97. He spoke in these terms for the colony as a whole in the 18th century, and his remarks appear equally valid for Québec in the preceding century.
59 Ibid., op. cit., p. 277. For a definition of roof types, *see* Yves Laframboise, op. cit., p. 277.
60 Georges Gauthier-Larouche, op. cit., pp. 33, 35–37; *see* particularly the table on page 35, which juxtaposes immigrants' geographic origin and roof pitch in various regions in France.
61 Peter N. Moogk, op. cit., pp. 22–23. In that passage Moogk was quoting from *L'Architecture Françoise des Bastimens Particuliers* by Louis Savot, which was republished in Paris in 1685.
62 Readers can find information about the use of these materials in Robert-Lionel Séguin, op. cit, pp. 37–39, and Pierre Mayrand, "Les matériaux de couverture en Nouvelle-France aux XVIIe et aux [*sic*] XVIIIe siècles," *APT*, Vol. 2, Nos. 1–2 (1970), pp. 70–71. For more on thatching, *see* Pierre Rastoul, "La chaumière québécoise," *Bulletin de culture matérielle/Material Culture Bulletin*, No. 21 (1977), pp. 19–41.
63 For a brief review of these imported materials, *see* Pierre Mayrand, op. cit., pp. 70–73.
64 Peter N. Moogk, op. cit., p. 56.
65 Pierre Mayrand, op. cit., p. 70.
66 Peter N. Moogk, op. cit., p. 103.
67 Robert-Lionel Séguin, op. cit., pp. 4, 7, 19.
68 Marc Lafrance, "Étude sur l'évolution physique," pp. 53–54, 63–64.
69 In Table 16 the houses were divided into three arbitrary categories: small, up to 500 square *pieds*; medium, up to 1000 square *pieds*; and large, over 1000 square *pieds*. The square footages shown in Table 16 are averages and apply to the ground floor only; the figures do not include upper storeys or lofts. For example, the average area of small houses in the town of Québec between 1663 and 1690 was 342 square *pieds* on the ground floor.
70 Yves Laframboise, op. cit., p. 22.
71 Carl Bridenbaugh, op. cit., pp. 8–11. For a brief background on the towns mentioned, *see* my chapter on demography.
72 Ibid.

Chapter IV
The People and the Town
Population and Labour Force

1 On colonization efforts prior to the creation of the Compagnie des Cents-Associés, *see* Marcel Trudel, Le Comptoir, pp. 151ff.

2 Table of population of Canada 1608–1700 taken from information published with the 1931 census of Canada as reproduced in Hubert Charbonneau, *Vie et mort de nos ancêtres, étude démographique* (Montréal: PUM, 1975) (hereafter cited as *Vie et mort de nos ancêtres*), p. 30.

3 Émile Salone estimated that at least 200 people were killed in the first Iroquois war; op. cit., p. 98.

4 The rate of increase between censuses is obtained using the formula 100(Pt-Po)/0.5(Pt+Po), where Po and Pt are the populations at the beginning and the end of the period under study. To find the average rate of increase, one divides the between-census rate by the number of years in the period; *see* Michel P. Paillé, "Accroissement et structure de la population à Québec au début du XIXe siècle (à propos d'un article de John Hare)," *Histoire sociale/Social History*, Vol. 9, No. 17 (May 1976), pp. 188–90.

5 Hubert Charbonneau, *Vie et mort de nos ancêtres*, p. 30; Allana G. Reid, "The Development and Importance of the Town of Quebec, 1608–1760," PhD diss., McGill University, Montréal, 1950 (hereafter cited as "Development and Importance"), p. 449. *See also* Table 18.

6 If one used the same period — 1628 to 1653 — for comparison of the annual average rates of increase for Québec and for the colony, the difference would be no more than 1.2 points: 7.4 per cent for New France, 6.2 per cent for Québec.

7 On these general observations, cf. the works of Trudel, Campeau, and Salone. *See also* Gabriel Debien, "Les engagés pour le Canada au XVIIe siècle vus de La Rochelle," *RHAF*, Vol. 6, No. 2 (Sept. 1952), pp. 177–233, and Vol. 6, No. 3 (Dec. 1952), pp. 374–407.

8 Allana G. Reid, "Development and Importance," pp. 36ff. The statistics on troop dispatch are from ANC, B, Vols. 11–13. These examples show the diverse make-up and sizes of the immigrant groups.

9 Table compiled by the French demographer Bunle and reproduced in Hubert Charbonneau, *Vie et mort de nos ancêtres*, p. 35. Net immigration after Lortie in ibid., p. 39.

10 Émile Salone, op. cit., p. 168. For Montréal the key years were 1653–62. *See* Louise Dechêne, *Habitants et marchands de Montréal au XVIIe siècle* (Paris: Plon, 1974) (hereafter cited as *Habitants et marchands)*, p. 44.

11 Hubert Charbonneau (*Vie et mort de nos ancêtres*, p. 221) found an average of 7.7 children per family. For birth and death rates *see* ibid., p. 34.

12 Marcel Trudel, *La population du Canada en 1663* (Montréal: Fides, 1973) (hereafter cited as *La population du Canada*), p. 11.

13 Carl Bridenbaugh, op. cit., p. 6. It is possible to compare the Québec of 1685 with the other towns in New France; its population was 11.2 per cent of that of the colony as a whole, versus 6.8 per cent for Montréal and 2.1 per cent for Trois-Rivières.

14 Allana G. Reid, "Development and Importance," p. 449.

15 The nature of the statistical data available does not permit establishing the average annual rate of increase for Montréal. The rate for Trois-Rivières was 5.2 per cent between 1681 and 1688.

16 Population statistics drawn from Carl Bridenbaugh, op. cit., p. 6. For the history of the various towns, *see also* John W. Reps, *The Making of Urban America; A History of City Planning in the United States* (Princeton: Princeton Univ. Press, 1965), pp. 140–75.

17 For the colony, my results resemble those of Jacques Henripin in *La population canadienne au début du XVIIIe siècle. Nuptialité, fécondité, mortalité infantile* (Paris: PUF, 1954), p. 19. The Université de Montréal's demographics research group put the excess of males in New France in 1666 at 70.0 per cent and 25.0 per cent in 1681. *See* Hubert Charbonneau, Yolande Lavoie, and Jacques Légaré, "Le recensement nominatif du Canada en 1681," *Histoire sociale/Social History*, Vol. 7 (April 1971), p. 81. Marcel Trudel (*La population du Canada*, pp. 61–62) reckoned there were 62.9 per cent men and 37.1 per cent women in the colony in 1663; women made up 38.5 per cent of the population in the capital region.

18 Lucien Campeau, *Les Cent-Associés*, p. 153.

19 Silvio Dumas, *Les filles du roi en Nouvelle-France. Étude historique avec répertoire biographique* (Québec: Société historique de Québec, 1972), pp. 34, 43.

20 Women made up about a third of all immigrants according to Louise Dechêne (*Habitants et marchands*, p. 102). However, Hubert Charbonneau and other demographers suggested that after 1667 there were as many female as male immigrants; *see* Hubert Charbonneau, Yolande Lavoie, and Jacques Légaré, op. cit., p. 81.

21 Silvio Dumas, op. cit., p. 122. This figure is Dumas's ten-year summation of data that do not apply solely to the town of Québec and extend to 1679. It is generally conceded that more boys are born than girls, the imbalance being corrected by males' greater infant mortality. Speaking of the 1681 census, Charbonneau pointed out that the sexes are more equally represented among those under 30 — a notable improvement over 1667, when the numbers were roughly equal only for those under 15.

22 Hubert Charbonneau, *Vie et mort de nos ancêtres*, p. 147.

23 For the "Québec government" the ratio was 105.6 men to every 100 women among those aged 25–29 as compared to 125:100 in the colony as a whole. Cf. Hubert Charbonneau, "À propos de démographie urbaine en Nouvelle-France. Réflexions en marge d'*Habitants et marchands de Montréal* de Louise Dechêne," *RHAF*, Vol. 30, No. 2 (Sept. 1976) (hereafter cited as "À propos de demographie urbaine"), p. 265; ibid., *Vie et mort de nos ancêtres,* pp. 161; Émile Salone, op. cit., p. 256; Louise Dechêne, *Habitants et marchands*, p. 100.

24 Married and widowed persons are taken together because they were not distinguished in 1688 and because the widowed represented such a tiny proportion of the married contingent. The expression "married persons" therefore includes widows and widowers.

25 The number of husbands in Québec in 1666 was put at 65, the number of wives at 55. The ten-wife deficiency can be explained: six men had wives in France, one married man lived alone, and three others' wives had been missed by the census. By 1681 the gap had shrunk to two: one man with a wife in France and another whose wife was missed by the census. As the 1688 census was not a nominal one, no data are available on the husband-wife imbalance for that year.

26 Hubert Charbonneau, *Vie et mort de nos ancêtres*, pp. 169–70. He mentioned that religious vocations displayed a contrary trend to that of the marriage mart: the greater the pressure to marry on eligible females, the more nuns were recruited.

27 ANC, B, Vol. 3, fol. 25v, Colbert to Talon, March 1671.

28 Quebec (Province), Législature, *Jugements et délibérations*, Vol. 1, p. 68, 28 Nov. 1663; Vol. 1, pp. 638–39, 20 Oct. 1670; Émile Salone, op. cit., pp. 169–70; Quebec (Province), Archives, *Ordonnances, commissions*, Vol. 1, pp. 104–105, 20 Oct. 1671. However, not too much stress should be laid on such regulations. Louise Dechêne (*Habitants et marchands*, p. 106) emphasized that despite the 1669 edict, Montréal women's attitude inclined to the norm for the period; she did not find any marriages that met these requirements. Hubert Charbonneau (*Vie et mort de nos ancêtres*, p. 190) found that only 2.0 per cent of men under 20 were married and fewer than 10.0 per cent of women under 16.

29 Raymond Roy, Yves Landry, and Hubert Charbonneau, "Quelques comportements des Canadiens au XVIIe siècle d'après les registres paroissiaux," *RHAF*, Vol. 31, No. 1 (June 1977), p. 56.
30 Louise Dechêne, *Habitants et marchands*, p. 102. In Montréal a third of the women married immigrants, something Dechêne found remarkable. For Hubert Charbonneau, though, that was no surprise; since women married from seven to eight years younger than men and at 17 or 18 outnumbered the men of 24 or 25, they were bound to marry immigrants. Hubert Charbonneau, "À propos de démographie urbaine," p. 268.
31 Émile Salone, op. cit., p. 283ff.
32 In Table 26, of the 79 persons of unknown age in the colony, 78 were said to be from Québec; in 1681, all of them were. We have the ages of all residents of the town for these dates, but it has not been possible to determine where the error crept into the figures reported in Canada, Dept. of Agriculture, *Census of Canada* (Ottawa: I.B. Taylor and Maclean, Rogers & Co., 1873–78), Vol. 4, pp. 2–23.
33 In 1681 the percentage of persons aged 21 to 40 dropped considerably, both in Québec and in the colony as a whole. In view of the slight decline in the 41-to-60 group in Québec, it is difficult to explain the drop in the first group. Naturally there were deaths and immigration was low, but the normal aging of the previous generation should have compensated.
34 For the entire colony, from 1640 to 1729, Hubert Charbonneau (*Vie et mort de nos ancêtres*, p. 165) estimated that the average age at marriage was 27.7 years for men and 22.0 years for women.
35 No age distributions are available for 1688 except for single persons, and at that only those over and under 15 for men or 12 for women are differentiated.
36 According to compilations made from the records of the Programme de recherche en démographie historique of the Université de Montréal.
37 The demographers say that a household is a physical unit; it refers to all those living under one roof. Gaël Olivier-Lacamp and Jacques Légaré, "Quelques caractéristiques des ménages de la ville de Québec entre 1666 et 1716," *Histoire sociale/Social History*, Vol. 12, No. 23 (May 1979), p. 67.
38 John Hare, "La population de la ville de Québec, 1795–1805," *Histoire sociale/Social History*, Vol. 7, No. 13 (May 1974), p. 27.
39 This social and occupational classification is a variant of that John Hare adopted (op. cit., p. 37). Woodworking trades include joiners. Labourers include boatmen, pilots, gardeners, sailors, and servants who were themselves household heads. Clerks and officeholders include bailiffs, constables, clerks per se, and the executioner.
40 Edward Shorter, *The Making of the Modern Family* (New York: Basic Books, 1977), p. 23.
41 In reckoning the number of children to a household, only families (those households headed by a married couple or a single parent) have been considered. For domestic servants, the results are based on all the data, including those for single persons, who, like the married, could have hired help.
42 ANC, C^{11}A, Vol. 2, fol. 157–157v, 3 Nov. 1665: bakers, brewers, ship's coopers (makers of barrels for beer and for the fur and fish sent to France), edge-tool makers, locksmiths, armourers, house carpenters and ship's carpenters, joiners, loggers, and makers of bowls and plates, charcoal makers, bricklayers and tilers, roofers in any material, tanners, leather workers, cobblers, bootmakers, hatters, furriers, and "several other trades of less importance or lacking the necessary materials."
43 When possible, the available information on trades given by the censuses of 1666 and 1681 has been augmented.
44 Non-resident volunteers were free men, day-labourers or not, not bound to a master. Although listed as non-residents, they did live in Québec all the same. They

were probably transients (outside merchants) or people not yet settled in the country.

45 Joseph-Noël Fauteux, *Essai sur l'industrie au Canada sous le régime français* (Québec: Ls.-A. Proulx, 1927), 2 vols.

46 In 1666, if joiners are included, the building trades accounted for 16.8 per cent of the labour force and in 1681 for 15.1 per cent.

47 This labour-force analysis is based on 229 contracts from construction industry records. Since some contracts were let to more than one workman, each entry has had to be treated individually. The contract entries for each mason, carpenter, joiner, and roofer has been tabulated from a total of 298 individual entries.

48 Throughout this section the term "entry" often recurs; it simply refers to a unit used in drawing up the statistics.

49 *DBC*, Vol, 1, 77.

50 Any information not found in the biographies consulted was compiled from Marthe Lacombe and Doris Drolet-Dubé, "Inventaire des marchés de construction," and René Jetté, *Dictionnaire généalogique des familles du Québec* (Montréal: PUM, 1983). For all individuals our chronology stops at 1690.

51 Raymonde Landry-Gauthier, "L'architecture civile et conventuelle à Québec (1680–1726)," thèse de maîtrise, Université Laval, Québec, 1976, pp. 149–50.

52 Antoine Furetière, op. cit., Vol. 2, s.v. "entrepreneur."

53 Figures provided by my colleague Yvon Desloges. They mainly relate to the hiring of masons; the hiring of joiners, for instance, was not considered.

54 A.J.H. Richardson, "Guide to the Architecturally and Historically Most Significant Buildings in the Old City of Quebec with a Biographical Dictionary of Architects and Builders and Illustrations," *APT*, Vol. 2, Nos. 3–4 (1970) (hereafter cited as "Guide to the Buildings in the Old City of Quebec"), p. 73.

55 *See* the list of hirings in Marthe Lacombe and Doris Drolet-Dubé, "Inventaire des marchés de construction," p. 446.

56 Data collected with the help of Yvon Desloges and apprenticeship records compiled by Marthe Lacombe and Doris Drolet-Dubé.

57 According to Antoine Furetière, an architect was someone who provided the plans and drawings for a building, who directed its construction, and who gave orders to the masons and other workmen under him.

58 For this particular contract, *see* Marthe Lacombe and Doris Drolet-Dubé, "Inventaire des marchés de construction," p. 171, No. 681.

59 *DBC*, Vol. 2, p. 436; Raymonde Landry-Gauthier, op. cit., p. 20.

60 For Couteron, Lavergne, and Duplais, all hiring figures come from handwritten index cards by Marthe Lacombe and Doris Drolet-Dubé. The hirings inserted in the inventory of construction contracts were also taken into consideration in their biographies.

61 Biographies were collected in A.J.H. Richardson, "Guide to the Buildings in the Old City of Quebec," and in the *DBC* for Pierre Ménage and Léonard Paillard, but similar biographical studies were unavailable for the others. For carpenters there will be no mention of hiring, as only one such contract has been found, that for the year 1686 in which Pierre Ménage and Jean Caillé hired two carpenters, one of whom was from Côte Saint-Michel. It may seem surprising that there should have been virtually no carpenter hirings, especially considering how prevalent hiring was with masons, but carpenters took on apprentices and so had no need to hire very many hands.

62 These data come from the *DBC*, Vol. 2, p. 529–30; A.J.H. Richardson, "Guide to the Buildings in the Old City of Quebec," p. 90; Marthe Lacombe and Doris Drolet-Dubé, "Inventaire des marchés de construction," and Lacombe and Drolet-Dubé's handwritten index cards.

63 Peter N. Moogk did not have at his disposal that excellent tool, Lacombe and Drolet-Dubé's "Inventaire des marchés de construction."

64 *DBC*, Vol. 2, p. 487.
65 A.J.H. Richardson, "Guide to the Buildings in the Old City of Quebec," p. 13. The Jacquet house is at 34 rue Saint-Louis.
66 *See* No. 484 in Marthe Lacombe and Doris Drolet-Dubé, "Inventaire des marchés de construction," p. 123.
67 Gacien is not mentioned in the *DBC*. In addition to the article already mentioned, A.J.H. Richardson provided additional information in "Early Roofing Materials," *APT*, Vol. 2, Nos. 1–2 (1970); *see* especially pp. 18–27. An inventory of the tools Gacien owned in 1682 is found on pp. 18 and 19.
68 From a handwritten hiring card by Marthe Lacombe and Doris Drolet-Dubé. The document was signed before Rageot on 6 Nov.
69 Michelon is mentioned in A.J.H. Richardson, "Guide to the Buildings in the Old City of Quebec," p. 82; however, no contract in his name is to be found in Marthe Lacombe and Doris Drolet-Dubé, "Inventaire des marchés de construction."
70 Hubert Charbonneau, "À propos de démographie urbaine," p. 268. However, this opinion was not shared by Louise Dechêne; she did not see any different population trend between Montréal and the country in the 18th century. Louise Dechêne, "La croissance de Montréal au XVIIIe siècle," *RHAF*, Vol. 27, No. 2 (Sept. 1973), p. 171.

Appendix B
Methodology Used in Analysing Construction Contracts

1 The rejects include 128 contracts for unknown sites, 126 contracts of different types (transport, supply of materials, erection of walls, miscellanea), and 33 contracts concerning fortifications as well as public and religious buildings.
2 Yves Laframboise, op. cit., p. 191.
3 Ibid., p. 83. For the definition of *colombage pierroté see* the section dealing with materials analysis in Chapter III.

Appendix C
Demography and the Labour Force Research and Methodology

1 Hubert Charbonneau and Yolande Lavoie, "Introduction à la reconstitution de la population du Canada au XVIIe siècle," *RHAF*, Vol. 24, No. 4 (March 1971), p. 489. The population in the Québec area increased enormously in 1667 as compared to the preceding year while that of the town itself showed an important decrease, which, according to these authors, indicates a change in the definition of the territory.
2 The original manuscripts are part of ANSOM, Dépôt des papiers publics des colonies, Registres de l'état civil, recensements et documents divers, G^1 460, Canada, Recensements (1666–1741). Montréal, Université, Département de démographie, *Répertoire des actes de baptême, mariage, sépulture et des recensements du Québec ancien* (Montréal: PUM, 1980), Vols. 1 and 6.
3 The most important are René Jetté, op. cit., 1176 pp., and Marcel Trudel, *Catalogue des immigrants, 1632-1662* (Montréal: Éditions Hurtubise HMH, 1983), 569 pp., as well as the different volumes of the *DBC*.
4 According to Hubert Charbonneau and Yoland Lavoie, op. cit., Québec had no more than 539 inhabitants in 1666, not 547. However, after eliminating census duplicates we still arrive at a population of 547 in 1666, even though my count of households is the same as Charbonneau and Lavoie's.

5 Canada, Dept. of Agriculture, op. cit., pp. 2–23.

6 I have not taken under-registration into account in my statistics because it was impossible to tell who had been left out. *See*, on this subject, Hubert Charbonneau and Yoland Lavoie, op. cit., pp. 503–508. In the 1666 census Québec accounts for the greatest number of omissions; its "real" population is likely to have been about 603.

BIBLIOGRAPHY

The town of Québec is not a new subject for study. The most important work is certainly Allana G. Reid's thesis, "The Development and Importance of the Town of Quebec, 1608–1760," written in 1950. I should also point out the studies done by Pierre-Georges Roy, *La ville de Québec sous le régime français*, and by Raoul Blanchard, *L'Est du Canada français, "Province de Québec."* In matters of town planning and urbanization, few authors have been interested in Québec. To my knowledge, no one has studied the concept of *ville* in New France, much less Québec.

The area of administration has given rise to numerous works, amongst others, Gustave Lanctôt's thesis, *L'administration de la Nouvelle-France*; R. La Rocque de Roquebrune's article "La direction de la Nouvelle-France par le Ministère de la Marine"; and André Vachon's book *L'administration de la Nouvelle-France, 1627–1760*. Of all these historians, only one, Gustave Lanctôt, showed any interest in town administration and only in a very brief article entitled "Le régime municipal en Nouvelle-France."

There have been some beginnings in one field of study, that of the urban landscape. I must first mention Marc Lafrance's "Étude sur l'évolution physique de la ville de Québec 1608–1763," and then Marcel Trudel's *Le terrier du Saint-Laurent en 1663* and *Les débuts du régime seigneurial au Canada*. In the area of construction, there are Yves Laframboise's *L'architecture traditionnelle au Québec. Glossaire illustré de la maison aux 17e et 18e siècles*; A.J.H. Richardson's works, of which the most important is certainly *Quebec City: Architects, Artisans and Builders*; and Peter N. Moogk's *Building a House in New France: An Account of the Perplexities of Client and Craftsmen in Early Canada*.

In the area of demography are numerous works. Jacques Henripin's *La population canadienne au début du XVIIIe siècle: Nuptialité, fécondité, mortalité infantile* dates back to 1954; Gabriel Debien's article "Les engagés pour le Canada au XVIIe siècle vus de La Rochelle" appeared in September 1952. Marcel Trudel published *La population du Canada en 1663* and Hubert Charbonneau gave us *Vie et mort de nos ancêtres, étude démographique*. The research group in historical demography, under the direction of Hubert Charbonneau and Jacques Légaré, at the Université de Montréal certainly deserves special mention for having published *Répertoire des actes de baptême, mariage, sépulture et des recensements du Québec ancien*. Its members have also published several articles, including Hubert Charbonneau and Yolande Lavoie, "Introduction à la reconstitution de la population du Canada au XVIIe siècle"; Hubert Charbonneau, Yolande Lavoie, and Jacques Légaré, "Le recensement nominatif du Canada en 1681"; Raymond

Roy, Yves Landry, and Hubert Charbonneau, "Quelques comportements des Canadiens au XVIIe siècle d'après les registres paroissiaux."

In my view, there are shortcomings in all of these documents. The town of Québec simply blends in with the rest of New France, some aspects of study are neglected, or there is very little interest shown in the 17th century. Except in the case of synopses, these authors have only touched upon one individual aspect of the city (concessions or house building, for example) and, like Allana G. Reid, have not considered Québec as a whole where all the components of urban life came into play.

Manuscripts

Canada. National Archives.
MG5, Ministère des Affaires étrangères, Paris, B1, Mémoires et documents, Amérique.

France. Archives nationales. Fonds des colonies.
B, Correspondance au départ vers les colonies.
C^{11}A, Correspondance à l'arrivée, Canada.
E, Personnel colonial.
F^{3}, Mélanges, Collection Moreau St-Méry.

France. Archives nationales. Section Outre-mer.
Dépôt des fortifications des colonies, Amérique septentrionale.
Dépôt des papiers publics des colonies, Registres de l'état civil, recensements et documents divers, G^{1} 460, Canada, Recensements (1666–1741).

Quebec (Province). Archives nationales à Québec.
AP-G-270, Archives privées, Ursulines, documents divers, 1660–1681.
Greffe de François Genaple.
Greffe de Pierre Duquet.
NF1, Ordonnances des gouverneurs.
NF4, Registres des intendants.
NF10, Procès-verbaux des grands voyers.
NF12, Registre des Insinuations du Conseil Supérieur.
NF25, Collection de pièces judiciaires et notariales.

Québec (City). Séminaire. Archives.
Documents Faribault.
Paroisse de Québec.
Polygraphies.
Registres A and B.
Séminaire 1 and 6.

Printed Sources

Boucher, Pierre
Histoire Veritable et Naturelle Des Moeurs & Productions du Pays De La Nouvelle France Vulgairement dite Le Canada. Re-edition of 1664 ed. La Société Historique de Boucherville, Boucherville, 1964. 415 pp.

Briquet
Code militaire, ou compilation des ordonnances des Roys de France Concernant les Gens de Guerre. Imprimerie royale, Paris, 1728. 4 vols.

[Canada. Department of Agriculture.]
Census of Canada.... I.B. Taylor and Maclean, Rogers & Co., Ottawa, 1873–78. 5 vols. Vol. 4: Censuses of Canada. 1665 to 1871. Recensements du Canada. Statistics of Canada. Statistiques du Canada.

Deidier, Abbé
Le parfait ingénieur françois, ou la fortification offensive et défensive, contenant la construction, l'attaque et la défense des Places.... 2nd ed. rev. and enl. Ch. An. Jombert, Paris, 1757. 340 pp.

De Merville
Ordonnance de la Marine Du mois d'Aoust 1681. Commentée & Conferée Sur les anciennes Ordonnances, le Droit Romain, & les nouveaux Reglemens. Guillaume Cavelier, Paris, 1714. 5 vols.

De Ville, Antoine
Les fortifications du chevalier Antoine de Ville contenans la maniere de fortifier toute Sorte de places ... avec l'ataque, et les moyens de prendre des places. Irénée Barlet, Lyon, 1628. 454 pp.

Jamet, Dom Albert, ed.
Les Annales de l'Hôtel-Dieu de Québec, 1636–1716. Hôtel-Dieu de Québec, Québec, 1939. 444 pp.

Jesuits
Relations des Jésuites. Éditions du Jour, Montréal, 1972. 6 vols.

Jesuits. Letters from Missions (North America).
The Jesuit Relations and Allied Documents: Travels and Explorations of the Jesuit Missionaries in New France, 1610–1791.... Ed. Reuben Gold Thwaites. Burrows Brothers, Cleveland, 1896–1901. 73 vols. Vol. 9.

Lahontan, Louis-Armand de Lom d'Arce, baron de
Mémoires pittoresques de la Nouvelle-France. 2 vols. Vol. 1: Voyages du Baron de La Hontan dans l'Amerique Septentrionale.... New edition by Éditions Élysée, Montréal, 1974. 376 pp.

Montréal. Université. Département de démographie.
Répertoire des actes de baptême, mariage, sépulture et des recensements du Québec ancien. Eds. Hubert Charbonneau and Jacques Légaré. Presses de l'Université de Montréal, Montréal, 1980. Vols. 1 and 6. Published by the Programme de recherche en démographie historique.

Quebec (Province). Archives.
Ordonnances, commissions, etc., etc., des gouverneurs et des intendants de la Nouvelle-France, 1639–1706 ... par Pierre-Georges Roy. L'Éclaireur, Beauceville, 1924. 2 vols.
Papier terrier de la Compagnie des Indes occidentales, 1667–1668 ... par Pierre-Georges Roy. L'Éclaireur, Beauceville, 1931. 378 pp.

Quebec (Province). Assemblée législative.
Édits, ordonnances royaux, déclarations et arrêts du Conseil d'État concernant le Canada. E.-R. Fréchette, Québec, 1854–56. 3 vols.

Quebec (Province). Législature.
Jugements et délibérations du Conseil Souverain de la Nouvelle-France. A. Côté and Joseph Dussault, Québec, 1885–91. 6 vols. Vols. 1–3.

Richebourg and Boismeslé
Histoire generale de la marine, contenant Son origine chez tous les Peuples du monde, Ses progrès, Son état actuel, & les Expéditions Maritimes, anciennes & modernes. Antoine Boudet, Paris, 1758. 3 vols.

Shortt, Adam
Documents relatifs à la monnaie, au change et aux finances du Canada sous le régime français. F.A. Acland, Ottawa, 1925. 2 vols. Vol. 1.

Tétu, H., and C.-O. Gagnon, eds.
Mandements, lettres pastorales et circulaires des évêques de Québec. A. Côté, Québec, 1887–93; Chancellerie de l'Archevêché, Québec, 1898–1955, 17 vols. Vol. 1.

Inventories

Lacombe, Marthe, and Doris Drolet-Dubé
"Inventaire des marchés de construction des Archives nationales à Québec, XVIIe et XVIIIe siècles." *History and Archaeology/Histoire et archéologie*, No. 17 (1977). Ottawa. 456 pp.

Quebec (Province). Archives.
Index des jugements et délibérations du Conseil souverain de la Nouvelle-France de 1663 à 1716 ... par Pierre-Georges Roy. N.p., Québec, 1940. 287 pp.
Inventaire des insinuations de la Prévôté de Québec ... par Pierre-Georges Roy. L'Éclaireur, Beauceville, 1936–39. 3 vols.
Inventaire des insinuations du Conseil souverain de la Nouvelle-France ... par Pierre-Georges Roy. L'Éclaireur, Beauceville, 1921. 325 pp.
Inventaire des procès-verbaux des grands voyers conservés aux Archives de la province de Québec ... par Pierre-Georges Roy. L'Éclaireur, Beauceville, 1923–32. 6 vols.
Inventaire d'une collection de pièces judiciaires et notariales conservées aux Archives judiciaires de Québec ... par Pierre-Georges Roy. L'Éclaireur, Beauceville, 1917. 2 vols.

Dictionaries

De La Poix de Fréminville, Edme de
Dictionnaire, ou Traité de la police générale des villes, bourgs, paroisses et seigneuries de la campagne. Gissey, Paris, 1758. 588 pp.

Dictionnaire biographique du Canada
Presses de l'Université Laval, Québec, 1966–. Vol. 1: 1000–1700; Vol. 2: 1701–1740; Vol. 3: 1741–1770.

Dictionnaire universel françois et latin, vulgairement appelé Dictionnaire Trévoux
4th ed. Les Libraires Asssociés, Paris, 1743. 6 vols.

Furetière, Antoine
Dictionnaire universel, Contenant generalement tous les Mots François tant vieux que modernes, & les Termes des Sciences et des Arts. 2nd ed. rev. and enl. by Basnage de Bauval. Arnoud and Reinier Leers, The Hague, 1701. 3 vols.

Guyot, M.
Répertoire universel et raisonné de jurisprudence civile, criminelle, canonique et bénéficiale. Panckoucke, Paris, 1783. 64 vols.

Jetté, René
Dictionnaire généalogique des familles du Québec. Presses de l'Université de Montréal, Montréal, 1983. 1176 pp. Published in collaboration with the Programme de recherche en démographie historique of the Université de Montréal.

Laframboise, Yves
L'architecture traditionnelle au Québec. Glossaire illustré de la maison aux 17ᵉ et 18ᵉ siècles. Éditions de l'Homme, Montréal, 1975. 319 pp.

Marion, Marcel
Dictionnaire des institutions de la France aux XVIIe et XVIIIe siècles. 2nd ed. A. and J. Picard, Paris, 1968. 564 pp.

Tanguay, Cyprien
Dictionnaire généalogique des familles canadiennes depuis la fondation de la colonie jusqu'à nos jours. Eusèbe Sénécal, Québec, 1871–90. 7 vols. Vol. 1.

Whittick, Arnold, ed.
Encyclopedia of Urban Planning. McGraw-Hill, New York, 1974. 1218 pp.

Studies

Baillargeon, Noël
Le Séminaire de Québec de 1685 à 1760. Presses de l'Université Laval, Québec, 1977. 459 pp. Les Cahiers d'histoire de l'Université Laval, No. 21.
Le Séminaire de Québec sous l'épiscopat de Mgr de Laval. Presses de l'Université Laval, Québec, 1972. 308 pp. Les Cahiers de l'Institut d'histoire, No. 18.

Barbeau, Marius
"Notre ancienne architecture." *La Revue du Québec industriel*, Vol. 5, No. 2 (1940), pp. 4–9.

Bardet, Gaston
L'urbanisme. 9th ed. Presses universitaires de France, Paris, 1977. 127 pp. Collection "Que sais-je?"

Beaujeu-Garnier, Jacqueline, and Georges Chabot
Traité de géographie urbaine. 3rd ed. Librairie Armand Colin, Paris, 1963. 493 pp.

Bilodeau, R.
"Liberté économique et politique des Canadiens sous le régime français." *Revue d'histoire de l'Amérique française*, Vol. 10, No. 1 (June 1956), pp. 49–68.

Blanchard, Raoul
L'Est du Canada français, "Province de Québec." Librairie Beauchemin, Montréal, 1935. 2 vols. Vol. 2. Publications de l'Institut scientifique franco-canadien.

Bordes, Maurice
"Les intendants de province aux XVIIe et XVIIIe siècles." *L'information historique*, Vol. 30, No. 3 (May–June 1968), pp. 107–20.

Braudel, Fernand
Civilisation matérielle et capitalisme (XVe–XVIIIe siècle). Armand Colin, Paris, 1967. 3 vols. Vol. 1, 463 pp. Destins du monde.

Braudel, Fernand, and Ernest Labrousse
Histoire économique et sociale de la France. Presses universitaires de France, Paris, 1977. Tome 1: De 1450 à 1660; Vol. 1: L'État et la ville.

Bridenbaugh, Carl
Cities in the Wilderness: The First Century of Urban Life in America, 1625–1742. 4th ed., Oxford University Press, London, 1971. 500 pp.

Brissaud, Jean
A History of French Public Law. Trans. R. Howell, intro. W.S. Holdsworth and J.H. Wigmore. John Murray, London, 1912. 922 pp. The Continental Legal History Series, Vol. 3.
A History of French Public Law. Trans. J.W. Garner, intro. H.D. Hazeltine and W.W. Willoughby. John Murray, London, 1915. 582 pp. The Continental Legal History Series, Vol. 9.

Brown, Clément
Québec, croissance d'une ville. Presses de l'Université Laval, Québec, 1952. 78 pp. Culture populaire, No. 4.

Burke-Gaffney, Rev. M.W.
"Canada's First Engineer, Jean Bourdon (1601–1668)." *Canadian Catholic Historical Association Annual Report*, 1957, pp. 87–104.

Campeau, Lucien
Les Cent-Associés et le peuplement de la Nouvelle-France (1633–1663). Éditions Bellarmin, Montréal, 1974. 174 pp. Cahiers d'histoire des Jésuites, No. 2.
La mission des Jésuites chez les Hurons, 1634–1650. Éditions Bellarmin and Institutum Historicum S.I., Montréal and Rome, 1987. 487 pp.

Caron, Ivanhoë
"Historique de la voirie dans la province de Québec."
Bulletin des recherches historiques, Vol. 39, No. 4 (April 1933), pp. 198–215.

Casgrain, H.-R.
Histoire de l'Hôtel-Dieu de Québec. Léger Brousseau, Québec, 1878. 612 pp.

Chapais, Thomas
Jean Talon, intendant de la Nouvelle-France. S.-A. Demers, Québec, 1904. 540 pp.

Charbonneau, André
"Les carrières de pierre dans la région de Québec sous le régime français." In *Exercices des métiers de la pierre et de l'argile*, ed. Jean-Claude Dupont, Célat, Québec, 1988, pp. 173–209. Cahiers du Célat, No. 9.

Charbonneau, André, Yvon Desloges, and Marc Lafrance
Québec; ville fortifiée du XVIIe au XIXe siècle. Éditions du Pélican and Parks Canada, Québec, 1982. 491 pp.

Charbonneau, Hubert
"À propos de démographie urbaine en Nouvelle-France. Réflexions en marge d'*Habitants et marchands de Montréal* de Louise Dechêne." *Revue d'histoire de l'Amérique française*, Vol. 30, No. 2 (Sept. 1976), pp. 263–69.
Vie et mort de nos ancêtres, étude démographique. Presses de l'Université de Montréal, Montréal, 1975. 264 pp. Démographie canadienne, No. 3.

Charbonneau, Hubert, and Yolande Lavoie
"Introduction à la reconstitution de la population du Canada au XVIIe siècle." *Revue d'histoire de l'Amérique française*, Vol. 24, No. 4 (March 1971), pp. 485–511.

Charbonneau, Hubert, Yolande Lavoie, and Jacques Légaré
"Le recensement nominatif du Canada en 1681." *Histoire sociale/Social History*, Vol. 7 (April 1971), pp. 77–98.

Debien, Gabriel
"Les engagés pour le Canada au XVIIe siècle vus de La Rochelle." *Revue d'histoire de l'Amérique française*, Vol. 6, No. 2 (Sept. 1952), pp. 177–233; Vol. 6, No. 3 (Dec. 1952), pp. 374–407.

Dechêne, Louise
"La croissance de Montréal au XVIIIe siècle." *Revue d'histoire de l'Amérique française*, Vol. 27, No. 2 (Sept. 1973), pp. 163–79.
"L'évolution du régime seigneurial au Canada. Le cas de Montréal aux XVIIe et XVIIIe siècles." *Recherches sociographiques*, Vol. 12, No. 2 (May–Aug. 1971), pp. 143–83.
Habitants et marchands de Montréal au XVIIe siècle. Plon, Paris, 1974. 588 pp. Civilisations et mentalités.

Delafosse, M.
"La Rochelle et le Canada au XVIIe siècle." *Revue d'histoire de l'Amérique française*, Vol. 4, No. 4 (March 1951), pp. 469–511.

Delalande, J.
Le Conseil Souverain de la Nouvelle-France. Ls.-A. Proulx, Québec, 1927. 358 pp.

Desloges, Yvon
"L'étude du passé urbain et ses nombreuses approches; un bilan historique." *Bulletin de recherches*, No. 197, Parks Canada, Ottawa, June 1983.

Desloges, Yvon, Alain Rainville, and Serge Saint-Pierre
"Building a House in New France. An Account of the Perplexities of Client and Craftsmen in Early Canada" [book review], *The Journal of Canadian Art History/Annales d'histoire de l'art canadien*, Vol. 4, No. 2 (1977/78), pp. 159–67.

Diamond, Sigmund
"Le Canada français au XVIIe siècle, une société préfabriquée," *Annales, Économies, Sociétés, Civilisations*, Vol. 16, No. 2 (March–April 1961), pp. 317–54.

Dickinson, John Alexander
Justice et justiciables. La procédure civile à la Prévôté de Québec, 1667–1759. Presses de l'Université Laval, Québec, 1982. 289 pp. Les Cahiers d'histoire de l'Université Laval, No. 26.

Dubé, Jean-Claude
"Origine sociale des intendants de la Nouvelle-France." *Histoire sociale/Social History*, Vol. 2 (Nov. 1968), pp. 18–33.

Duby, Georges, and Jacques Le Goff, eds.
Histoire de la France urbaine. Seuil, Paris, 1980. Vol. 2: La ville médiévale. Des Carolingiens à la Renaissance, 653 pp.

Dumas, Silvio
Les filles du roi en Nouvelle-France. Étude historique avec répertoire biographique. Société historique de Québec, Québec, 1972. 382 pp. Cahiers d'histoire, No. 24.

Eccles, W.J.
"The Background of Louis Buade, Comte de Frontenac." *Canadian Historical Association Annual Report*, 1954, pp. 20–27.
Frontenac; The Courtier Governor. 3rd ed. McClelland and Stewart, Toronto, 1972. 358 pp. Carleton Library, No. 24.

Faillon, Étienne-Michel
Histoire de la colonie française en Canada. Poupart-Darvyl, Paris, 1865–66. 4 vols.

Fauteux, Joseph-Noël
Essai sur l'industrie au Canada sous le régime français. Ls.-A. Proulx, Québec, 1927. 2 vols.

Filion, Konrad
"Essai sur l'évolution du mot habitant (XVIIe — XVIIIe siècles)." *Revue d'histoire de l'Amérique française*, Vol. 24, No. 3 (Dec. 1970), pp. 375–401.

Frégault, Guy
Le XVIIIe siècle canadien. Études. HMH, Montréal, 1970. 387 pp.

Gareau, Jean-Baptiste
"La Prévôté de Québec: ses officiers — ses registres." *Rapport de l'archiviste de la province de Québec pour 1943–1944*, Rédempti Paradis, Québec, 1944, pp. 51–146.

Gauthier-Larouche, Georges
Évolution de la maison rurale traditionnelle dans la région de Québec (étude ethnographique). Presses de l'Université Laval, Québec, 1974. 321 pp. Les archives de folklore, No. 15.

George, Pierre
Précis de géographie urbaine. 4th ed. rev. Presses universitaires de France, Paris, 1974. 286 pp.

Gottmann, Jean
"Plans de villes des deux côtés de l'Atlantique." In *Mélanges géographiques canadiens offerts à Raoul Blanchard*, Presses de l'Université Laval, Québec, 1959, pp. 237–42.

Goubert, Pierre
L'Ancien régime. 4th ed. Librairie Armand Colin, Paris, 1973. 2 vols. Vol. 1: La société; Vol. 2: Les pouvoirs. Collection U.

Hamelin, Jean
Économie et société en Nouvelle-France. Presses de l'Université Laval, Québec, [1960]. 137 pp. Les Cahiers de l'Institut d'histoire, No. 3.

Hare, John
"La population de la ville de Québec, 1795–1805." *Histoire sociale/Social History*, Vol. 7, No. 13 (May 1974), pp. 23–47.

Harouel, Jean-Louis
"Les fonctions de l'alignement dans l'organisme urbain." *Dix-huitième siècle*, No. 9 (1977), pp. 135–49.

Harris, Richard Colebrook
The Seigneurial System in Early Canada: A Geographical Study. 2nd ed. University of Wisconsin Press, Madison, 1968.

Heers, Jacques
L'Occident aux XIVe et XVe siècles; Aspects économiques et sociaux. Presses universitaires de France, Paris, 1970. 419 pp.

Henripin, Jacques
La population canadienne au début du XVIIIe siècle. Nuptialité, fécondité, mortalité infantile. Presses universitaires de France, Paris, 1954. 129 pp. Institut national d'études démographiques, travaux et documents, cahier No. 22.

Lachance, André
"La criminalité à Québec sous le régime français: étude statistique." *Revue d'histoire de l'Amérique française*, Vol. 20, No. 3 (Dec. 1966), pp. 409–414.
La justice criminelle du roi au Canada au XVIIIe siècle, Tribunaux et officiers. Presses de l'Université Laval, Québec, 1978. 187 pp. Les Cahiers d'histoire de l'Université Laval, No. 22.
"Les prisons au Canada sous le régime français." *Revue d'histoire de l'Amérique française*, Vol. 19, No. 4 (March 1966), pp. 561–65.

Lafrance, Marc
"Étude sur l'évolution physique de la ville de Québec, 1608–1763." Manuscript on file, National Historic Sites Directorate, Canadian Parks Service, Ottawa, 1972. 150 pp.
"Évolution physique et politiques urbaines: Québec sous le régime français." *Revue d'histoire ubaine/Urban History Review*, année 1975, No. 3 (Feb. 1976), pp. 3–22.

Lamontagne, Roland
"L'influence de Colbert sur l'oeuvre de Jean Talon." *Revue d'histoire de l'Amérique française*, Vol. 6, No. 1 (June 1952), pp. 42–61.

Lanctôt, Gustave
L'administration de la Nouvelle-France. 2nd ed. Éditions du Jour, Montréal, 1971. 177 pp.
Histoire du Canada. 4th ed. Librairie Beauchemin, Montréal, 1964. 3 vols.
"La participation du peuple dans le gouvernement de la Nouvelle-France." *Revue trimestrielle canadienne*, Sept. 1929, pp. 225–39.
"Le régime municipal en Nouvelle-France." *Culture*, Vol. 9, No. 3 (1948), pp. 255–83.

Landry-Gauthier, Raymonde
"L'architecture civile et conventuelle à Québec (1680–1726)." Thèse de maîtrise, Université Laval, Québec, 1976. 193 pp.

Lareau, Edmond
"Les syndics d'habitation sous la domination française." *Revue canadienne*, 2nd ser., Vol. 19, No. 3 (1883), pp. 129–40.

La Rocque de Roquebrune, R.
"La direction de la Nouvelle-France par le Ministère de la Marine." *Revue d'histoire de l'Amérique française*, Vol. 5, No. 4 (March 1953), pp. 470–88.

Lavedan, Pierre
Géographie des villes. 2nd ed. Gallimard, Paris, 1959. 341 pp.

Histoire de l'urbanisme. 2nd ed. rev. Henri Laurens, Paris, 1959. 3 vols. Vol. 3: Renaissance et Temps modernes.

Lavedan, Pierre, and Jeanne Huguenay
L'urbanisme au Moyen Age. Arts et métiers graphiques, Paris, 1974. 184 pp. Bibliothèque de la Société française d'archéologie, No. 5.

Lepetit, Bernard
"L'évolution de la notion de ville d'après les tableaux et descriptions géographiques de la France (1650–1850)." *Urbi*, Vol. 2 (1979), pp. 99–107.

Marsan, Jean-Claude
Montréal en évolution. Historique du développement de l'architecture et de l'environnement montréalais. 2nd ed. Fides, Montréal, 1974. 423 pp.

Mathieu, Jacques
"Les causes devant la Prévôté de Québec en 1667." *Histoire sociale/Social History*, No. 3 (April 1969), pp. 101–11.
"La vie à Québec au milieu du XVIIe siècle, étude des sources." *Revue d'histoire de l'Amérique française*, Vol. 23, No. 3 (Dec. 1969), pp. 404–24.

Mayrand, Pierre
"Les matériaux de couverture en Nouvelle-France aux XVIIe et aux [*sic*] XVIIIe siècles." *APT Bulletin: The Association for Preservation Technology/Association pour la préservation et ses techniques*, Vol. 2, Nos. 1–2 (1970), pp. 70–74.

Méthivier, Hubert
Le siècle de Louis XIV. 7th ed. rev. Presses universitaires de France, Paris, 1975. 126 pp. Collection "Que sais-je?"

Miville-Deschênes, François
"Les lois de la construction et de la propriété des édifices dans la Coutume de Paris." Term paper, Université Laval, Québec, 1976. 36 pp.

Moogk, Peter N.
Building a House in New France: An Account of the Perplexities of Client and Craftsmen in Early Canada. McClelland and Stewart, Toronto, 1977. 144 pp.

Mousnier, Roland
Les hiérarchies sociales de 1450 à nos jours. Presses universitaires de France, Paris, 1969. 196 pp. Collection Sup.
La plume, la faucille et le marteau. Institutions et société en France du Moyen Age à la Révolution. Presses universitaires de France, Paris, 1970. 404 pp. Collection Hier.

Mumford, Lewis
The City in History: Its Origins, Its Transformations, and Its Prospects. Harcourt, Brace & World, New York, 1961. 657 pp.

Olivier-Lacamp, Gaël, and Jacques Légaré
"Quelques caractéristiques des ménages de la ville de Québec entre 1666 et 1716." *Histoire sociale/Social History*, Vol. 12, No. 23 (May 1979), pp. 66–78.

Ouellet, Fernand
"Propriété seigneuriale et groupes sociaux dans la vallée du Saint-Laurent (1663–1840)." In *Mélanges d'histoire du Canada français offerts au professeur Marcel Trudel*, Éditions de l'Université d'Ottawa, Ottawa, 1978, pp. 183–213.

Paillé, Michel P.
"Accroissement et structure de la population à Québec au début du XIXe siècle. (À propos d'un article de John Hare)." *Histoire sociale/Social History*, Vol. 9, No. 17 (May 1976), pp. 187–96.

Perrot, Jean-Claude
Genèse d'une ville moderne, Caen au XVIIIe siècle. Mouton & Co. and École des Hautes Études en sciences sociales, Paris and The Hague, 1975. 2 vols. Civilisations et Sociétés, No. 44.

Petit-Dutaillis, Charles
Les communes françaises. Caractères et évolution des origines au XVIIIe siècle. 2nd ed. Albin Michel, Paris, 1970. 379 pp.

Provost, Honorius
"La Canoterie. Essai de petite histoire." *Le Canada français*, Vol. 28, No. 10 (June 1941), pp. 1059–68.

Rastoul, Pierre
"La chaumière québécoise." *Bulletin de culture matérielle/Material Culture Bulletin*, No. 21 (1977), pp. 19–41.

Reid, Allana G.
"The Development and Importance of the Town of Quebec, 1608–1760." PhD diss., McGill University, Montréal, 1950. 475 pp.
"The First Poor Relief System of Canada." *Canadian Historical Review*, Vol. 27, No. 4 (Dec. 1946), pp. 424–31.
"Intercolonial Trade During the French Regime." *Canadian Historical Review*, Vol. 32, No. 3 (Sept. 1951), pp. 236–51.
"The Nature of Quebec Society During the French Regime." *Canadian Historical Association Annual Report*, 1951, pp. 26–36.
"Representative Assemblies in New France." *Canadian Historical Review*, Vol. 27, No. 1 (March 1946), pp. 19–26.

Reps, John, W.
The Making of Urban America; A History of City Planning in the United States. Princeton University Press, Princeton, 1965. 574 pp.

Richardson, A.J.H.
"A Comparative Historical Study of Timber Building in Canada." *APT Bulletin: The Association for Preservation Technology/Association pour la préservation et ses techniques*, Vol. 5, No. 3 (1973), pp. 77–102.
"Guide to the Architecturally and Historically Most Significant Buildings in the Old City of Quebec with a Biographical Dictionary of Architects and Builders and Illustrations." *APT Bulletin: The Association for Preservation Technology/Association pour la préservation et ses techniques*, Vol. 2, Nos. 3–4 (1970), pp. 3–144.

Richardson, A.J.H., et al.
"Early Roofing Materials." *APT Bulletin: The Association for Preservation Technology/Association pour la préservation et ses techniques*, Vol. 2, Nos. 1–2 (1970), pp. 18–27.
Quebec City: Architects, Artisans and Builders. National Museum of Man and Parks Canada, Ottawa, 1984. 583 pp. Mercury Series, No. 37.

Roy, Joseph-Edmond
"La cartographie et l'arpentage sous le régime français." *Bulletin des recherches historiques*, Vol. 1, No. 2 (Feb. 1895), pp. 17–40.

Roy, Pierre-Georges
"Les épidémies à Québec." *Bulletin des recherches historiques*, Vol. 49, No. 7 (July 1943), pp. 204–15.
"Le premier recensement nominal de Québec." *Bulletin des recherches historiques*, Vol. 37, No. 6 (June 1931), pp. 321–31.
"Le procès de l'abbé de Fénelon devant le Conseil Souverain de la Nouvelle-France en 1674," *RAPQ, 1921–1922* (Québec: Ls.-A. Proulx, 1922).
La ville de Québec sous le régime français. Rédempti Paradis, Québec, 1930. 2 vols.

Roy, Raymond, Yves Landry, and Hubert Charbonneau
"Quelques comportements des Canadiens au XVIIe siècle d'après les registres paroissiaux." *Revue d'histoire de l'Amérique française*, Vol. 31, No. 1 (June 1977), pp. 49–73.

Saint-Germain, Jacques
La Reynie et la police au Grand Siècle d'après de nombreux documents inédits. Hachette, Paris, 1962. 342 pp.

Salone, Émile
La colonisation de la Nouvelle-France, étude sur les origines de la nation canadienne française. New ed. Boréal Express, Trois-Rivières, 1970. 505 pp.

Séguin, Robert-Lionel
La maison en Nouvelle-France. Musée national du Canada, Ottawa, 1968. 92 pp. Bulletin No. 226.

Shorter, Edward
The Making of the Modern Family. Basic Books, New York, 1977. 371 pp.

Smailes, Arthur E.
The Geography of Towns. 3rd ed. Aldine Publishing, Chicago, 1968. 160 pp.

Sulte, Benjamin
"Recensement de 1681." In *Histoire des Canadiens français, 1608–1880*, Wilson, Montréal, 1882, Vol. 5, pp. 53–57.

Teisseyre-Sallmann, Line
"Urbanisme et société: l'exemple de Nîmes aux XVIIe et XVIIIe siècles." *Annales, Économies, Sociétés, Civilisations*, 35e année, No. 5 (Sept.–Oct. 1980), pp. 965–86.

Thomson, Jean R.
"An Evaluation of Judicial Fees in Cases Brought Before the Sovereign Council, 1663–1690." *Revue du Centre d'Étude du Québec*, Vol. 3 (May 1969), pp. 9–18.

Traquair, Ramsay
The Old Architecture of Quebec. A Study of the Buildings Erected in New France from the Earliest Explorers to the Middle of the Nineteenth Century. Macmillan, Toronto, 1947. 324 pp.

Trudel, Marcel
Atlas de la Nouvelle-France. Presses de l'Université Laval, Québec, 1968. 219 pp.
Catalogue des immigrants, 1632–1662. Éditions Hurtubise HMH, Montréal, 1983. 569 pp. Cahiers du Québec.
Les débuts du régime seigneurial au Canada. Fides, Montréal, 1974. 313 pp. Collection Fleur de Lys.
Histoire de la Nouvelle-France. Fides, Montréal, 1966. 554 pp. 2 vols. Vol. 2: Le Comptoir, 1604–1627.

La population du Canada en 1663. Fides, Montréal, 1973. 368 pp. Collection Fleur de Lys.

Le terrier du Saint-Laurent en 1663. Éditions de l'Université d'Ottawa, Ottawa, 1973. 618 pp. Cahiers du Centre de Recherche en Civilisation canadienne-française, No. 6.

Vachon, André

L'administration de la Nouvelle-France, 1627–1760. Presses de l'Université Laval, Québec, 1970. 87 pp.

"La restauration de la Tour de Babel, ou 'La vie à Québec au milieu du XVIIe siècle.'" *Revue d'histoire de l'Amérique française*, Vol. 24, No. 2 (Sept. 1970), pp. 167–250.

Warden, G.B.

"L'urbanisation américaine avant 1800." *Annales, Économies, Sociétés, Civilisations*, 25e année, No. 4 (July–Aug. 1970), pp. 862–79. Special issue on history and urbanization.

Zolvany, Yves

"Esquisse de la Coutume de Paris." *Revue d'histoire de l'Amérique française*, Vol. 25, No. 3 (Dec. 1971), pp. 365–84.